Hand in Hand

with the Messiah

Letters from the Messiah

by
Debra Stuart Sanford

CCB Publishing
British Columbia, Canada

Hand in Hand with the Messiah:
Letters from the Messiah

Copyright ©2014 by Debra Stuart Sanford
ISBN-13   978-1-77143-196-5
First Edition

Library and Archives Canada Cataloguing in Publication
Sanford, Debra Stuart, author
Hand in hand with the messiah : letters from the messiah
/ by Debra Stuart Sanford. -- First edition.
Issued in print and electronic formats.
ISBN 978-1-77143-196-5 (pbk.).--ISBN 978-1-77143-197-2 (pdf)
Additional cataloguing data available from Library and Archives Canada

Book design by Kevin O'Keefe.

This book may be ordered from: **www.AlephTavScriptures.com**

Publisher: CCB Publishing
                British Columbia, Canada
                www.ccbpublishing.com

DEDICATION

THIS book is dedicated to my children who are a gift from Heaven: Jennifer, Jessica, Jason, Jordan, Justin, and also the children that have been added to me: Josh, Michael, Joshua, Chloe, Madelyn, and Tobey Samuel. I feel blessed everyday to have been given such treasures.

ACKNOWLEDGEMENTS

I want to personally thank my husband, William Sanford, for his constant encouragement. Without his support and loving devotion this book would not have been published.

PREFACE

HAVE you ever imagined what it would be like to live during the time that the Messiah lived? Have you ever wanted to sit at the feet of the Messiah and hear His teachings? What would it be like to walk hand in hand with Him down the seashore? You could ask him any question, and He would answer you. You could look into His Eyes and see your Creator in the flesh. You could see His compassion and love being poured out on all those around Him. You could watch as He changed lives before your eyes. You could share in the celebration when the blind, deaf, mute, crippled, diseased, or demon possessed were healed and restored. What a glorious day it must have been for these people and their families! So great was My desire to look into His Eyes and share these moments that I was urged by His Spirit to begin an intensive study of the Gospels. I began to examine the Scriptures verse by verse to catch a glimpse of the Messiah. I wanted to know how He lived when He walked among us. I wanted to know how He wants me to live every day. My journey through the Gospels changed the way I look at My Life. The Messiah became vivid in My Mind. I wanted to be like Him and pour out love to everyone like He did. I wanted to become His Hands and Feet. I wanted to walk hand in hand with Him every day. I invite you to take the same journey that I did through the Gospels to catch a glimpse of the Messiah as He walked on earth. You can break the Gospels apart over the course of a year for an intensive study or you can shorten the study to meet your needs. Be led by His Spirit as to how you will use this book, because it is only an avenue to lead you into a deeper walk with Him. Enjoy your journey hand in hand with the Messiah.

SERVANT of the Most High,

DEBRA Stuart Sanford

INTRODUCTION

"HAND in Hand with the Messiah" is a unique collection of 365 letters written by the Messiah to give you insight into the compassion and love that He has for His People. Each daily letter holds a message for you that is inspired by Scripture. Each page helps you grasp deeper understanding into the character of the Messiah as He walked upon this earth. As you travel through the Gospels and examine each step the Messiah took, you will desire to take those same steps that He took spreading love and compassion to all people that cross your path. Allow the Messiah to speak to you through these letters and become real in your life. You will become the Hands and Feet of the Messiah. Enjoy your journey hand in hand with the Messiah!

"TAKE My yoke upon you and learn from me, for I am gentle and humble in heart, and you will find rest for your souls. For My yoke is easy and My burden is light." *Matthew 11:29-30*

Matthew 1:1-17

My Beloved, My Birth had been prophesized for many years. My People were looking for their Messiah, their King. They had searched the scriptures for signs about My Coming. They knew the season must be near. The prophets had given many signs to look for along the way. I came through the seed of Abraham, Isaac, and Jacob just as I promised that I would come. I said that I would be from the tribe of Judah, the son of David. David was promised a king that would reign forever through his line of descendents. I chose a very humble girl named Mary, who was engaged to Joseph, to bring My Spirit forth. She received the news gladly that she would give birth to Me. The task that I gave Mary and Joseph to bring Me into this world would not be easy for them. They would have to flee for their lives many times. Satan wanted to stop My Birth and kill My Flesh before I could ever begin My Ministry to My People. Satan was constantly at the gate trying to harm Mary and Joseph. My Angels guarded them and protected them. My Angels told them when to flee and when to stay and rest. My Spirit was placed in a fleshly body, so I could come to earth to tell you about Me. I wanted to walk among My People. I loved you so much that I wanted to be close to you and share in your laughter. I wanted to tell you the Truth and release you from the bondage of deception. I carefully guarded over all those in My Line of descendants. I carefully guarded over those who would hear the news about Me and receive Me. Are you afraid today? Do not be concerned about anything. I am guarding you and keeping you safe from the evil one. You do not ever have to be afraid. You are guarded by My Angels. Remain in peace.

Matthew 1:18-25

My Beloved, I sent My Angel to talk to Mary and tell her that she was going to conceive a child filled with My Spirit. She was willing to do what I told her to do and be a humble servant. When Joseph found out that she was pregnant he wanted to put her away privately, so she would not be shamed. She had told him that an angel came to her and told her that she would conceive a child filled with My Spirit. Joseph did not know what to think about this, so as he was sitting quietly pondering her words I sent My Angel to him to tell him what to do. I told him to take Mary to be his wife and care for her. I told him to name the baby Yahshua (Hebrew name for Jesus). I told him that He would save the world from their sins. Joseph still did not understand exactly what was happening, but he received it by faith and took Mary into his house and cared for her tenderly. Are you struggling with a problem today? You may not understand the situation that you are going through. If you call on My Name, I will help you try to understand what I am doing in your life. You must trust Me and believe in Me knowing that I will only bring you good things.

Matthew 2:1-12

My Beloved, there were a group of men who searched the stars for the coming Messiah. They knew the time and region. They saw the star form, and they set out to bring the child gifts. They came from the east in the land where Daniel had worshipped Me while he was in Babylon. Daniel had taught the men under him to look for the Savior that would come. This Savior would be a king and rule his people. Daniel wanted to bring Him gifts and worship Him. He wanted to see this King who would save his people from their sins. Daniel did not live long enough to see Me in the flesh, but the men he taught continued his search and brought Me the gifts Daniel wanted to send Me. The men had been searching for awhile to find Me. They even went to King Herod to see if he had seen this new born King. King Herod had the priests search the scriptures to find where I would be born. The scriptures told the priests that I would be born in Bethlehem, so the Magi went to find him there. The Magi rejoiced to find Me and look upon My Face. Angels surrounded Me caring for Me. There was a great Light around Me. The Magi prostrated themselves and worshipped Me. They gave their very expensive gifts to Me suitable to give a king. They did not understand why I was living in such lowly surroundings. I revealed to them in a dream that King Herod wanted to kill Me. They departed and took another route home, so they would not encounter King Herod. They were given understanding that My Kingdom had not yet been revealed, but when I ruled as King that the entire world would bow to Me. They had spent many days searching for Me, and they were rewarded with insight into My Kingdom. Are you searching for Me? If you search for Me with all your heart, I will give you insight into My Kingdom. I will show you hidden things, so you can be strong and mighty and overcome everything that comes your way.

Matthew 2:13-15

My Beloved, Mary and Joseph were overwhelmed that the Magi would travel so far to worship Me. Their hearts were filled with joy! This confirmed inside of them that they ware caring for a very special child. The Magi were warned to go another way home to escape King Herod. I also sent an angel to Mary and Joseph to warn them about King Herod. I told them to escape into Egypt, and I would shelter them there. The expensive gifts were given to Mary and Joseph at a time when they were very poor. Now they had to escape into an unknown country and live until I told them to return. These gifts sustained them and helped them establish a suitable place to live, so they would remain safe from King Herod. Living in Egypt was very difficult for Mary and Joseph. They were used to living in a land that served Me, and now they were in a pagan land. They did not understand the customs of the people. They depended on Me to help them. Both were righteous people who were grieved by the people of this land and their pagan ways. They stayed where I told them to stay until King Herod died. I sent an angel to tell them when they could leave the country. They waited patiently everyday for the return of the angel to tell them when they could leave to go home. Are you waiting for something to happen in your life? I have heard your prayers. I have not forgotten you. You may be waiting patiently today for Me to tell you when you can go back home. You are in exile just like Mary and Joseph were in exile far from their home. I will call you to come out and come back to the Land. I will call all the exiles to return home to My Land and live together in peace. Listen for My Call!

Matthew 2:16-18

My Beloved, King Herod was watching and waiting everyday for news of this new king. He and his administration were very upset over the birth of a new king. Would this king try to rule over them? Would this new king cause the people to rise up and rebel against him? Would this new king have powers to support him that he did not know about? The priests also were very upset to hear that King Herod wanted to kill their Messiah. The priests were praying for My Safety. They were fasting and praying and wanting angels to intervene for this little child. After a long period of time King Herod sent messengers over the area to find out where the Magi had gone. The local people told his messengers that the Magi had been there and then left. They told the messengers that they did not see a king. The local people were trying to hide where the baby had gone. When the messengers told the king that the Magi had returned to their country, he was furious. Herod used the time that the Magi had calculated finding the formation of the star and sent a decree to kill all the babies two years old and under. Herod was going to stop the rule of this king. He did not want anyone to rule over him and try to destroy his kingdom. There was great weeping in My Land. These young children were slaughtered by King Herod's soldiers. There was blood in the street as men and women tried to save their children from destruction. The Land was in mourning. This was My Hand of judgment on My People to punish them for the innocent blood they had shed in the Land. My People did not service the poor in the courts as they should and many were killed for the sake of the rich. They had also taken children from their parents to use them as their personal slaves. The religious leaders did whatever they wanted to do in the name of the Temple. This was an abomination to Me, and they had to pay the price for their sins. You will also have to pay for your sins while you are on earth.

Walk in righteousness, so you and all your house will prosper.

Matthew 2:19-23

My Beloved, eventually King Herod died and his reign of terror was over. The people rejoiced over his death. I sent an angel to Joseph to tell him to come back to the Land. He rejoiced over the message to come home. It had been a long time since he had seen his family. He longed to return to the Land. He was afraid that I would still be in danger and did not want to go back to Bethlehem. I sent an angel to tell him to go live in Galilee in a town called Nazareth. Mary and Joseph had to start over again in a new place. They were in a place that they had not lived before. This was a more remote place away from many of the soldiers of the king. They found a place to live there, and they blended with the local people there. At least they were not in exile with the pagan people. At least they could worship Me with the people around them. At least their family could come see them and surround them with their love. Soon they began to prosper there, and they felt settled. They never knew if they would have to leave again or go back to Egypt. They constantly were concerned about My Safety. They thought that someone still may want to kill Me. They had to trust Me to care for them. They called on My Name constantly for help. I heard their prayers, and no harm came to them. Are you fearful about your safety today? Call on My Name and I will help you. I will send you My Spirit to comfort you and give you peace. You do not ever have to be afraid, because I will guard over you. No harm will come to you as long as you trust in Me to care for you.

Matthew 3:1-12

My Beloved, I called John to go before Me and prepare the way. John told the people that they needed to repent, because the Messiah was coming. John told them that they must be clean and walk in righteousness, so I could see their good deeds when I returned. The people came from all over the area to be baptized by John. The people would repent of their sins and be baptized in water to cleanse them of their past sins. They were told to go and sin no more. Even the religious leaders came to be baptized to show that they too wanted to be ready for the Messiah when He returns. John was outraged over them coming to be baptized. He knew that they came for a show for the people. He knew that their hearts were not grieved over their sins. They were not repenting, but displaying their acts of righteousness to the people. John called them snakes or deceivers. He told them that unless they repent and bear the fruit of righteousness that they would be burned up in the Lake of Fire. John told them about Me, and that I would arrive soon. The area was ready for Me to come to them. They were waiting for My Arrival. Are you ready for My Arrival? Have you cleansed yourself and made yourself ready for My Return? Look at yourself, and repent of your sins. Walk in righteousness for the Master of the Home will return home to see which of his servants are obeying him, and which ones are disobedient servants. I will bless you for your faithfulness and destroy those who are not walking in My Ways.

Matthew 3:13-17

My Beloved, John was a faithful servant, and he prepared the way for Me. He told many to repent of their sins and get ready for My Coming. The whole area was expecting Me to come to them soon. When John saw Me walking towards him his spirit leaped inside of him. He rejoiced to see Me again. John assumed that I was coming to immerse him in water, but I surprised him. I wanted to be an example to My People that I wanted them to be water baptized. John was reluctant to baptize Me, but I told him that this was right in My Eyes. After he immersed Me in water the door of heaven was opened. My Spirit from heaven came down in the form of a dove and hovered over My Head. My Spirit announced that I had been pleasing through My Obedience. I came to earth and humbled Myself. I gave up My heavenly throne and descended to earth to walk among you and teach you about Me. I came to save you from your sins. Heaven testified that it was very pleased with Me, and all men should listen to Me. Are you listening to Me? Are you obeying Me? Walk humbly beside Me, and do as I tell you to do. Do not rebel against Me, and I will prosper you greatly. I will give you peace, love, joy, and comfort. You will walk hand in hand with Me all day, and rejoice in My Presence.

Matthew 4:1-11

Many times you will have temptations, but be on guard and know that the evil one will come to tempt you when you are weak. He will be watching and know just when to send the temptation. He always wants to show those that look on that you are unworthy of inheriting My Kingdom. He wants to prove that I AM wrong in My Decision to choose man as My Heir to the throne. The evil one is created. He is limited in his reasoning and insight and cannot see ahead. I know what you will become. I know those who will follow Me and want to serve Me with all their hearts. Do you love Me enough to serve Me all day long? Do you love Me enough to lay down your life and follow after Me not giving into your flesh but being led by My Spirit? The evil one is always watching to bring you into sin. Keep your eyes open, and do not let him catch you unprepared. If you do fall into sin, then repent quickly. Get back on the right track, so your punishment will be small. If you continue down the wrong road for a long time, then you will have to pay a heavy price for your sins. The sins of the flesh are not satisfying. You will always want more. The satisfaction that walking hand in hand with Me is far greater than you could ever imagine. Weigh them in the balance, and you will find that the rewards of walking with Me far outweigh walking in the flesh.

Arise, My Beloved! Arise! Walk in the things of Me.

Matthew 4:12-17

My Beloved, I was tempted in the desert by Satan. He came to Me as a light. He wanted Me to look upon him and worship him. He could tell that I could see who he was and what his plan was for Me. Satan did not know My Power in the flesh. He came to test My Strength to stand firm as he does to every man. I stood firm and was found faithful, then I was ready to minister to the people around Me. I came to the area around Galilee thus fulfilling the words of the prophet. I taught the people to repent of their sins for the Kingdom of Heaven had come to them. The people saw a great Light! Some of them received the Light, and others could not receive the Light. Are you sharing the Truth with others? Some will receive it, and some will not receive it. Do not be concerned about whether they receive the Truth of not. With love and compassion you have told them the Good News about Me coming to save them from their sins. If they reject your words, they reject Me, not you. You are just the messenger. You are My obedient servant who is bringing a message from Me to those who are lost. You are just the vessel who is poured out onto them. When they reject Me, they reject eternal life and their salvation. This is their choice. Every man will make this choice and decide whether he wants to love Me and hold Me or turn his face away from Me. Do not reject the man who has rejected your words from Me. Continue to pray for him, because the seed has been planted. I will water it, and it may grow. You have been obedient, so know that you have completed what I have asked you to do. This is all I ask of you, and you will be rewarded.

Matthew 4:18-22

My Beloved, I came to teach My People about what they must do to enter the Kingdom of Heaven. I came to Simon Peter and Andrew his brother. I called to the men and asked them to follow Me, because I wanted to make them fishers of men. I did not choose these men randomly. I knew their heart and what they would give up for Me. I knew that they would love Me and adhere to Me. They gave up their livelihood, but I gave them great treasure. They learned from Me, and when I left they continued telling the Truth about Me. I also came to James and John with their father in his fishing boat. I called to James and John to come follow Me. They had other brothers working with their father, but I only called these two men to leave their father. I knew they would cling to Me and serve Me. I chose these men from the beginning of time. I knew who My Disciples would be and how they would serve Me. These men were created and anointed and set apart for service to Me. They may seem like common fisherman, but they were much more than this. They were far above the average man. They were strong and courageous and ready to stand against persecution. They were not taught by the religious leaders of the day, so I could fill them with the Truth and they would receive it. Did you know that I have chosen you from the beginning? Do you know how special you are? You may not feel like you are special, but you have been anointed to serve Me in a special way. Draw close to Me, and I will show you the purpose I want you to fulfill. If you do not hear My Voice, then seek Me and you will find Me. Know Me, and you will be fulfilled. You will want to complete the task ahead, and do the best you can so you can please Me. You are chosen. Rejoice in this!

Matthew 4:23-25

My Beloved, I took My Disciples and began to teach in all the synagogues on Sabbath. Huge crowds began to follow Me bringing all the ones who needed to be healed. News spread all over the area and even into Syria. People were desperate for a healer and deliverer. They would bring their sick long distances, so I could heal them. They came by faith believing that I would heal them. I never turned anyone away. They left rejoicing and dancing! They learned about My Love and compassion. They heard the Good News about the Kingdom of Heaven coming to earth. They were convicted of their sins, and they repented. They were taught a better way to worship Me. I told them about the bondage of the laws of the religious leaders. I told them that Moses told them not to add or subtract from My Laws. I showed them a better way to live, and they received it gladly. My Disciples listened to My Words and learned from Me. They assisted Me with the people to handle the crowds. They grew to love Me and would do anything for Me. They knew that I was the Messiah sent to earth to save man from destruction. You have that same chance today. You can learn from Me and grow to love Me. You can serve Me and be My Hands and Feet. Do you want to make a difference in the lives of others? Stay strong, and do not give up. The way may be difficult at times, but I will help you overcome.

Matthew 5:1-12

My Beloved, you are blessed if you want to follow after Me. You will not be liked by others. You may be mocked or persecuted, because you love Me and want to serve Me. They cannot understand My Ways. They cannot see the right path to follow, because they do not have a heart that wants to serve Me. If you love Me, you will want to keep My Laws and follow in My Ways of loving kindness and tender mercies. If you love Me, you will love others. You will want to give generously to others. I spoke to My Disciples, and they listened to My Voice and followed closely next to me. If you want to be My Disciple, you must hear My Voice and follow next to Me. You will have to wait on Me to guide you. You cannot be impulsive, but you must be patient. You must want to rest in My Presence and watch My Hand move for you and open doors for you. You will want to listen and hear My Instructions for you. You will know that I AM guiding you, because you will see things change around you. You will have peace as you walk forward. You are My Beloved, and I will help you as you walk in the path I have made for you. Do not be concerned about men, because they will always be present. They may not say kind words to you, but they will know you are walking in the Light. They will shun you and turn their eyes away from you, so their sins will not be made apparent by the Light. Are you letting your Light shine brightly? Shine brightly on those around you. Let your Light fill the path before you, so you can always know the path to travel. You are My Beloved, and

I will always be right beside you hand in hand with you.

Matthew 5:13

My Beloved, you are the salt on this earth. You are the one who brings flavor to life. Your touch can heal those around you. Your words can bring strength and encouragement. Your walk is an example to others, so they will change their ways. What happens if you lose your flavor and you do not give anything back to those around you? What happens if you are in sin and do not want to follow after Me? You will be worthless and have no flavor and should be thrown onto the ground. You no longer have any worth unless you are obeying Me and doing what I want you to do. Listen and stand upright, so you can do as I tell you to do. Listen and think about your actions. Do you want to set a bad example for those around you? Do you want to have others look at you and you lead them astray? You will be held responsible for your actions. Do you want to pervert My Words by not speaking the Truth about My Laws? You will have to pay the price for teaching others lies about My Ways. You must be the one who brings life to those around you. You must remain steadfast and not bend. You must forgive those around you who mock you. If you continue to walk uprightly, then I will bless you with overflowing blessing. You will receive more than you could ever imagine. Be bold. Be brave. Be strong!

Matthew 5:14-16

My Beloved, you are the Light of the world. You are to shine brightly for all men to see your loving kindness and tender mercy. You are to glow and allow those who are lost and destined to know Me to come to you and find the answers to all their questions. You are the one who will guide their way and be a light to their path. You are the one who will light the darkness and expose the sins of others. You will see clearly the road ahead and know where to walk and when to turn to the right and the left. If you hide your light, how will the world know how to come to Me? If you hide your light and do not show others My Love and kindness, then how will they be convicted of their sins? Your love and kindness will help them to see how they are selfish and arrogant. They will see their sins, because of your love. You cannot turn your back on the world. You must expose yourself to them, so they can see in the darkness. The darkness is so dark unless you show them My Face-My Love and kindness. If you do not want to help others, then you do not know Me at all. If you do not want to love those around you, then you do not really know who I AM. If you love those around you and want to help others, then you are My Beloved and you will know all that I need you to do to touch the people around you. You will care, and it will be given back to you. If you give, I will bless you in all you do. Do not be afraid. Give and I will give back to you.

Matthew 5:17-20

My Beloved, I did not come to destroy the Law, but to fulfill the Law. I did not come to take away the Law, but to make sure all the Laws and promises came to pass. I did not come to destroy all My Commandments. I came to make a way for you to keep My Commandments. Do you obey all My Commandments today? My Spirit lives within you to prompt you and urge you to keep My Commandments. I came to tell the false teachers and prophets not to make more laws, but to allow My People to keep My Commandments that bring life. I did not want My People to carry a heavy burden upon their shoulders. My People cry out to Me for life and deliverance and freedom from the burden of sin. If My People did not have My Laws, they would not know the way to walk in righteousness. They would be lost in a sea of guilt and pain. My People were given My Laws as guidelines to conduct their life, so they could have strong boundaries that would keep them righteous. My People have suffered for many years not knowing My Laws and how to live their lives. They are lost, but I AM bringing Truth back to them, so they can keep My Sabbaths and feast days and rejoice in My Covenant. My People have been denied the knowledge of My Laws, but now My People are coming into the Truth and the Light is dawning. My People are being set free from the bondage of false teachers and prophets. My People want to know Me, and they cry out to Me. I hear their cries and know that they want to serve Me, but they can't without the Truth. I will bring Truth to their houses, so they can rejoice and know Me and be at one with Me. Rejoice and be glad that I love you so much that I give you Truth and you can see clearly. If only you could see ahead and know that I will restore all My Laws on the Last Day, and My People will rejoice in them.

Matthew 5:21-26

My Beloved, do you hold anger in your heart, but forgive your brother. Are you angry with your brother? Have you forgiven your brother for his sin against you? Go to him quickly and resolve the argument with your brother. You will then be guiltless when you come before Me presenting your petitions. Listen carefully to your bother when he explains himself to you, so you can hear what he is saying and resolve your differences. Do not hate your brother who loves Me and wants to serve Me. If you love Me, then you must be at peace with all men and put aside all your differences. You must do all you can to compromise with your neighbor, so you can live peacefully side by side. You must not stray from what is right, but you must give a little and not want everything your way. A righteous man wants to give to others and does not want to hold onto the things of this world. He does not pile up possessions, but he piles up good deeds that he does for others out of love and compassion for them. If a man wrongs you, go to him and work out your differences without going to a judge and involving the court. If you have tried all you can do to make the man do what is right and he will not listen, then you must involve the court. You must do what is right in My Eyes. If a man wants to sue you, then go to him and try to reason with him and pay him the amount of restitution that is fair. Do not go to court unless you have exhausted all your efforts, because the court is a worldly institution and you do not need to be there. You are my Beloved, and I will judge between you and him. I will press hard on the person until he does what is right. It may take some time, but trust Me to do the right thing. I will bless you for listening to My Voice and obeying My Wisdom. Be strong and be brave and end all arguments as soon as they begin, and you will live at peace and walk in My Ways.

Matthew 5:27-32

My Beloved, I told you not to commit adultery. I told you not to lust after others who are not your spouse. I have told you that even if you look at others with lust in your heart, then it is just as if you have already committed adultery. If you dwell on this person who you lust over, then eventually you will make up reasons within your heart to commit adultery with this person. You can justify in your own mind why you should leave the person you are in marriage covenant with. If this person has left you and does not want to come back or if this person has committed adultery with another and broken your marriage vow, then you have a reason to leave this person. You must stay with the person and work out your difficulties. You must do what is right in My Eyes. You think that you know what is best for you. You think that you know that you should be able to love who you want to love, but I have given you this person for a reason in your life. If this person is not a believer and does not want you to serve Me, then you may leave the person because you are not equally yoked. If this person is not a believer but will allow you to worship Me and serve Me, then stay and be an example to this person and love this person. One day this person may come to Me and serve Me also. Do you allow My Spirit to rule over you? Do you allow lust to control your flesh? As you journey along in this life you will come to crossroads, and you will have to decide which direction you will go. If you choose to be led by My Spirit, then you will be greatly blessed. If you choose to be ruled by your flesh, then you will suffer loss. You must listen to My Voice and follow Me. I am the Way.

Believe in Me.

Matthew 5:33-37

My Beloved, you have heard My Laws that say keep your oaths to Me and not to swear falsely. You are not to say that you will do something knowing that you will not do it. If you say that you are going to do something, then you must do it or I will count it against you. I will have to punish you for your unrighteousness. You are righteous people and you must always tell the truth and walk in honesty. You must let others know that you will be responsible and can be counted on to keep your promises. You must not lie to others, but you must continue to walk in the way of light and shed light on others around you. You may not know what lies before you, so do not say I will do this or that. Just say that if I AM willing that you will do what you say you will do. Do not swear by anything. Your words must be honest and truthful, and then men will believe what you say and not make you swear an oath to them. Can you be trusted? A man who can be trusted is a man who has great wisdom and power. Others will put large tasks in his hands and he will be successful. He will work diligently and not give up until the task is done. When I give you a task to do, then do it diligently and walk in integrity and never go back on your words. Your words are like gold. You must make sure they shine, and you always do what you say you will do. You are My Beloved, so shine brightly for Me.

Matthew 5:38-42

My Beloved, are you holding a grudge against your brother? Love your brother even when he is wrong. If he comes against you and wants you to do something that is not right in your eyes, then do it for him instead of arousing your anger against him and becoming angry in your heart. If you can work together, then work together. If you cannot work together, then do what he wants you to do and do not be absorbed in your anger. If he asks you to do something against My Laws, then he is not your brother. If he asks you to borrow your car or to mow his lawn, and you think that this is unreasonable for you to do, then do it in love and shower him in kindness. He will see your light and be convicted by your righteousness. If he is not your brother, then do not do what he asks you to do. If he has authority over you, then you must submit to him. My People have had enemies ruling over them for many years, and they place burdens on them and make their life unbearable. The Roman soldiers would make My People carry their heavy packs for a mile, but I told My People to do it in love and carry it another mile for Me. The soldiers wanted to make My People angry and upset and mock them and sneer at them, but a righteous attitude cannot be looked down upon. The light of your love will convict others and cause them to repent. Think of these things when you are in a difficult situation and hold my Words in your heart, so you will not sin against your brother or those in authority over you.

Matthew 5:43-48

My Beloved, do you love those around you? If someone hates you, then pray for him. I will hear your prayer and touch his heart and change him. If he sees you continuing to be loving and kind even when he is hateful, this will be a strong example of your loving kindness. You will cast hot burning coals upon his head. He will be convicted by your love, and you will leave a searing mark on him. If you try very hard to be kind to someone and he will not allow you to come near him and be a friend to him, then you have done your best. I will reward you for your efforts and bless you. You must never give up on anyone. Continue to love him and be kind to him, even if he is not a close friend. Sometimes others do not see your worth or value. Sometimes they do not know who you are. You are My Beloved, and there is no one more valued by Me than My Children. You must know that even though men will persecute you, I stand beside you. No man can harm you. No man can come near you. I put a guard around you and keep you close to Me. When in danger, call on My Name and I will save you. I will send angels to comfort you and protect you. I will send angels to you, so you will not be led astray. Think of these words and call on My Name and have faith. I will bring you into only good things.

Matthew 6:1-4

My Beloved, do not tell others about your acts of charity or what you give to others. Keep all your good deeds secret, and then I will reward you in secret and give to you generously. If you tell others about your good deeds and they give you praise, then you have received your reward. I can give you a greater reward than what men can give you. Once you understand My Ways, then you will understand how important it is that I reward you and not men. If you take a man to court, then whatever the judge gives you as punishment is what you will receive. If the judge finds you guilty in a lawsuit and makes you pay a fine, then you have paid for your crime. Whatever the judge makes you pay is what your restitution will be. You have gone to an earthly judge, and he has set the penalty. I will not extract any further penalty. If you do not go to court and the man takes from you, then I will give back to you and the man will have to pay for his crime against you. Has someone wronged you and restitution has not been made? Ask Me to help you, and I will right the wrong against you. I will always balance the scales. Keep on doing good deeds and do not tell anyone about them, and I will bring blessings to your house. I will give to you generously, because you look to me for your praise and not to men.

Matthew 6:5-13

My Beloved, when you pray do you ask for what you need? Do not repeat to Me endless prayers from books, but pray to Me what is on your heart. If you need food, then ask Me for food. If you need shelter, then ask Me for shelter. Whatever you need, then ask Me and I will provide for you. Do not chant or say the same words over and over. Do not meditate on words or phrases. Come to Me boldly like you would a child coming to his father. Ask Me knowing that you will receive. I will help you through any difficult situation. I taught My Disciples how to pray, so they would not pray like the hypocrites. I do not want you to stand before men and pray eloquent prayers that have no meaning to you. Stand up with a humble heart and cry out to Me, and I will hear you. Those who want praise from men for their prayers will not receive an answer to their prayers. If you come before Me in secret and talk with Me through faith, then you will receive what you ask for. Remember that My Timing is perfect and even though you may think that I have delayed, I know what is best for you and will answer your prayer when the time is right for you. Trust Me and I will bless you with whatever you need.

Matthew 6:14-15

My Beloved, have you forgiven those who have tried to harm you? If you forgive those who are mean to you and hurt you, then I will forgive you when you are mean to others and hurt them. If you will forgive others when they take from you, then I will forgive you when you take from others. If you say mean things to others and you want to be forgiven, then go to them and ask them to forgive you. If they forgive you, then I will forgive you. If they do not forgive you, then you have gone to them with a humble heart and the burden will be on them until they forgive you. If others stand in the way of what you want to do, look to Me and I will remove them. If they are standing in your way, because I put them there to stop you from going through this door, then ask Me to show you another route for you to take. If your children do not honor you and you are very bitter against your children, then go to your children and pray with them and make peace. No matter what they have done in the past, you must make peace with them. If they continue not to honor you even after you have gone to them and prayed with them, then turn them over to Me, and I will discipline your children for you. If your mate does not respect you, then go to your mate and pray together and find a way to make peace between you. If your mate continues to disrespect you, then turn him over to Me, and I will discipline him for you. Turn all those who will not forgive you over to Me, and I will deal with their hearts. You continue to forgive, and I will forgive you.

Matthew 6:16-18

My Beloved, do you fast and pray for those you love? When you fast, I want you to go about your day as you usually would and do not tell anyone what you are doing. Do not be a person that boasts about how much you fast, because that will be all the reward that you get. If you fast in secret and pray in secret, then I will see what you do and reward you for fasting and praying for others. When you fast, come to Me with your requests and let them be known to Me. Declare your petitions, and I will hear them. If you fast for others, then wait on Me to move on them and never give up on praying for them. If you continue to fast and pray I will move on their hearts, and they will change before your eyes. If you have prayed for someone for many years, do not give up hope. I hear your prayers and know that you are diligent, and I will reward you. The more you pray for others, the more I will bless you. A humble man prays for others and desires to see them prosper and have success. A proud man only wants for himself to prosper and have success. If you love others, you will want to see them be blessed. If you love others, you will pray for them and fast for them. Do not be boastful or proud, but love those around you, and I will bless you greatly.

Matthew 6:19-24

My Beloved, do you serve Me or the world? You cannot serve Me and the world also. You must serve Me and not be concerned about the world and how much money you can make. I want you to have money to provide for all of your needs. Do not look for a job that pays a certain amount of money or do not look for a way to make lots of money. If you seek Me first, then I will guide you to the right job for you. If you seek Me first, then I will guide you to the business opportunity for you. Some people cannot be given a large amount of money or they would soon forget about Me and My Ways. Some people can be given a large amount of money, and they will not turn from Me. They look at money as a way to bless others. They are not stingy but giving. If you have little money, maybe it is because you cannot handle wealth. If you do not have the money needed to buy your basic needs like food, clothes, shelter, and transportation, then you may be in sin and need to repent. I bless those who are obedient and want to do what is right. If you are not obeying My Laws and not doing as I tell you to do, then turn aside from your sins and do what is right. You will see that I will bless you greatly.

Matthew 6:25-34

My Beloved, are you worried about the things in this world? Trust in Me to care for you. Trust in Me to guide you. Trust in Me to show you the hidden ways, so you can walk hand in hand with Me. Walk close to Me, and I will tell you secret things that others do not know. Did you know that you have a perfect life? Did you know that I have created this life for you and its perfect? Every day is perfect for you, so you can be transformed into My Image. The purpose of this life is to transform you into a glorious creature that all the heavens long to see and know. The purpose of this life is to strip away all the flesh and focus on My Spirit. If you love Me, then you will know that I will only do good things for you. I will give you all that you need. You do not have to worry about food, water, shelter, or clothes. I will provide all of it for you. Do not be afraid, but ask Me when you are lacking and I will give generously to you. Be kind and generous to others, giving from your heart. I will give back to you, so you will never be lacking in anything. If you love Me, you will want to give to My Children. Do not be afraid, but be thankful that you have so much to give. If you draw closer to Me, then you will be able to stand firm and not bend. You will rest in My Presence and dwell in My eternal peace.

Matthew 7:1-5

My Beloved, the way that you judge others is the way that I will judge you. If you judge others harshly, then I will judge you harshly. If you have no mercy on others, then I will have no mercy on you. If you are merciful to others, then I will have mercy on you. If you do not judge others harshly, then I will not judge you harshly. If you look at others and condemn them, then I will condemn you also. If you judge your brother, then you should stop first and judge yourself. Look at your own faults. Is there any man that is perfect? Is there anyone that does not have faults? You are human and all humans are not perfect. If you look at a man and try to find his faults, then you will find some faults. If you look at a man and want to find his strengths, then you will find his strengths. Look at your brother with eyes of love and compassion, so I will look at you with eyes of compassion. Judge yourself and look carefully at how you should change and glorify Me. I want all My Children to shine the Light of My Presence within them. I don't want to see My Children fighting with each other, but I want to see My Children loving each other and supporting each other. I want My Children to live in harmony with each other. I want My Children to have mercy on each other. I want My Children to live in peace without contention being at one with Me and with all their brothers. Let My Spirit of peace reign in the midst of you.

Matthew 7:7-11

My Beloved, do you ask Me for whatever you need? Ask Me, and if you believe that I will give it to you, then you will receive it. Ask Me when you need food. Ask Me when you need encouragement. Ask Me whenever you need healing. Ask Me when you need a friend. Ask Me and I will give it to you, if you believe that I will bring it to you. You must trust Me to bring you what you need. If you ask for something that would not benefit you, then I will not give it to you. If a baby asks for candy and you know this is not good for the baby, then you will not give it to the baby. Instead you will give the baby good food to eat that will nourish his body. The baby wants the candy, but you know that nourishing food will be better for the baby. When I look at you I know what lies ahead and what you will need. I give you what you need to mold you and make you into My Image. If you struggle against Me, then you will suffer loss. If you are content with what comes your way, then you will be greatly blessed. Not all bad things are really bad. I bring situations along your way to test you and perfect you. You must not be afraid, because I will mold you into My Image. I will break you, if you are not humble. If only you wait on Me and trust Me, I will perfect you and make you whole.

Matthew 7:12

My Beloved, do you treat others as you would like them to treat you? Treat others with respect and dignity not placing one person above the others. Do not cater to the rich or despise the poor. Do not give generously to a man that is not deserving of your gifts to obtain favor. Give generously to the poor who need your help knowing that they cannot ever repay you. Treat others in a way that you show them appreciation when they do what is right. Do not side with those with authority, if they are in the wrong. Do not look to obtain power, but look to obtain grace in My Eyes. If you treat all men as equals and each man is worthy of receiving your love and compassion, then you will know what it is like to walk in My Ways. I want you to be My Hands and Feet. I want you to love those around you and let your light shine brightly. I want you to be at peace with all men and live in harmony with them. Do unto Me and not unto them, and then I will bless you. Put love above all things.

Matthew 7:13-14

My Beloved, do you walk in righteousness and not waiver? The road to eternal life is narrow and difficult. Many will give up. They do not want to have a disciplined life that is shaped by My Laws. They want their own way and want to do whatever seems right in their eyes. Those who seek for the path that leads to eternal life seek for My Wisdom and Grace. They seek Me daily for help, so they will know the way to travel. They are at one with Me and live in harmony with those around them. They are not filled with bitterness and anger. They want to bring love and peace to others. If you want to walk down the narrow path, then you must love those around you and be kind in all your ways. If you seek Me first and do what I tell you to do, then you will rejoice and be glad that I have given you so much. Once you come to the end of your journey in this life, you will arrive at My Throne Room and you will rejoice that you see Me face to face at last. In your glorified bodies you will be free from the flesh and will no more desire the fleshy things. This struggle that you constantly battle against the flesh prepares you for the life in My Eternal Kingdom. Your newly shaped bodies will be mighty and magnificent. You will be a joy to all who see you. You will be the image of Me!

Matthew 7:15-23

My Beloved, beware of those who say they are from Me and yet they do not bear good fruit. Are they walking in love, compassion, understanding, and mercy? Do they long to put others' interests before themselves? If they are greedy and stingy and wanting personal power or gain, then they are not from Me. My Disciples do only what I tell them to say and only what I tell them to do. If they do not want to walk in My Ways, then I will tell them to get away from Me. Only My Children who love Me will walk in My Ways of love and compassion. Only My Children will want to obey Me and long to serve Me. Only My Children will be brave and strong in these Last Days and stand firm not doubting Me or lacking faith. Only My Children will endure to the end. Others may cast out demons in My Name and heal the sick in My Name, but they are not from Me. They are deceived, because they do not know Me. They are lost and toss here and there. They have no anchor. I AM the only anchor. I AM the only firm foundation. I AM and I AM. I AM the first and last. I know all things, and I will bring you into Truth and count you as My Own. You will walk hand in hand with Me and inherit My Kingdom.

Matthew 7:24-27

My Beloved, are you standing on a firm foundation? Do not be like the foolish man who built his house on sand and had no foundation. When the storm came it washed his house away. Stand on the Rock that never moves or bends. Stand on Me and My Ways and never depart from them, then you will stand even when the storm comes. You will never be shaken. Even when you hear bad news, you will not be moved. You will have faith in Me and know that I AM faithful to help you and protect you. You will become strong and mighty. You will not whither when others talk to you and condemn you for My Name's sake. No, you will rise up and speak boldly, because you know who I AM. You will not allow anyone to shake your firm foundation. Only when you believe in Me and know who I AM will you be able to overcome. Many men may tell you all sorts of things that are not true. When you hear the Truth, then you will believe it and adhere to it. You will know Truth, when it comes to your door. You will be strengthened by it. You will know that it has come from Me, and you will rejoice in it. I love you so much My Beloved, and I AM beside you in every storm. Just call on My Name and I will reach out My Hand and grab you and pull you up to a stronger place.

I AM faithful until the end.

Matthew 8:1-4

My Beloved, a man came to Me and asked me to heal him, so he could be clean and go back into the Temple to praise Me. I looked at the man and saw that he was sorry for his sins. He wanted to come back into My Presence once again. The man asked Me if it was My Will to heal him to please allow him one more chance. I healed the man and made him clean from all his sins. He had paid for his sins and humbled himself and turned away from his sins. I told him to keep My Laws and go to the priest. The priest would examine him and pronounce him clean, so he could enter the Temple once again. Once he was pronounced clean I told him to bring the sacrifice required as a thanksgiving offering. The man did as I told him to do, and this pleased Me. The man was surrounded by people asking him questions about how this happened. The man told the priests about what I had done for him. They were fearful of who I AM. They could not receive Me as the Messiah. They wanted to rule over My People and not have to be ruled by Me. They were greedy sinful men who loved power and fame. They wanted their own way and refused to see the Light in front of their eyes. Do you see the Light in front of your eyes? Can you see the miracles happening around you? What is keeping you from following Me?

Matthew 8:5-13

My Beloved, I came to heal the sick and raise the dead and minister to those who were lost. I came to the sick and hurting to allow them to see the Light and know who I AM. I came to those who wanted to know the Truth, and many received Me. Even some of the ones who were against My People came to Me and could see the Truth. One of the Roman officers came to Me to heal his orderly who was paralyzed and suffering. The officer could not bear to see his orderly suffer any more. Out of desperation he sought for a way for him to be cured. He came to Me and heard My Words, and he saw how I healed others. He knew that I came to the Jews and not to his people, but he came to Me humbly and asked for Me to have mercy on his orderly. He came believing in Me. He asked Me to help him knowing that I had the power to heal, and I said that I would heal his orderly. The officer knew he was not worthy of My Help, so he told Me not to come to his house, but just to send someone to touch his orderly and he would be whole. I sent My Angel to his orderly to touch him and he was whole. The officer could see passed the natural into the supernatural and knew I had others who helped Me. He was blessed that His eyes were open. I blessed his family after him, and they all served Me. Trust in Me and I will open your eyes to My Ways. I will give you the faith to believe, so you can also receive the blessings being poured out from My Hand. Do you trust Me to heal you? Do you trust Me to care for you?

Do you really trust Me with all your heart?

Matthew 8:14-22

My Beloved, are you following Me and not looking back at the past? I wanted My People not to go back to their homes and become involved in their old man-made traditions or pagan traditions. I wanted them to follow Me and not look back. I wanted them to see My Face and not the face of men. I wanted them not to think about those who try to pull them back into the world. You must love them and care for them, but not to the point of giving into the enemy and going back to your old ways. I came to heal the sick and raise the dead. Only a man that serves Me with his whole heart can follow in My Ways and do what I did. He cannot be afraid of men, but he must fear only Me and know who I AM and walk in My Ways. If you love Me, you will serve Me. If you love Me, you will want to do what I did. You will seek Me and find Me and long to be like Me. You will see what I see. You will speak what I speak. You will perform acts of kindness as I did. You have My Authority, so call on My Name and if the person is worthy of receiving healing, then I will heal him. I will have mercy on him and raise him up. Be wise when you call on My Name to heal someone. Not all men will be healed. They must repent from their sins and turn towards Me, and then I will heal them.

Matthew 8:23-27

My Beloved, I tried to teach My Disciples to trust Me during the short time that I was with them. They could see only in the natural in the beginning, but soon they began to trust Me and could see into the spiritual realm. They were just children and had to be taught. They had been corrupted by man-made doctrine and did not see clearly. Are you corrupted by man-made doctrine? Do you know My Laws and My Ways? My People have been deceived, and think that they must keep the holidays that man has created. They do not even know My Feast Days or My Timetable. They are blinded and only My Light can open their eyes. They are walking around blindly, and they feel that they know My Ways. They cannot see, because the darkness is so great. They cannot see, because the spirit of religion is so heavy upon them. They are in great darkness, and it will take a great Light to open their eyes. I will send an outpouring of My Spirit, and they will be shaken and see at last. They will know who I AM, and they will cry out in anguish that they have been lost and wandering for all long. They are My Beloved, so I will not leave them in darkness forever. Soon they will see and cling to Me. They will rejoice in the Truth that has come their way. Rejoice that I have given you so much.

Matthew 8:28-34

My Beloved, as I walked on this earth I released many from the bondage of the evil one. The evil one sends his messengers to inhabit men and terrorize them and overtake them. They rule over them until they have no will of their own. The soul of the person is hidden by the strength of the demon within him. A person can fight against the demon and eventually be set free, if he does not give into his ways. Some men are too weak to fight against them, but fall into their lies and deception. Demons tell men lies so they will sin against others and themselves. Demons like to get men to harm themselves and harm others. There are many demons. As one demon takes hold of a man, then others come to join him. Demons want a host to live in. I came to two men consumed by demons. The demons terrorized those who came near them. The men lived in a cave like animals and anyone who came near them they hurt. The whole area knew not to ever come near these men. The demons knew Me, because I had cast them into exile. The demons were afraid I would send them to the abyss, so they asked Me if they could go into the pigs. I allowed them to flee into the pigs. The pigs went crazy and ran off the cliff. The loss was extensive to the owner, because he lost his whole herd of pigs. The people in the area asked Me to leave, because they did not know who I AM. They thought I had demonic powers. They did not understand, but the men who I set free did understand My Powers and who I AM. Do you know who I AM? Will you trust Me to set you free from demonic forces? Will you trust Me to deliver you from the evil one? Ask Me in My Name, and I will deliver you from all darkness.

Matthew 9:1-8

My Beloved, I walked upon this earth among My People, but My People could not see who I AM. Some of the people had trust in Me and believed in Me. Some of them brought Me a man who was paralyzed. I looked upon them and saw their trust in Me and healed the man. I told him that his sins were forgiven. The sins of his parents were the cause of him being paralyzed. The teachers of the Law were upset with Me, because I said that his sins were forgiven. They thought I was blaspheming, because they did not know who I AM. I told them that I had authority given to Me by the Eternal One, but they could not comprehend what I was saying. I told the man to get up and go home. The man listened to Me and went home rejoicing. All the people who saw this miracle praised Me and blessed My Name. The teachers of the Law condemned Me, because they thought I was walking in deception and wanting to lead the people astray. They could not see the Truth, because they were blinded by the traditions of men. Can you see the Truth? Do you know who I AM? Do you want to really know Me? Put aside the traditions of men and search My Scriptures for the Truth. Ask Me to guide you, and I will.

Matthew 9:9-13

My Beloved, I came to heal the sick and teach the Truth to those who were deceived. I came to those in pain and suffering. I came to those who needed to see clearly and wanted to follow Me. When I came to Matthew he immediately stopped what he was doing and followed Me. He saw a great Light, and he knew what he saw was good. He could see the Truth in Me, and he wanted to know Me. I knew before I ever asked him to be My Disciple that he would follow Me. He was tired of his life as a tax collector. He wanted a better life. These are the people that I called, because they wanted a different life. They wanted to know the Truth and walk in it. When I sat at the Philistine's house the tax collectors and other sinners wanted to sit around Me and hear My Words. The religious leaders scorned Me and wanted to know why I sat with these people. I told them that I came to help those who needed help. Those who are sinners need to learn to walk in the Way. Are you helping those in sin? Do not shun them, but love them. Have compassion on them, and one day they will see the Light inside of you. If they are searching, they will come to you and want you to help them find the Way. You will be there to help them and support them. Your love and compassion will overcome the things of the world. You will be able to be a beacon to them in a dark world. They will see your Light and come to you searching. They will find what they are looking for. Hold fast and do not waiver. I will send to you those who need you in the hour that they need you. Hold firm!

Matthew 9:14-17

My Beloved, John's disciples were watching Me and wondering what My Mission would be. John had told them that I was the One that they had been looking for. John's disciples watched what I did and could not understand why I asked My Disciples to fast. This was unheard of during this time and place. While I was with My Disciples they would rejoice that I was with them. They could fast after I was gone. I AM the Bridegroom, and I AM waiting for My Bride. Are you preparing to be My Bride? Are you allowing Me to perfect you into My Image, so you can be in harmony with Me? We will be married at the marriage supper, and you will be in covenant with Me forever. You will be able to know Me intimately like a groom knows his bride. No one else can experience this but you. You are My Beloved. I created you to become one with Me and be transformed into My Image. You will be given My Authority and know who I AM. All will acknowledge you are the Chosen Ones. You will stand beside Me and stand firm. You will not turn aside from Me, but you will always face Me and long to hear My Voice. You will love Me with all your heart, and there will be no other more important to Me than you. When I was with My Disciples, I was the New Voice-the new way. I brought Truth back to My People. You can't take an old wine skin filled with the traditions of men and put a part of Me in it. No, you must create a new wine skin (a new creature) and fill it with My Spirit. I created you brand new when you accepted Me as your Master-your King-your Father-your Teacher. I created you new, and I filled you with new wine. You became a new creature that I can rejoice in. Rejoice and be glad that I recreated you, and gave you My Love and compassion to share with others around you. Rejoice and be glad that I love you so much.

Matthew 9:18-19, 23-26

My Beloved, an official came to me and asked Me to come heal his daughter, because she had died. He had heard of Me raising the dead, and He trusted in Me to heal her. I came to his house and already the mourners were there. They were ready to prepare her for burial. The man would not allow anyone to touch her until I had come to see her. I told everyone to leave the house. I took the girl at the hand and breathed life into her. She opened her eyes and saw My Face and she smiled. The man saw his daughter come to life again, and he wept with tears of joy. The man worshipped Me and praised Me proclaiming Me as his Master. He ran outside and told every one about the miracle, and the news spread throughout the region. The people began to flock to see Me knowing that I was a great healer. I healed the body, but I also healed the soul and filled the person with new life. I AM the beginning of a new life in you. You can look all around you, but you will not find anyone who loves you and wants to bless you more than Me. Do you see My Blessings all around you? My Blessing is tailored for you, so it fits you well. My blessing will shape you into My Image and prepare you for the coming days. Dark days are coming! Rejoice that I love you, and My Angels are around you. Rejoice that My Hand covers you and protects you. Happy are those who love Me and trust Me. Great will be their reward. Come to Me, My Beloved, and I will heal you and restore you. The wounds from the past will be healed, and you will be strong and mighty once again. Do not trust in men, but trust in the hands that care for you. Trust only in Me.

Matthew 9:20-22

My Beloved, I walked on this earth and many saw Me and loved Me and wanted to cling to Me. There was a lady who had a hemorrhage that she struggled with for twelve years. She had spent all she had trying to be healed. She was constantly unclean, so she could not go into the Temple into My Presence. She was miserable and cried out to Me. When she saw Me she knew that I would heal her. She felt the presence of My Love and compassion. She drew close to Me and did not want to bother Me. She thought that if she could touch My Robe-the hem-the end-the Tzitzit-that she would be healed. As soon as she touched Me I felt her trust, and healing flowed out to her. I turned to look at her and she was afraid. I told her that she was healed, because she had faith to believe. She had courage to come near Me and touch Me. Are you brave enough to come near to Me to touch Me? Do you have enough faith in Me to believe that I can help you? Are you sick? Come to Me and believe in Me. Are you lacking and without? Come to Me and I will supply for you. Are you bitter, angry, resentful, and unforgiving? Come to Me and I will help you forgive. I will bring you peace. Are you broken-hearted? Come to Me, and I will heal your wounds from the past. I will help you focus on the future and not look to the past. I will help you be able to leave your past behind and your wounds will heal. Whatever you need from Me I will give it to you, if you will call on Me and trust Me to do it. I do not want you to come to Me whining and complaining. I want you to come to Me with courage and trust and believe in Me. You are My Beloved. Would I withhold anything that you needed from Me? If you do not receive what you asked for, then you do not need it. It is not good for you, and I will provide better. I will show you a different way to walk, because I love you.

Matthew 9:27-31

My Beloved, as I walked among My People, two blind men came to Me. They followed Me into the house asking Me to heal them. I asked them if they believed that I could heal them, and they confirmed with their mouth that they believed that I could heal them. I saw their faith in Me. I saw that they were desperate, and they saw hope in Me. They had heard about the other healings that I had performed, and they rushed to Me so I could also heal them. They wanted My healing touch, and they got more than that. They saw their Creator face to face. They did not know that their Creator was restoring what he had created. They were so filled with joy that they went around the whole area praising My Name and giving thanks to Me. They glorified Me to those around them. They were blind and now they could see. They were blind and handicapped, but now they would work and be prosperous. Now they would not be scorned by society, but they would have honor. Their family rejoiced with them. They all came to Me rejoicing and thankful. They all called on My Name as their Messiah. They shared the Good News with all they saw, and I counted it as righteousness. I told them not to tell anyone, but their joy was too full to hold it back. Sometimes your joy is too full that you want to share with others what I have done for you. Have you confessed your sins to Me and received My Spirit? If you have, then you have so much to rejoice over. If you are My Child, then you should rejoice every day and be glad that I have given you so much. You should have no fear, but you should have complete trust in Me that I will care for you and direct your path. I love you so much. Cling to Me, and I will set you free from the burdens of this world. You will see them all as blessings to change you into My Image. You will see with eyes of wisdom. You will rejoice all your days.

Matthew 9:32-34

My Beloved, a man came to Me who could not speak. He had been bound by the evil one since birth with a demon who would not allow him to speak. He came to Me desiring to be set free. He had heard about My Miracles, and he had hope in Me. He trusted Me to overcome the ruler of this earth and set him free. When he came to Me he looked into My Eyes, and he saw freedom. He felt the demon trying to hold onto his home that he had for so many years, but his trust in Me expelled the demon. I told the demon to leave, and the man was set free. He had peace at last, and he was free to speak the words he had longed to speak for so many years. The people were amazed that the man could speak. They had known this man for years and knew he could not speak. Great was their rejoicing! Even as the people rejoiced the Pharisees said that I was ruler over the dark ones. They saw how I released him from a demon. They did not want to accept Me as the Messiah. They wanted to lessen Me in front of the people, so I would have no value to them. They were blinded by the evil one, and they never could see. They did not want a Messiah to come unless he came to overthrow their enemies. They did not want Me to say love your enemies, and be kind to those who persecute you. They wanted someone different. Do you want someone different? Do you want a god who only gives gifts that you want? Do you recognize Me for who I AM? I AM your Creator and I AM creating a new creature within you, so you can rule with Me eternally in My Kingdom of Light. Rejoice that I have chosen you, and accept what I AM doing inside of you. I will test you and form you into My Image, because I love you. Rejoice and be glad that I AM making you stronger and wiser everyday by the troubles that you endure. Accept what I AM doing inside of you. Be brave and strong and courageous. I AM always beside you.

Matthew 9:35-38

My Beloved, I walked among My People. I healed them and I washed them clean by My Presence. I touched My People, and they knew they had been touched. My Disciples watched Me as I walked among My People. They saw how I had compassion on My People even in their sins. They saw Me as I healed them and restored them to a life without pain and suffering. They watched as I taught My People My Words. They watched as I gave them insight into My Words. I taught the scriptures, and they were amazed that I had so much wisdom. They did not know that I AM the Eternal One wrapped in flesh. They did not know that I AM the only One that can bring them new life. I AM the only One that can bring them salvation. As I walked among them I could see that they were troubled and lacking a leader to guide them. Their religious leaders were corrupt and blinded. They had lost sight of the Way to righteousness. They had lost the path that leads to Me. They had made so many new laws for My People to carry that they were burdened down and grievous. I wanted to release My People from that burden. I wanted to set them free to be led by My Spirit. If you love Me, you will seek after Me and find Me. I will show you the narrow way that leads to life. I will help you overcome the evil one. I will help you walk in My Presence. I will help you see the Lighted way. Rejoice that I have given you so much. Do you know the way to walk? Do you need Me to guide you? Ask Me to help you, and I will open your eyes. I AM in your midst.

Matthew 10:1-15

My Beloved, I chose My Disciples. I chose those who would want to serve Me. I looked at their hearts and saw how they received Me. I chose those who would be faithful. I chose those who would want to give up everything for Me and do My Will. I told them to go to the lost sheep from the tribes of Israel. These are the ones who are My Children. They are the ones who are chosen, but they were living in exile and did not know the Truth. When My Disciples came to a city they spoke the Truth and those who were My Children received the Truth and accepted Me as their Messiah and Savior. They accepted Me and wanted to walk in My Ways. I told My Disciples to heal the sick and drive out demons and set My People free from the bondage of the evil one. I told them not to take any provisions with them, because My People would take care of them. They would provide all that they needed. If they came to a town that rejected them, then they would curse the town and judgment would come upon it. This town rejected the ones I sent to tell them about Me. They rejected Me and judgment came to them. If they stayed in a house with one of My Children, then they must leave a blessing of peace on the house. My Presence would abide with them, and I would bless them greatly. My Disciples knew that I was with them, because wherever they went I protected them and kept them safe. I provided food and shelter for them. They were never alone. I sent My Angels with them to prepare the way before them. I AM always with you. I guard and protect you. I give you My Peace. Do you want to be My Disciple and follow after Me doing My Will? If you are My Disciple, you will receive great rewards in My Kingdom. You will be greatly blessed by My Hand. You will see My Face and know Me in the Kingdom to come, because you are My Beloved.

Matthew 10:16-20

My Beloved, are you afraid of the future? Do not be afraid of anything, because I AM with you always. Do not be afraid, but be bold and brave and courageous. I AM always there to give you advice and direction. I will send My Angels to help you and fight for you. I AM always near and know what you need when you need it. If you will call on My Name, then I AM beside you to guide you. There will be people that hate you because you love Me. Rejoice that they can see the Light inside of you, and you are a testimony to them. Great will be your rewards. If you have to stand before government officials to state your case, know that I will speak through you. You will not have to be concerned about what you will say. I will put you before them as a witness for Me. Even if they rule against you, you have been obedient, and I will deliver you from their oppression. If you will hear My Voice when I tell you to leave a certain place, then you will be able to flee to a safe place. Eventually the whole world will be against you, and the only safe place will be on My Land. There I can keep you safe. You will be surrounded by armies, and I will destroy them all by the breath of My Mouth. I will return to you and live among you. You will see My Face and know Me. You will be righteous before Me, because I will be your Teacher. I will show you My Ways and how to walk in My Laws and be at one with Me in peace and harmony. If you are young and do not understand My Ways, call on My Name to teach you. I will teach you by My Spirit. I will give you great wisdom and allow you to see into the future. If you are old, it is not too late to learn from Me. I will show you great things in My Words. You will rejoice that I love you so much and have brought Truth to your house.

Matthew 10:21-23

My Beloved, do you have family members who are against you, because you follow Me? There will be conflict in the midst of families. Those who hate Me will rise up against My Beloved Ones. They will fight against My Chosen Ones. They will want to kill all of them. I will put My Hand up to shield them, and they will not be harmed. If you continue doing what is right in My Eyes even if others do not like what you do, I will protect you and keep you safe. I will shelter you. I will show you the way. I will be your guide through difficult situations. You will be persecuted by many, because you love Me and want to serve Me. If you are persecuted in your town, then flee to another town. I will protect you and guide you along your path. If I call you to Israel, My Land, then you will be safe there. You can go from town to town in My Land during the troubled days ahead, but I will protect you in each of those towns. People may mock you and ridicule you, but remain strong. They are mocking and ridiculing Me not you. They hate Me. They hate the Light. They hate the Truth, because it exposes their sins and shows them the darkness inside of them. They do not want to be exposed, but they want to go their own way and have no one interrupt them. They think they are gods and can do as they please. They are their own gods, but I will fight against these false gods and have victory over them and anyone who serves them. You must serve only Me, and then you will have peace and not live in darkness. You will be encompassed with a great Light, so you will see all around you clearly. You will have no fear, because you know that I AM with you and no harm can come to you. I AM always beside you guarding you and protecting you. I AM faithful.

Matthew 10:24-27

My Beloved, are you afraid of what men will say about you? I will expose all the sins of men. Do not be afraid when men accuse you of things that are not true. I will bring Truth to the surface, and it will expose those who come against you. If they say that you are from the evil one because your beliefs are different from the traditions of men, then be brave and strong and know that I will bless you for your continued walk in righteousness. Do not be afraid when men look down at you and say you are less than they are. They do not know your value. Only I know your value, and I will guard over you as a precious jewel. Men are blinded unless they walk in the path that leads to the Light. If a man falsely accuses you, then put the offense in My Hands. I will bring to light the truth and expose the person who has falsely accused you. If you are governed by men who want to harm you because of how you believe, then leave that place quickly. I will take you to a new place where you can live in peace. There are places all over the world where I can keep you safe. You do not have to live under the rule of a man who hates you. Ask Me to take you to a new place, and I will hear your prayers and show you another place to live. If men want to harm you, really they only want to harm Me. They want to destroy the Light within you, so they cannot see their sins. They want to hide in the dark, but I will expose them no matter where they are. If you cling to men, you will stumble and fall. If you cling to Me, I will bless you and keep you close to Me. I will give you only good things and protect you wherever you go. Just trust in Me to show you the way.

Matthew 10:28-33

My Beloved, are you afraid of men? Do not be fearful of men, but fear Me who has the power to throw you in the Lake of Fire and consume your body and soul. I AM the life giver. I give life, and I take it away. I will give eternal life to My Children who prove themselves worthy to enter My Kingdom of Light. My Children serve only Me, and they confess My Name and tell others who they serve. They are Light to many people of their loving kindness. They are at one with Me and want only to serve Me all their days no matter what men may say about them. If authorities or rulers try to come against you, then call on My Name and I will deliver you from them. Listen to My Voice, and I will guide you. If you choose to stay where you are and not listen to My Voice, then you will have to endure hardships. If you are willing to give up anything for Me and leave when I say leave, then you will find a safe haven. Those who do not trust Me will be lost in exile among those who hate you. If you are My Servant and you hear your Master calling you out of bondage, then pack up your things and leave. You will be called when times are good to leave. After the days become difficult and you have ignored My Call, then you will suffer with your family. You must listen to Me in good times and bad times. You must confess your love for Me to all men. I will deliver you from evil men, and I will hold you in My Arms of Love. If you fear Me and follow Me, then your load will be light and your journey will not be difficult. Trust in Me, and I will keep you safe.

Matthew 10:34-42

My Beloved, do you love Me more than anyone else? If you love Me more than anyone else, then you are worthy of entering My Kingdom. If you love your mother or father more than Me and you follow after their traditions to honor them instead of honoring Me, then you are not worthy of entering My Kingdom. If you love your sons and daughters more than Me and do what they want you to do instead of following after Me and obeying My Laws, then you are not worthy of entering My Kingdom. You must love Me with all your heart and be obedient to all My Laws, and then you will be counted worthy of bearing My Name and reigning with Me and becoming joint heirs with Me. You will be at one with Me, and I can bless you. Many will cling to their family and not cling to Me. Many will cling to the traditions of men and not cling to Me. They will want the respect and praise of men and not be concerned about Me and My Ways. If you really love Me, you will not be concerned about men but about Me. I have already said that people in your own household will turn against you and turn you into the authorities. When the authorities put pressure on them to turn in those who rebel against the government, then they will turn you in as a rebel. They will think that they are doing you a favor, but they will take you to your death. They will never see you again. You must decide who you will serve and follow. If you are listening to My Call, you will hear My Voice when I call you out of Babylon. I will say, "Come" and you will come to Me. Rejoice that you hear My Voice and are obedient, so I can deliver you from this dark place and take you to another place of Light. Rejoice that I love you so much.

Matthew 11:1-19

My Beloved, John came to point My People in the right direction to tell them that I was on My Way. John came as a prophet and he lived in the desert. He was a simple man and he loved Me greatly. I came robed in garments of higher quality. I sat among the tax collectors and sinners, and I told them the Good News. They judged John harshly, and said he had a demon. They judged Me harshly and said I was king of the demons. They hated us, because we were filled with Light and wanted only to speak Truth. John was the one who was prophesized to come before Me. John was given to men by Me to prepare them for Me. I came to receive the men who John had turned towards Me. I took them by the hand and took them out of the world and allowed them to know who I AM. Do you want to follow Me? You must walk away from the world and into the Light. Men did not respect John or Me. They wanted to do what they wanted to do and not respect things that come from Me. Lift your eyes up and see clearly what I have to say to you. Walk in My Ways and be strong. Man will try to come against you like they came against John and Me. They killed us both, because they hated the Truth we spoke. I rose from the dead and came back to deliver you from the evil one and make you free. I came to show you a better way to walk in Me. You do not have to be burdened down by the things of the world. Accept what I have given you and be glad that you have only what you need. You will be content and happy when you walk simply and humbly before Me. Rejoice that I show you Truth, and you can see clearly the path ahead. If you love Me, you will want to follow Me. You will seek Me diligently and hear My Voice and walk in My Ways. Keep your eyes on Me, and I will give you all you need to walk in Me. I will supply all you need and develop you into a glorious creature. John could not even imagine what I had in store for him in the Kingdom of Light. You will be a changed creature filled with My Glory. Rejoice that I love you so much.

Matthew 11:20-26

My Beloved, I did miracles everywhere I went as I walked among My People. I saw the hearts that believed in Me and trusted Me. I reached out and touched them and made them whole. Many people mocked Me and said that I did miracles because I was the king of the demons. Many rejected Me for who I AM. I cursed the towns that rejected Me. When their enemies came in, the towns were destroyed along with all their inhabitants. These towns were not restored, just like Sodom and Gomorrah have not been restored. I walked among them, and they rejected Me and all the good things that I did for their people. There were some towns who received Me, and I blessed them. I made a way out for the people of the town when their enemies came in and took over. I told them in advance, and they were able to leave the area. I sent a messenger to them to instruct them when to leave and where to go. Do you think that I will leave you all alone? I will send messages to you to guide you. If you hear My Voice, then I talk to you all day long. You must find Me in the stillness. You must find Me in the secret places. You must know who I AM. I can do all things. I can open any door. I will bless you greatly. If you come to Me and abide in Me and love Me, then I will make a clear path for you and you will be able to see ahead. I will take you by the hand and help you stay on the path. I will show you My Face shining brightly on you. You will feel My Presence all day. You will know My Presence and walk in it. You will know when you are out of My Presence and off the path, so you can get back on the path quickly. I will guard and protect you, because I love you so deeply.

Matthew 11:27-30

My Beloved, are you struggling with your life? Are you burdened with sorrow? Come to Me, and I will bring you comfort and rest. I will allow you to rest on My Bosom, and I will hold you. I will comfort you in My Arms of Love. I will lift the sorrow from you. You will see clearly the days ahead and how I will bless you. If you are grieving over a loved one, then you must honor him with your grief. He will rest in My Arms until you see him again at the Day of Judgment. Your loved ones will be judged on that day. If they are righteous and wanted to walk in My Ways, then they will enter My Kingdom of Heaven and walk with Me for eternity. If they are not righteous and wanted to go their own way, then they will be thrown into the Lake of Fire and will be no more. They were tested and found not faithful while they were on this earth. They were tested and tried, and they were found lacking. If you are burdened with sin, then repent and walk in My Ways. My burden is light and easy. You can keep My Laws. I have not made them difficult to keep. Man has added to My Laws, and now they are a heavy yoke. Keep only the Laws given to Moses, and do not add to them or take from them. Do as they say to do. They are simple and easy to keep. If you are seeking Me, you will find ways to please Me, and I will show you how to walk in My Ways. I will show you the way to walk hand in hand with Me. Come to Me, those who cannot rest. Come to Me if you are making difficult decisions. I will give you wisdom for each decision you have to make. Come to Me if you cannot sleep or your work is heavy and you have too much responsibility. I will show you how to decrease your work load, so it is easier to manage. Come to Me and let us talk together and I will show you great things.

Matthew 12:1-8

My Beloved, do you want to keep the Sabbath and not work? What should you do when your brother needs your help on the Sabbath? You must love your brother, and help him when he needs you. The greatest commandment is to love your brother. This commandment is more important than all the other commandments. If you are hungry on Sabbath, then eat. If you are sick on Sabbath, then go to a doctor. Do not condemn your brother, because he violates the Sabbath. I want you to rest and not work. I want you to commune with Me. Sometimes there will be situations that arise that are out of the ordinary, and you must take care of them. If you need to help someone that needs you, then you must help them. I will bless you, because you helped them when they needed you. If someone wants you to go to a restaurant or go shopping on My Sabbath Day for your own pleasure, then I count it against you if you violate My Sabbath Day. You did not need to help your brother go to a restaurant or shop. You must think about what is important, and call upon my Name and ask for My Wisdom and advice. I will help you make the right choice, because I love you so much. I will show you the hidden way. I would rather you have compassion than bring Me sacrifices. If you have compassion on the poor and your brother, then you are giving more than the required sacrifice. You are giving your life to others, and I will bless you greatly.

Matthew 12:9-15

My Beloved, I walked among My People, and many of them wanted to accuse Me of something. They wanted to cast blame on Me. They wanted Me to leave and go far away from them. They were blind without a shepherd. They were blind following the blind. They had the Truth in the midst of them, and they could not see the Truth because the darkness was so great in them. The Light walked among them, and they shunned the Light and wanted Me to be far away from them. I healed a man whose hand had shriveled due to lack of use. He could no longer use it. He yearned to be healed. He wanted to be restored. He called out to Me to help him, and I had compassion on him and I restored him. The religious leaders questioned what I did. "Should you heal on the Sabbath? Isn't that work?" they cried. If you do good things on Sabbath to help someone, then I will bless you. If you help the sick or feed the poor, then I will bless you. You must not seek your own pleasure on the Sabbath, and do what you want to do to benefit yourself. If you will do good things to benefit others, then I will bless you greatly. Do not become bound up in laws, but remember the greatest of My Commandments is to love others. If you will love others, then I will bless you greatly. You have learned My Ways when you can walk in compassion and have mercy on others. It will not be easy to always walk in love. People will offend you, and you will be disgusted by their sins. Look at the heart and allow My Love to flow through you. I will allow you to be a vessel poured out – a vessel to bring healing and encouragement. Are you reaching out your hands to others? If you are, then I will reach My Hand out to you.

Matthew 12:16-21

My Beloved, I came to walk among My People. I had compassion for them and healed them of all their diseases. I delivered them from their demons. I restored their souls. I allowed them to see Truth, and the Light walked among them. They were not aware of who I AM. I was clothed in flesh, but I knew them. I touched those who wanted to follow Me. I had many followers who walked with Me. I cared for all of them and taught them, and then I sent them out to tell others about Me. I gave so much to them. I gave them strength and understanding into My Words. I gave them the insight to understand who I AM. I walked alongside them even when others tried to harm them. I helped them at every turn in the road. I told those who I touched and healed and restored not to tell anyone of what I had done for them. I wanted them to be quiet, but they could not keep quiet. They wanted to tell everyone. They wanted to lift up My Name, so everyone could know about Me and find Me and draw close to Me. Have you found Me? Are you walking in My Ways? Even today I heal My People and restore My People. I make all broken things new. I can heal you and restore you. I can make you like new. When you walk hand in hand with Me, I touch you and soften you and make you a new creature. I will form you into My Image. I will make you whole once again just like I created you in the beginning. Hold onto Me, and I will set you free from the things of the world.

Matthew 12:30-32

My Beloved, do you stand up for Me? If you are not for Me, then you are against Me. If you are not seeking after righteousness, then you are seeking after the things of the world. If you are not seeking to obey My Laws and walk in My Ways, then you are seeking to disobey Me and not follow My Ways. If you are seeking after the traditions of men, then you are not seeking after Me and My Words. If you are seeking to be rich, famous, or have power over others, then you are seeking after the wrong god. I want you to be loving, kind, tenderhearted, and forgiving. I want you to be humble and ready to obey and ready to lay down your life for the sake of another. The greatest commandment is to love others. If you do not love others, then you do not love Me. If you reject Me and My Son, you cannot be forgiven. If you turn and repent from your sins, you can be forgiven. If you reject My Spirit dwelling within you, then you reject Me and My Salvation. There is no repentance for this. You must receive My Spirit within you and be led by My Spirit and commune with My Spirit, or you will not be forgiven. You will be lost and lacking. You will not be a part of Me. You will stand before Me on Judgment Day, and I will find you guilty of rejecting Me. I will not have mercy on you. I will send you to the Lake of Fire, and you will be no more. You will not stand in My Presence anymore. There will be no more time for you to repent. You have missed your opportunity at that point to serve Me here on this earth. You must choose today who you will serve. If you choose to serve Me with all your heart, then you will live with Me eternally. You will walk hand in hand with Me as My Beloved.

Matthew 12:33-37

My Beloved, are you watching carefully over the words you speak? You are judged by the words you speak. You will stand before Me on Judgment Day and tell Me why you were mean and harsh. You will give account of every evil word that you said to others. You will be judged by your heart. If your heart is good, then you will have good fruits-kindness, joy, peace, and love for others. If your heart is not good, then you will produce bad fruit-jealousy, resentment, bitterness, and hatred for others. You will be judged by how you treat others. If you love others, you will be blessed. If you are mean, angry, bitter towards others, you will suffer loss. You will have to pay the penalty for hurting others. If you want to be like Me and serve Me, then you must love those around you. No one is perfect. Expect people to make mistakes. They will not make the right choices sometimes. They will be influenced by others to do evil. They will learn from their mistakes and change. If they continue to walk in their old ways and not repent, then you will know that they have rejected Me and My Ways. I have mercy on people for a while, but then I punish them. They will feel my Hand upon them to correct them. If they listen, then they will not suffer loss, but they will be blessed. If they do not listen, they will have to suffer under My Hand of corrections until they repent and do what is right. Watch carefully over the words you speak. Guard your tongue well. You will have to enter the narrow gate. Only those who desire to walk in righteousness will enter My Kingdom of Heaven. Only those who want to serve Me will enter and sit beside Me in My Kingdom. You must be found worthy to enter My Kingdom, so guard over yourself and I will help you overcome.

Matthew 12:38-42

My Beloved, I came and walked among My People, but the religious leaders came to Me wanting Me to prove Myself to the people by showing a miraculous sign. I was not going to prove Myself to these religious leaders. Whatever I presented to them, they would deny and mock Me. The only sign they would have is what the prophet Jonah gave to My People as a sign. Jonah in his disobedience spent three days and three nights in the belly of a whale and was brought back to life, so he could go preach to the wicked city of Nineveh. I through My Obedience laid down My Life and spent three days and three nights in the belly of the earth. I arose and brought all the captives back to My Bosom. Those who have ears to hear, then listen to My Words. I laid down My Life for you. I shed My Blood for you. I took on your sin, so you could live with Me in My Kingdom for eternity. I wanted you to be at one with Me forever. You are my beloved, and I will care for you all the days you live on this earth. I know that the sins of those around you grieve you. I know your heart is heavy. I know you desire to leave this place and return to the Land that I have promised to give you. It will be soon!! Be strong and brave, and do not grow weary in doing what is right. Does your flesh feel heavy and difficult to bear? I will give you the ability to overcome the flesh and use self-control. You will tell your flesh what to do. You will not be governed by the flesh. You will hold onto Me and want only to please Me. You will be full of My Spirit and be moved by My Spirit. You will not ask for a sign, but you will ask for Me to guide you. I will bring you sign markers along the way to let you know you are on the right path. I will guide you and keep you safe always.

Matthew 12:43-45

My Beloved, the evil one roams the earth to see who he can deceive. He sends all those who serve him to find bodies that they can inhabit and rule to do evil. Many on this planet are completely ruled by the evil ones. These servants are ruthless. They are under a false illusion that has been generated by the evil one. They think that if they can prove that My Children are not worthy to enter My Kingdom that they will be restored to My Kingdom. This is a lie. I chose My People knowing that they would be made mighty by living in the flesh. I knew the seed of righteousness would grow and prosper within them, and they would be filled with love and compassion for others. They would turn from evil and want to do good things. I chose My Children knowing that they would bring Me great joy and happiness due to the life of obedience that they lived. They praise Me with their mouths, and their hearts are bent towards Me. They desire only to do what is right. They listen to My Voice, and they want to serve Me and please Me. The evil ones want to destroy, and My Children want to build up. The evil ones want to deceive and lie and My Children want to restore the Truth and set those who are bound in darkness free from the lies they have been told. My Children will rule this world, and the evil one hates the thought of this. He wants to rule the world and all worlds, but his time is short and he will be cast into the Lake of Fire. He will be judged and found unworthy to enter My Kingdom. My Children will be judged and found worthy to enter My Kingdom of Light. Do you love Me and want to serve only Me? If you love only Me, you will be able to stand in My Presence of Light- unapproachable Light. I AM a being without form or shape. I fill all things and know all things and create all things. You cannot see My Face, so I wrapped My Son-part of Me-in flesh so you could have an image to look upon. He has always been. He stood beside Me during creation. We are one and yet My Son is separate or an extension of Me, so you can relate to Me and know Me. You are My Beloved. Soon you will come to the wedding chamber, and we will be at one at last. Rejoice in these things.

Matthew 12:46-50

My Beloved, do you obey Me? If you do as I tell you to do, then you are part of My Family. You are the ones who will dwell in My House in My Kingdom. You are the ones who will rule with Me and reign with Me in My Kingdom. If you do not want to follow Me, then you will be cast away from Me. You will stand before Me on Judgment Day and be sentenced with the wicked. You will not receive mercy, because you rebelled against Me and wanted to serve yourself. You wanted to set yourself up like a god and do as you please. You must want to do My Will. My Will is to do good things for others. You must love others as you would love yourself. You must make sacrifices for others, so they can have what they need. If a man needs you, then go to him and help him. Do not take from those around you, but give to those around you. My Laws are built on loving others and doing good things for others. If you do not love, then you do not know Me. I AM Love. My Kingdom is built on love and compassion. Follow Me and walk in My Ways, and then you will become at one with Me and part of My Family of Light. No one can understand My Words unless they are following Me. Many mock Me and turn against Me. Only those who want to follow Me have understanding into what I am asking them to do. Open your eyes, and open your ears and listen. You will hear My Voice and follow closely to Me. You will be rewarded on the Last Day for your faithfulness.

Matthew 13:1-9, 18-23

My Beloved, I taught My People in parables, because only those who wanted to serve Me would seek Me out and look for understanding. So it is today. Those who really want to know Me will find Me and seek for answers to their questions about My Words. If you listen to My Voice, I will tell you what you need to know so you can grow and blossom. If you love Me, you will find the way to Me and search for Me with all your heart. I told My Disciples about the parable of the sower. If a man hears My Words (the seed) but the evil one comes and steals My Words from him by his lies, then he cannot receive Me. If a man hears My Words that has a rocky heart that does not have faith in Me that I will take care of him in troubled times, then he will lose what he has received and lose sight of Me. If a man has a thorny heart, then he worries about the things of the world. He desires to have wealth and fame and authority. The things of the world choke out My Words, and he does not receive Me. If a man has a pure heart that receives My Words, he will love to hear My Words and learn from Me. He will produce fruit. He may produce 100 times as much fruit as others around him. He may produce only 60 times as much as the others around him. He may only produce 30 times as much as the others around him. He will be rewarded by the fruit that he produces, and he will be greatly blessed. How much fruit are you producing?

What will your reward be?

Matthew 13:10-17

My Beloved, I taught the multitude in parables, and they did not understand. They did not understand, because they did not want to hear. They did not want to listen to the Truth, and they did not want to obey Me. They laughed and mocked Me, and they turned away from Me. I saw their hearts. Is your heart bent towards Me? If your heart desires to serve Me, then you will want to learn and listen and understand. You will want to be at one with Me. If your heart is not bent towards Me, then you will not want to hear. You will turn your face away from Me and rebel against Me. You must not be like the stiff-necked people of old. You must be aware of the times ahead and how the days grow darker. You must have your eyes open and listen to My Words, so you can see the path ahead. Many people listened to My Words on earth and did not understand, but some came to Me seeking to find Truth. They followed after Me and wanted to know Me and what I was saying. They became My Disciples, and they stayed close to Me and learned from Me. If you love Me, you will become My Disciple. You will want to follow My Teachings and walk in My Ways. You will know that I have called you to come after Me. You will know that you are blessed by Me. You will not be afraid of tomorrow, but you will have faith in Me and trust Me to care for you even in the darkest of days.

Matthew 13:24-30, 36-43

My Beloved, I told the people parables and only those who wanted to learn more came to Me and asked Me to teach them. I told them about the end of the age when there would be judgment for all of those who ever lived on earth. I told My People that at the end of the age, I would judge everyone. I will throw into the Lake of Fire those who rebelled against Me. The ones that the evil one sowed in the wheat field are the ones who I will root up and cast into the Lake of Fire. The angels will gather them up and kill all those who turned against Me and did not want to serve Me. If you want to serve Me, then you will enter My Kingdom of Light and be joint heirs with Me. I told My People that I am the one who sows the wheat, and the evil one sows the weeds. If you want the things of the world, then the evil one will consume you. You will always think of the things of the world and be happy to sin against Me. You will be rooted up at the last day and be thrown into the Lake of Fire. If you want to follow Me and love Me, then I will hold you close to Me and you will never be far from Me. I will guide you and direct you. You will want only the things of Me. I will judge your heart and if you are found lacking, then you will not be able to be part of My Kingdom. Do you want to be part of Me? Only those who want to be in harmony with Me will be able to sit at My Side and be in My Kingdom of Light. Look up and see Me and join with Me, and you will be spared on the Last Day. You will be gathered into My Kingdom and reign with Me forever.

Matthew 13:31-32

My Beloved, the Kingdom of Heaven is like a small seed that is planted in the hearts of men. Some will accept the seed, and it will grow and prosper. Some will reject it, and it will die. Each man will decide how much he will accept the Truth. Each man will be judged how he wanted to deny his flesh and follow Me. He will be judged according to his works. Man will want to do what the flesh wants to do. The Truth within him is at odds with the flesh, and it will rise up and overcome the flesh. Each man will be judged how much he submits to the Truth and denies the flesh. This little seed will grow and fill the earth. Many will come to the Tree of Life and find comfort in its branches. Many will be given all they need and be well provided for under its branches. Many will cling to the roots of the Tree of Life as an anchor in the storms of this world. You will be judged by how you adhere to the Tree of Life and want to follow Me and walk in My Ways. Do you really want to serve Me? If you want to serve Me, then you will want to draw close to Me and find how to please Me. Follow My Spirit, and I will lead you always even in the darkest of days.

Matthew 13:33-35

My Beloved, I spoke in parables to My People to fulfill what the prophets wrote about Me. The prophets said that I would talk to My People in parables and tell them secret things that have been hidden from the beginning of the universe, but they would not understand. I gave hidden knowledge to those who came to Me while I walked on earth and asked Me to explain the parables. I had a plan from the beginning. I could see ahead and knew what would happen. I saw that Adam and Eve would be deceived, and I used this to My Advantage. I used My People's time on this earth to test them and find out if they would be worthy to enter into My Kingdom. I used all the sins of My People to form them into creatures of Light that will reign with Me eternally. I spoke to them in parables, but those who wanted to love Me came near to Me and found Me and asked Me about the hidden knowledge. The others mocked Me and turned their faces away from Me. I could see that they were blinded and did not want to see. Do you really love Me? If you love Me, you will draw close to Me and seek Me and find Me. You will commune with Me and read My Words and find secret things hidden in them. I am unveiling the scriptures in these Last Days. Those in exile are going to come home soon. They need the Truth written within them to help them endure to the end. Be strong. Be brave. I will come soon.

Matthew 13:44-46

My Beloved, the Kingdom of Heaven is the most valuable thing you can obtain in this life on earth. There is nothing of greater value. Men of the world try to acquire great wealth, but this will all pass away at My Coming. I will roll back the heavens and come in power and might. I will destroy all the wicked ones and stand supreme over all men on earth. I will proclaim My Majesty, and all men will bow to Me. I will bring My Chosen ones to My Side. The rebellious ones will be cast away from Me and brought to their punishment for rejecting Me. My Kingdom will stand forever. If you love Me, you will seek Me and find Me and guard over your relationship with Me. There is nothing more valuable than knowing Me and walking with Me. You are walking with the King of the Universe. I have given you the privilege of holding My Hand and allowing Me to guide you, so you are never alone. You always have Wisdom to guide you, and you always have the protection of My Right Hand. The Kingdom of Heaven is in your midst, but only those with seeing eyes can obtain it. Do you long for the things of the spirit? You must focus on Me and want to abide in Me. You are a people of faith who see with spiritual eyes and not the eyes of the world. Be strong. Be brave. Stand firm. I am coming soon! The Kingdom of Heaven is yours. You have received a great treasure!

Matthew 13:47-50

My Beloved, I taught My Disciples about the things to come. I taught them old things from My Words that I had given Moses and the prophets. I clarified My Words, so they would understand. They had been taught so many things that were not true. They had been taught by religious leaders who had added to My Laws and placed a heavy burden on My People. My People struggled under the weight of it. I wanted My Disciples to know that My Laws give life and do not bring death. They are not a burden but liberty. They bring love and peace and not destruction and sadness. My People were dying under the weight of the burden that the religious leaders had placed on them. Their life was being taken away. I came to restore their life. I gave My Life, so they could have life again. I gave My Life, so they would be free from the weight of sin and be free to know Me and walk with Me. I gave My Spirit to them, and they were full and satisfied. No other god had ever done that before. I gave My Disciples understanding to the words of Moses and the prophets, but I also gave them insight into the future. I will give you insight into the future, if you ask Me to unveil it for you. Do you know that I AM coming soon? You must return to My Land, and no longer walk in exile. I will show you what lies ahead for you and help you make decisions for the future. I AM your guide in this life. Rely on Me, and rejoice that I love you

so much.

Matthew 13:51-57

My Beloved, do you believe that I can change a man? A town watches a boy grow up into a man, and they remember all the things that the boy did as he grew up. He may have done some foolish things, and they are not forgotten. When the man changes and walks in the things of Me, then the town only remembers the foolish things the boy did. They cannot see the man who has emerged and now walks in Me. Do not remember the child, but look at the adult who has emerged. Trust Me that I have changed him into the person that now serves Me. When I walked on earth the people looked at My humble background, and they knew that I did not have in-depth teaching with the rabbis. They wondered how I could have gained so much wisdom. They saw My mother and sisters and brothers, and they knew they were not special. They could not understand how I could gain power to have Wisdom from heaven. They could not see anything but My Flesh. They could not see who I AM. They could not trust in Me and believe in My Words, because they saw Me as a man from humble beginnings. I always walked in the Spirit, but they could not see this either. They were blinded and not trusting in the One who created them. They were looking for the Messiah, and when I came they could not see Me. They were looking for a king, but I came as a servant. I want you to look past the flesh of a man. Look into the heart of a man and find the good there. I want you to be understanding and patient with men. I want you to look for the things of the spirit within them. I want you to support them and pray for them. If you will do this for your brothers, then you will be rewarded by Me. You will see My Presence in them, and you will rejoice. Stay focused on Me, and I will bless you greatly.

Matthew 14:1-14

My Beloved, My cousin John was born before Me. He was a righteous man who told the people about My Coming. He was consumed with My Presence. He wanted the world to know that I would come to save them from their sins, if they only believed in Me. He had been under assault by men from an early age, because the message that he brought to the world was not received. He lived in the desert, and My People knew he was a prophet. He came to My People to deliver them a message from Me. Some would listen and receive, but others mocked him. John told Herod of his sin with his wife, and his wife hated John for it. When Herod's wife had the chance to get rid of John, she rejoiced. The voice telling her of her sin was gone, but the sin was still there with her. She could not escape My Judgment that came from destroying My Prophet, My Voice to My People. John's disciples were grieving and came to Me and told Me what happened. I also wept over his death. I went away to be quiet and alone and mourn the death of My Cousin. My People followed Me. They were lost without a shepherd. They cried out to Me, and I healed them. I had compassion on them, because I knew their loss of John their beloved. I knew the oppression that they were under. I wanted them to rejoice and be set free, so I healed them. I touched them and made them whole. My Beloved, will you come to Me and rejoice in My Presence? I will touch you and heal you. I will help you in whatever you need. Just look to Me as your source. I will fulfill My Covenant with you and deliver you from all your sorrows and grief. Trust in Me to deliver you, and I Will.

Matthew 14:15-21

My Beloved, My Disciples wanted Me to send the people away to find food to eat. It was a remote place with no food and many were hungry. I wanted the people to stay and hear My Words for them. I wanted to explain the scriptures to them and give them wisdom that had not been taught. This crowd was a mixture of many different types of people. There were religious leaders who had much and common people who did not have much. There were Romans and other nationalities. There were wealthy merchants and poor traders. They had heard about Me and all the miracles I had done. They wanted to come see what I was doing. Some came to be healed. Some came for entertainment. Some came to hear My Wisdom. Some came because others wanted them to come hear Me. They came to see Me with all kinds of reasons at a certain point in time. They did not know that they were seeing their Creator wrapped in flesh. They did not know that they were seeing the Messiah that would redeem them from their sins. Some came to mock Me, but others came to adhere to Me. I had compassion on them and fed them all no matter why they came to see Me. I wanted to touch each of them and let them know about Me. Many saw, but only a few could understand who I AM. Many came, but few left with the Wisdom that I wanted them to receive. Even today many hear, but few want to receive. Nothing has changed in this world, except now you have My Spirit to guide you. Now you have My Presence all the time. Now men who seek Me will find Me no matter where they live. Are you rejoicing in Me today? Rejoice that I have given you so much. Rejoice that I have reached My Hand out to you this very day.

Matthew 14:22-33

My Beloved, I sent My Disciples away in the boat, because they were tired and needed rest. I wanted them to have some time away from all the people and relax. I stayed with the crowds and then told them to go home to their families. I left them, and went to a remote area and prayed. I needed to have peace and quiet to renew My Strength. You too must pull away from the crowds and come to Me and be quiet and still and listen to Me. I listened in the stillness and found solitude. The creatures around Me rejoiced in My Presence. You must rejoice in Me and My Presence. You must walk away from all men and come be still before Me, so you can regain strength. My Disciples were far away from Me and a storm came up on the lake. I saw their troubles, and I walked towards them. When they saw Me walking on the water, they were afraid. They thought I was a demonic presence trying to impersonate My Form. Peter wanted to test the spirit. He asked Me to let him walk on the water, if it truly was Me. He began to walk on the water. He was strong, but the waves were fierce and made him doubt My Strength in the midst of the storm. I AM your Strength even in the midst of a storm. Call on Me, and I will allow you to walk on water and not be shaken. You will walk beside Me and not be moved. Are you keeping your eyes on Me and not the storms in your life? Trust in Me, and I will help you overcome all things in this life.

Matthew 14:34-36

My Beloved, everywhere I went people followed Me and begged Me to heal them. They knew that I had healed others, and they wanted to be healed also. Imagine if someone walked on your earth today, and everyone who touched him was healed. There would be great crowds of people that would come to him just hoping that he could heal them. The people who were healed would call all their relatives and tell them to come find the One who heals. Everywhere I went people were desperate to be healed. They did not have trained doctors to give them medicine. They had no hospitals to help them. They had a few herbs that grew in the area. There were no surgeons. These people were desperate to get help. They knew they would be healed if they just touched the Tzitzit on My Garment. I allowed all those who wanted to be healed to come touch My Garment, and they were healed. They rejoiced and cried and were thankful. They wept before Me and held at My Feet in praise and worship. They did not know who I was. They only knew Me as a healer. Even My enemies could see that I had great power, but they told the people that it came from the evil ones. They tried to deceive the people. Those who were healed felt My Presence, and they knew it was not the evil ones who healed them. They knew that a divine power had touched them. They left Me rejoicing and went to tell others the good news. Soon it was hard for Me to go anywhere, because crowds of people came to Me to be healed. I had to stay in remote areas where only a few people knew where I was. I wanted the people to come to Me and hear My Words and receive them. Only a few received Me and knew that I was the Messiah in flesh. Will you come to Me this day and hear My Words and draw close to Me? Find out for yourself who I AM. Touch My Garment, and be healed from all your sins and be made whole.

Matthew 15:1-9, 12-14

My Beloved, I told My Disciples to listen to My Words and obey them. I told them not to listen to the rules of men who add or take away from My Scriptures. If you read My Scriptures and learn My Laws and follow them, then you will not stumble and fall. Even today the religious leaders have added to My Laws and given the people a heavy burden to carry. My Laws are simple and not hard to carry. If you listen to Me and hear My Voice, then you will not be blinded by the traditions of men. You will pull away from their false doctrine. They will fall down and not get up, because they have turned from the Truth. The evil ones try very hard to have men turn from the Truth. The righteous man stays on the path and clings to My Words. The man that goes astray clings to the words of men. He clings to the words of religious leaders and pastors and preachers and does not cling to Me. You must wash away all that they say. If you do not see it written in My Words, then cleanse it from your heart. You will never go astray or be deceived. You will walk a straight path and not stumble and fall. You will know who I AM and keep your eyes on Me. Do you walk a different path than those around you? Be strong, because you walk in the path that leads to life. You will walk towards Me and My Kingdom of Light.

Matthew 15:10-11, 15-20

My Beloved, I told My People that it is not what you eat that makes you unclean, but it is what comes out of your mouth or what you say that makes you unclean. My People were so set on rules and regulations. They rated their sins by what they did. I wanted them to know that what was in the heart was what made a man. I wanted them to know that if they dwelled on evil thoughts and sexual things that they would be unclean. They did not look at the heart of a man, but how he kept My Laws. You cannot judge a man by how he keeps religious laws. He still may have mean and hateful thoughts within him. He may not be able to forgive others. He may hold grudges. He may want to harm someone. He may want to commit adultery. Only I know the heart, but you can judge others by the words they speak. If they are kind and loving and giving to others, then they will speak kind, loving, caring words. You will know them by their fruits. You will know if they walk in peace and joy. They will be content and not complain. Many religious men are very unhappy. They know traditions and how to keep them, but they do not know Me and follow in My Peace. If you really know Me, you will be in harmony with Me and walk hand in hand with Me. We will commune together, and you will enjoy walking in My Ways. Are you afraid of the future? Trust Me in all you do, and you will remain at peace and will always be content.

Matthew 15:21-28

My Beloved, as I walked on this earth I was looking for My Children who were lost and did not know My Name. I was looking for the tribes of Israel that had left Jerusalem and worshipped in another place. I came to seek them and show them the way to find Me. The tribes of Judah and Benjamin had stayed in the area around Jerusalem and had continued to worship in the Temple. The rest of the tribes left in anger due to the high taxes of Solomon's son who took over after Solomon died. My People were lost and without a shepherd, so I came to bring them back into the fold. When a woman not from any of the tribes of Israel came to Me, I was reluctant to help her. She was not following My Ways and none of her ancestors had ever followed Me. She continued to beg Me to heal her daughter from the demons that had possessed her. She saw how others were delivered, and she came to Me in desperation. She would not stop holding onto My Feet and begging for mercy. In compassion for her grief I healed her daughter, and the woman turned to Me and served Me. She had not known Me, but she saw a Great Light in her midst. She was drawn to the Light and trusted Me. Are you a light to the world around you? Do you bring love and kindness to others? If you are My Child, then you will have compassion on others and love them just as I loved others as I walked on this earth.

Matthew 15:29-31

My Beloved, I walked among My People and had compassion on them. I sat on a large hill and crowds of people came to Me. I healed the sick and the lame and the crippled. I healed the blind and the mute. The people were amazed to hear the mute speaking and the blind seeing. These people had not talked or been able to see before. They came to Me in desperation. There was no one to help them. They came crying out to Me. I told the crowds that I would heal them all if they sat quietly. I took them one at a time. The crowds rejoiced over each one that was healed. They sat and waited their turn each one hoping that he would be healed and restored. They looked into My Eyes and received their healing. They came believing and knowing that I would touch them and heal them. They wanted to see Me and be close to Me. They were in the midst of My Presence. All the people were amazed and shouted in joy. I wanted My People to understand who I AM and receive Me. Very few saw the miracles and believed that I was the Messiah. Very few wanted to follow after Me. They wanted the miracle, but they did not want to follow in My Ways. I had compassion on them no matter what they would do in the future. I healed them knowing they would not follow My Ways. What about you? Do you want the miracles and blessings, but do not want to cling to Me and walk in My Ways? Do you still cling to manmade traditions? Is it too hard for you to walk in My Laws? Turn your eyes to Me and repent. Draw near to Me and cling to Me, and you will be blessed.

Matthew 15:32-39

My Beloved, many people came to hear Me teach the scriptures. They came wanting to know more about My Words. They knew that I had wisdom. They had never heard the scriptures being taught with such clarity. Great wisdom came to all who would listen. Great wisdom was found in the explanation that I gave them. They searched for answers, but I had all the answers. They came crying to Me when I gave them the Truth. They came to Me weeping, because they had found the good news. They believed that I would come back to them and fill them up with My Spirit, and I did. They believed in Me, and I brought life to many. If you love Me, you will follow My Laws and walk in My Ways. I gave to this people who had been with Me for three days. I blessed the food we had and multiplied it. After the people were filled physically and spiritually, I send them away. I had given them all that I had. I gave them freely from My Hand. Do you give freely to others? If you have some to give to others, give freely. If you have none, then love those around you. You must always give love to others. I loved all the people around Me, and I cared for them. I want to care for you.

Matthew 16:1-4

My Beloved, when I walked the earth many men tried to trap Me, so they could say to the people that I was a liar and a fraud. I knew what they were thinking. I created them. I knew that their heart was wicked. I knew that they were evil and had wicked intentions. I knew them, but they did not know Me. They did not desire to know Me. I was a threat to them. I wanted the people to see the Truth, and they wanted the people to continue in worthless laws and regulations. They did not seek to find the Truth. They wanted to live as they wanted to live. They wanted to have all the people under their authority and force the people to do as they pleased. They liked the power they had over the people. I never intended My People to be enslaved in laws. I wanted them to live by My Laws, but walk in liberty and truth. When I told the religious leaders about their sins, they did not like to be rebuked. They wanted to have the respect of all men even at the expense of leading the people into error. They wanted to continue in their corruption. I came to tell My People not to listen to them, but to walk in My Ways. Some of the people listened to My Words, but others continued to be enslaved by the religious leaders. Beware of the religious leaders. Do you follow a man or are you led by My Spirit? Be led by Me. They were looking for a sign to show them that I could do a miracle. The only sign you need is the sign of Jonah. He was dead three days and three nights in a fish and rose again, so he could preach to Nineveh. My flesh was in the grave for three days and three nights, so I could bring salvation to My People and set you free from the bondage of sin. Look to Me, and I will guide you continually.

Matthew 16:5-12

My Beloved, My Disciples did not understand much of what I was doing. They saw Me feed the five thousand people, yet they were upset when they forgot bread and did not have anything to eat. They were blaming each other for not bringing the bread to a remote area where there was no food. They did not look to Me to feed them. I could call bread down from heaven at any time, but they still did not see Me as Creator of the Universe. Only until I ascended into heaven did they understand that I AM Creator of all things and in charge of all things. I tried to teach them My Ways. I wanted them to guard against the teaching of the religious leaders. The religious leaders had changed My Ways and My Laws and created a heavy burden for the people to carry. The religious leaders wanted power over the people, but I wanted My People to know Me and be comforted in My Presence. The people were afraid to break away from the religious leaders, because they would forbid them from going into the Temple. The people wanted to worship Me in My Presence, but the religious leaders would not approve for them to enter the Temple. That was My Temple! The religious leaders needed My Approval concerning who worshipped Me in My Temple. The people were lacking walking in darkness without a leader. I was a great Light to them, and many saw Me and wanted to follow Me. They wanted to please Me and create a new way to live. Are you afraid that you will be shunned in your church for speaking the Truth? Turn away from man and always walk in My Ways. You will please Me and walk in harmony with Me.

Matthew 16:13-20

My Beloved, I asked My Disciples who they thought I was. They told Me that the people thought I was John or Elijah or Jeremiah or one of the other prophets brought back to life to bring a message to them. The people did not realize who I was. They were sheep without a shepherd. They needed someone to guide them. I asked My Disciples who they thought I was. Peter said that he thought I was the Messiah. His eyes had been opened! He could receive in his heart that I was the One that he had been waiting to rule earth and bring salvation to the people. I was pleased that Peter had been given such a revelation. I told him that he had the keys to My Kingdom of Light. He was able to open the door and come in and dwell with Me. Do you know who I AM? If you trust in Me and want to serve Me, then you too will receive the keys to My Kingdom. You will enter into My Kingdom of Light and dwell with Me eternally. You will rule beside Me. You are the one that I have chosen to be My Heir. You are My Chosen One, and no one can overtake you and destroy you. They may destroy the flesh, but they cannot destroy who you are. You are wrapped in My Arms of love and protection. I will keep you close to Me all the days of your life, and you will live with Me forever.

Matthew 16:21-23

My Beloved, I told My Disciples that I must go to Jerusalem and die, but I will come back to them after three days. I told them that I had to suffer before the High Priest and religious leaders. I told them that My Blood would be on the heads of the religious leaders, and they would suffer loss by rejecting Me. I told them that I would bring new life to My People, and that My Spirit would dwell in them forever. I told them all these things and they heard Me, but they did not understand what would happen to Me. Peter caught a glimpse of My Suffering, and he rebuked Me. He told Me that I did not have to endure this suffering, but I rebuked him. He was looking at My Words from a physical stand point, not a spiritual stand point. He saw with his fleshly eyes and not My Eyes. Peter wanted to spare Me suffering under the hands of the religious leaders. He despised them and wanted Me to be free of them. He did not understand that I would bring liberty to many enslaved in the hands of the evil one. I set the captives free, and I restored the earth back to Me. I came to redeem the world and begin a new life for My People. Now My People can commune with Me all day long. Are you looking at the world through fleshly eyes like Peter did? I AM always with you. You do not have to be afraid. I will bring you comfort at all times. I died that you may be at one with Me.

Matthew 16:24-28

My Beloved, I told My Disciples to give up their own life –all their hopes and desires- and follow Me. If you put aside what you want and only do what I tell you to do, then you will be rewarded. You must not desire the things of the world that pass away so quickly. If you will focus only on Me, then all you need will come to your house. Do not desire a fancy house or expensive clothes or designer shoes. Do not desire a fast or luxurious car. Do not desire to have power or wealth or fame. Do not desire to have your children in places of power or wealth or fame. Do you want your children to walk in My Ways? You must put your children in My Hands and allow Me to guide them. Even if your children walk in a different path than I have taken you, they will be blessed in the path I have chosen for them. You do not ever have to fear. I will always take care of your children. If you are angry that you do not have control over your children, then put them in My Hands. I will guide your children and form them into My Image and transform them into beings of Light. Do you desire the things of the world? You should lay down your life and pick up a new life in Me desiring the spiritual things. If you desire My spiritual gifts, then you will do well. If you desire to touch Me and hold close to Me, then you will draw near and I will tell you secret things. I AM coming soon. I will come in My Glory. All men will bow at My Feet. All men will know who I AM and magnify My Name.

Matthew 17:1-8

My Beloved, I wanted My Disciples to know who I AM. I told Peter, James, and John to come up the mountain with Me, so we could be alone. My Divine Presence came upon them. I AM the Light and am perfect. I AM Love and compassion. I came and talked in the midst of them. I brought My Friends, Moses and Elijah and we talked together. My Disciples were afraid and fell down in fear wondering "Who is this that talks with Elijah and Moses? Who is this that transforms into Light? Who is this that walks with us and talks with us and yet He is divine?" I spoke with them from heaven and told them, "This is My Son in whom I am well pleased. Listen to him." I wrapped Myself in flesh, so I could walk among My People. I wanted My Disciples to see My Divinity. My Disciples were overwhelmed with what happened, but I told them not to talk about it with anyone until I had suffered and died and rose again. My Disciples kept these things in their hearts and shared it later with the other disciples. They were faithful men who I could trust. I could build a firm foundation upon men such as these. Are you faithful? Can I build a firm foundation on you? Will you bend and break under stress? Will you stand firm in the midst of a storm? I AM here to help you at all times. I love you.

Matthew 17:9-13

My Beloved, I walked and talked with My Disciples and tried to explain what I was doing. I wanted them to know My Purpose for coming to earth. I wanted them to know that I wanted to save them from their sins and bring salvation to a lost dying world. My Disciples listened to My Words and they grasped Truth, but it was much deeper than that. It was so deep that they would not understand in full until they departed from this life. My Disciples wanted to learn from Me more than anyone else did. They were constantly asking Me questions. I mentored them and showed them the way to go. Not one of them rejected Me except for Judas. My Disciples asked Me if Elijah had come or should they look for another. I told them that John the Baptizer had the spirit of Elijah in him. He was the one who would prepare the way for Me. He gave up his life for Me. He pointed all men to Me. He wanted all men to believe in Me, but some could not believe in Me. Some were baptized to find favor with those looking on. Some were not baptized, but mocked him as knowing nothing. It is the same world today. You will come to Me, if you love Me. You will reject Me, if you hate Me. You may say you are from Me, and yet you do not know Me. I look at the heart and judge the person. I know if you love Me or not. I know if you want to draw close to Me. Are you looking only for Me? I want you to be in harmony with Me, so I can give you a depth of understanding that you have never known before. Be faithful and continue to seek Me. Rejoice that I love you so much!

Matthew 17:14-21

My Beloved, one day a man came to Me with a boy who was possessed by a demon. The demon would make him go into fits and hurt himself. The man was grieved over his son and came to My Disciples to heal him. My Disciples did not know what to do. They rebuked the demon, but the boy was not set free. The man came to Me, so I could help him. He desperately wanted his son to be healed. He had seen the demon hurt the child time and time again, and he could not bear to watch it any longer. I knew his heart and how he grieved over the child. I rebuked the demon and it left. I was angry with My Disciples, because they did not trust in Me enough to believe that the demon would leave in My Name. They doubted My Deity. They doubted Me. I was angry, because they were with Me every day and saw miracles every day, and yet they did not believe in Me. Do you believe in Me to do miracles? If you believe in Me with all your heart, you could ask whatever you wish and it would be done for you. The problem is that you see with physical eyes, and you do not know who you are. You do not realize that you are My Child. You have power and authority over all things, if you walk in My Will for you. The evil one knows this and keeps you in deception, so you cannot see clearly. Soon I will bring you out of exile and bring you back home to My Land. Once you are on My Land you will be able to see and know things that you never have known before. You will want to be in My Presence always and always walk in My Will. You will be free from those who walk in darkness. You will walk in the Light, and you will be free to worship Me and praise Me all day long. You will be liberated from the world and walk in My Ways as led by My Spirit. What glorious days it will be for My Children!

Matthew 17:22-23

My Beloved, I tried to tell My Disciples that I would be betrayed and put to death by those who hated Me. The religious leaders plotted against Me and wanted to kill Me, because they thought I was leading My People astray. They were the ones lost in darkness and could not see. The evil one had blinded them. Now they walked in so much pride that they could not see clearly. They thought I was evil. Instead I was bringing righteousness to My People, so they could walk hand in hand with Me. I tried to tell My Disciples about the future events, but they did not want to hear these things. They were very sad that I had to die. They did not understand about Me coming back to life after three days. This was unheard of. Yet they had seen Me raise the dead back to life. I AM the Giver of Life. I hold the breath of life, because I AM the life spirit. No one has life unless I give it to him. I give and I take. I told My Disciples that I would overcome death, so they would not be afraid. Are you afraid of the future? I will tell you the future also, so you will not be afraid. I want you to know future events and things I will ask you to do. I want you to be prepared. I tell you that you will come back to My Land again. All My Children will be gathered from all over the earth to My Place of residence. I have chosen this Land as My Own, and I marked it for Me. You will be called. When I say, "Come to Me!" then come quickly. I will bless you there.

Matthew 17:24-27

My Beloved, the collectors of the Temple tax came to Peter and wanted him to pay his tax for the year. Peter was troubled over this and wanted to know what I would say about this. I knew his thoughts before he ever arrived back home. I asked him if a king should make his sons pay taxes. He told Me that the sons should not pay taxes, but only the others under the authority of the king. I wanted Peter to know that I AM King of the Universe, but while on earth I AM a servant to man. I told Peter that I AM King and he is My Son, and he really does not have to pay taxes. While he was on earth he would have to pay taxes to those in authority over him. All My Sons and Daughters are being tested. They are in the form of servants. I came in servant form to teach you how to walk on this earth. I told Peter to go catch some fish, and the fish would have a coin in his mouth. Peter gave the coin to the collector to show him that His King could produce his taxes from any source. Do you believe that I can provide for all you need? All you have to do is believe in Me and trust Me, and I will provide all you need. You will have to walk in humility here on earth. You must walk in love and compassion. Even though you are My Sons and Daughters, your time has not come. You will reign with Me in the next kingdom. You will have authority over all things. You will rule over many for eternity. You will be tested and found worthy to enter My Kingdom of Light. Rejoice and prepare for the days ahead.

Rejoice that I love you so much!

Matthew 18:1-11

My Beloved, I told My Disciples to watch out for the traps set by the enemy. The evil one sets traps for My Children to bring them into deception and turn them away from Me. My Children love Me and want to serve Me. They listen to My Voice at all times or they will fall into deception. It is very easy to fall into deception, if you are listening to what a man tells you to do or allowing him to interpret the scriptures for you. If you are reading the Scriptures and allowing Me to guide you to Truth, then you will not fall into deception. Cry out to Me to bring Truth to your house, and I will. No man has all the Truth. Man has a little Truth, and when I return I will give him all the Truth and set him free from deception. The evil one plants deception everywhere you go. Have you fallen into deception? Be careful that you guard over yourself and do not fall into the traps of movies, TV shows, computer games, worldly books, and any other thing that may cause you to turn from My Scriptures and searching My Words for Truth. If you desire the things of the world more than searching My Words, then you are ripe for deception. You must not allow your flesh to rule you. Be humble and serve Me, and I will bless you greatly.

Matthew 18:12-14

My Beloved, every one of My Children is very precious to Me. I love everyone from the youngest to the oldest. I see an accumulation of generations in each one of My Children. Each one is special and has special characteristics. Each one is very valuable to Me. I see Myself in each of them. They are My Children and will be heirs to My Throne. They will be My Hands and Feet. They will be the only ones who I entrust My Authority. They will be great in My Sight. You must be bold and courageous while you are here on earth to fight against the flesh and the evil one. Pressure is on all sides. You must be strong and brave and walk in My Ways. You must be kind and good before Me. You must want to please Me and serve Me. If you turn away from Me, I will follow you and I will find you and bring you back to My Fold. Every one of My Children I watch over very carefully. I AM the good Shepherd and you are My Sheep. I keep you in a pasture that is fenced around with My Presence. No one can touch you. No one can come close to you unless I give him permission. Do you really love Me? If you love Me, you will rest close to Me and want to know more about Me. You will be in tune to My Spirit and hear My Voice and know who I AM. I AM always with you. I AM never far away. Lean on Me, and I will make you strong. Do not be deceived by what your eyes see, but call on My Name and I will show you a better way to walk on this earth.

Matthew 18:15-20

My Beloved, if you see your brother in sin, go to him and confront him about his sin privately. Ask him to stop sinning against Me. If he will not listen to you, then take two men that he trusts and honors and go talk to him about his sin. If he denies his sin or thinks that it is not a sin, bring him before your group of believers and let them decide. If he still does not repent, then he will be cast out of the believers and be considered a nonbeliever. He will be left outside the fold where the wolves are, and he will suffer loss. If your brother is in sin, then pray that My Hand will be on him to bring repentance to him. I will hear your prayer for him and touch him by My Hand. If you are praying in agreement with other believers, then I AM with you in the midst of you. Pray in agreement with others, so your prayers will be great lights before Me. You do not have to be in the same room. You can be on opposite ends of the earth as long as you are praying in one accord with each other for the same request or the same petition. I will hear your prayers and send My Angels to fight on behalf of you. I will cover you with My Presence as you pray, and you will be kept safe from the enemy. He will not hinder your prayers from coming up before Me. Are your prayers being hindered? Some places are so dark that My People who live there have their prayers hindered. If you live in such a place, call out to Me to help you. I will answer you, and take you to a safe place where you can be heard.

Matthew 18:21-35

My Beloved, I told My Disciples to continue to forgive their brothers who believe in Me and trust Me to guide them. You must forgive all men especially those who walk in the faith. My Disciples were astonished by My Words. Were they really supposed to continue to forgive someone who does them wrong time after time? I want all men to walk in peace with forgiveness in their hearts. I want men to have compassion on others and treat them with love and fairness. Are you having a hard time forgiving someone? You must put the past behind you. You must be able to see the man for what he is. He is only flesh and he will make mistakes. He will not ever be perfect. If he harms you because of his own errors, then his intention was not to harm you. If he hurts you maliciously, then he is not of Me. One of My Children would not harm someone out of hatred. My Children love those around them and want to see them prosper. If you love others, then I will deliver you from sin and punishment. If you love others even though they do not love you, I will bless you greatly. You must love those around you, and then you will receive forgiveness from Me. I will compensate you for all you have lost.

Matthew 19:1-12

My Beloved, I told My Disciples that a married man must not divorce his wife unless his wife commits adultery and leaves him. If the wife commits adultery and then repents and wants to stay with her husband, then her husband must forgive her and allow her to stay. If his wife continues to commit adultery, then she has not repented and should be sent away. If the man commits adultery and wants to stay with his wife, then his wife must forgive him and stay with her husband. If her husband continues to commit adultery even after he begs her to stay, she is no longer commanded to stay with her husband. She is free to go, because her husband did not repent. Do you want to marry someone? Ask yourself if you love this person enough to never desire anyone else. If you can answer yes to this question, then you should marry the person. If you are not sure, then you must wait until you are very sure that this is the person for you. You must look for someone that loves Me and wants to serve Me, or you will suffer loss in your relationship. You must commit to Me in a pure relationship where you both are serving Me. Do not think that you can serve the world and keep a marriage pure. You both must want to do what is right in My Eyes. Think about these things before you get married. I will guide you to the right person for you, and then you will always live in peace.

Matthew 19:13-15

My Beloved, great crowds came to Me and I healed all of them. They even brought their children to Me, so I could bless them and heal them. My Disciples could see that I was tired and wanted the children to be taken away from Me, but I looked into the eyes of the children and knew they wanted to draw close to Me. My Heart was filled with compassion for them. I could see the heart of every child and how he would serve Me or turn away from Me. I could see all their past ancestors within them calling out to Me. I could see their innocence. Some of the children that I touched that day remembered My Touch and wanted to serve Me. They looked into My eyes and saw Me. They had found their Creator. They had found the One who could guide them. They looked into My eyes and saw peace. They wanted to stay in that peace. It may have been years later that they understood who I was that they touched that day. It may have been many lonely days between that special day that they looked into My eyes until they received My Spirit within them. They never forgot My Face or My Touch. Have you looked into My Eyes and felt My Touch? Do you know My Presence? Do you rely on Me to heal you and comfort you and guide you? I AM the only One who can give you everything that you need. I want you to draw close to Me and know who I AM. I AM the only One who can bring you an abundant life. I can give you gifts that no one else can give you. I can form you into a glorious creature of Light. I will give you great rewards, if you follow only Me. I will give you a great Kingdom to live in with Me forever. You will no longer suffer, but you will live in total contentment. You will no longer struggle with your flesh, but you will live in peace and worship Me continually for all the good things I have done for you.

Rejoice that I have chosen you as My Own.

Matthew 19:16-30

My Beloved, a young man came to Me to find out what he had to do to receive eternal life. He had heard Me teach and he wanted to live eternally. He knew that by keeping My Commandments that he could obtain righteousness. He asked Me what commandments he should keep. I pointed him back to the laws of Moses. He told Me that he had kept all of these since he was a child. He wanted to know how he was still lacking. I could see in his heart that he loved his wealth and affluence. I could see that he would not give up everything to serve Me. I could see that he wanted eternal life, but not at the price of giving up his worldly possessions. He loved the world more than he loved Me. My Disciples questioned Me about this man. I told them that he must give up his earthly life to earn an eternal one. My Disciples had given up everything to follow Me. They served Me daily and learned from Me. I taught them how to walk in My Footsteps. I told them that I had twelve thrones reserved for them in My Kingdom. Each one of them would rule over one of the tribes of Israel. They had given up their lives to follow Me, and now they would rule with Me eternally. Have you given up your life to follow Me? Do you obey Me? Do you listen to My Voice and obey My Commandments? I will give back to you 100 times what you give up here to serve Me. You are My Beloved, and I will give to you generously in My Kingdom.

Matthew 20:1-16

My Beloved, I told My Disciples a story, so they could understand the Kingdom of Heaven. I am the owner of the Land. I give to each man as I choose to give to him. I told each man that they would receive a certain pay if they worked for Me. Some came in the early morning and others came late in the afternoon. Each man worked hard for Me, so I was generous with the ones that came late and gave them the same wage. It is the same way for My Kingdom. Some may start working for Me when they are a child and seek to please Me all their life. Some may come to Me with they are in their 20s or 30s. Some may come to Me when they are in their 40s or 50s. Some may come to Me in their old age. I continue to seek those who want to come to Me. When a man surrenders his heart to Me and wants to serve Me no matter how old he is, I will accept them gladly and reward him with eternal life. Each man is given the same reward no matter how many years he has served Me. If you think this is unfair, then you must consider that I also reward you for your services during the years of your life. If you have many years serving Me, then your rewards will be much greater than a man who came to Me in the latter part of his life. You must judge your life daily and see what you need to do to serve Me. How can you please Me? How can you be a Light to others? How can you focus on Me and listen to every word I say? Once you listen to Me, you will find your life rewarding and you will take great joy in living. You will be blessed greatly in My Kingdom where all things will come to Light at last.

Matthew 20:17-19

My Beloved, I told My Disciples that I would be taken to the High Priest and falsely accused for crimes that I did not commit. They will hand me over to the Roman soldiers who will beat Me and mock Me and execute Me. My Disciples cried out to Me to stop all this. They wanted Me not to go to Jerusalem. They wanted Me to stay in the remote areas, so no one would find Me. They wanted Me to arise and pull My Army together and fight against their enemies. They did not realize that there was judgment on My Land for the sins of My People. Their enemies came into My Land to judge My People and make them pay for their sins against Me. The religious leaders hated Me just as they will hate you. They will not want to hear what you say. They will mock you and call you misled or deceived. You are carrying a heavier burden than they are, because you are walking against the current. You are being worn away as you walk away from the world and closer to Me. You will know that I AM always with you. I will lead you steadfastly, and you will know exactly where to turn. Never lose faith in Me, but always keep your eyes on Me no matter how dark the days get. I AM faithful. I AM beside you. Call on Me, and I will answer your prayer. Do you think that I am not answering your prayers? Even if it does not look like I am answering your prayer, I hear your requests. You must believe that I care enough about you to give you only the best-only what you need. Rejoice that I have this insight and can mold you into a glorious creature of Light.

Matthew 20:20-28

My Beloved, one of the mothers of My Disciples came to Me and bowed before Me asking Me to favor her sons in My Kingdom. I could see that she wanted her sons to have power and fame, but I wanted her sons to be servants and to love others. She did not understand this kind of logic. The other disciples were upset that this mother would come to Me and ask favor for her sons over them. They all loved Me and served Me and did just as I asked them to do. They wanted to serve Me with all their heart. There was not one disciple that I put before the others. They were all mighty men that there chosen by Me, because I knew they would not bend and would overcome in the end. These men would be the pillows in My Kingdom on earth. They taught others what I taught them. They were an example of love and righteousness to those around them. They were the ones who helped the other believers be able to stand firm in the days of trouble. I have a special place for these men in My Kingdom. They will each rule over one of the twelve tribes. You will see them and honor them in My Kingdom. They gave up their life to serve Me. Will you give up your life to serve Me? Will you do as I tell you to do? Will you suffer the wrath of men that hate Me to serve Me? Will you teach your children My Ways and not allow them to slip into the world? Will you study My Words and find Wisdom in them? Will you walk in love with all men no matter how they treat you? Do you want to be an example of righteousness to all those around you? What will you give up for Me? Whatever you give up for Me, I will give it back to you in overflowing measures because I love you so much.

Matthew 20:29-34

My Beloved, two blind men had heard about Me and knew that I could heal them. They sat by the road hoping that I would come their way. They heard the crowd coming and the voices shouting to make way so I could pass. They cried out to Me for help. I heard the others in the crowd tell the blind men to stop shouting that I had no time for them. The blind men shouted even louder and cried out in desperation to Me. I stopped and could see that they wanted to be healed. I asked them what they wanted, because you have to ask Me to be able to receive from Me. They asked Me to heal them, and I had compassion on them. They lived in a dark world and could see no light. A great Light had come to them, and I wanted them to see Me. I wanted them to see My Face and follow in My Ways. I touched their eyes and the darkness fell away and Light came into their world. They rejoiced and were glad while the crowd looked on in wonder and amazement. I had taught the crowd to have mercy on even the lowest of people. Even the blind men had value. Do you value all men and want to give them love? All men should be valued and be able to walk in freedom. Treat all those around you the same. Love each person and have compassion on him. Reach your hand out to the lowest of persons, and I will bless you greatly. Loving someone is the greatest gift you can give to another. Love others, and I will give you great gifts in return.

Matthew 21:1-11

My Beloved, I told two of My Disciples to go get a donkey with its colt and bring it to Me. I wanted to fulfill what had been written by the prophet, so the people could see that I was the Messiah. I was leaving evidence everywhere I went for those who had eyes to see and ears to listen. My Disciples brought the donkey and colt to Me. I rode on the donkey and the colt followed with My Possessions. I told the people that I had come to save them, and they believed Me. As we went towards Jerusalem the people begged Me to deliver them from the Romans. They wanted to be set free. They wanted to come to Me and be a part of Me. The religious leaders wanted to silent them and bring Me to destruction. My People had seen the miracles I had done. They knew where to find Me, and they followed Me daily to hear My Words. They loved Me and believed in Me. If you want to know Me, you must follow in My Ways. If you love Me, you will follow close to Me and walk beside Me. The religious leaders of the day did not want to know Me. My People wanted to be close to Me and crowded around Me. They did not want to let Me go. Do you really want to hold onto Me? Do you believe that I AM the Messiah? Do you believe that I have come to save you and set you free? Rejoice and be glad that I have given you the insight to believe in Me.

Matthew 21:12-13

My Beloved, I went to My Temple and all I could see were business men who wanted to make a profit on My People. They were there to sell animals for sacrifices at an inflated price. They had money changers who converted the money into coins for the Temple. They had all sorts of merchants who wanted to sell My People their items. This disgusted Me. I was furious that these people were allowed to come to My Temple and prey on My People. I knocked over all their tables and benches and drove them out of My Temple with a whip. They were furious and went to the leaders of the Temple. The leaders did not want Me to come back there again. How could they stop Me? The people were walking with Me and talking about all the miracles I was doing. The people would be upset and turn against the leaders, and they could not allow that to happen. I went and did as I wanted to do. I did not let the leaders keep Me from doing My Work on this earth. Should you allow others to stop you from doing My Work on earth? If you see injustice, try to stop it. If you have no way to stop it, then pray that I will intervene and stop those who try to take Truth away from My People. I will change the way the leaders look at things and protect you. You must seek to walk in Truth, and do not allow anyone to hinder you from doing this. You may not be able to change a whole system, but you can change one person at a time.

Matthew 21:14-17

My Beloved, I drove all the money changers and business men out of the Temple. They were driven out of My Temple, so My People could come in and reside in My Presence without men trying to rob them. My People surrounded Me in the Temple, and I healed all of them who wanted to be healed. The little children cried out to Me to deliver them from those who oppressed them. The religious leaders were furious. Even though they saw all the miracles that I was doing, they focused on the children magnifying My Name and bringing praise to Me. The religious leaders came to Me and told Me to stop them, but I declined. I allowed the little ones to praise Me and bring honor to My Name. The religious leaders were angry and wanted to bring harm to Me, so I left that place. The religious leaders were leading My People into a ditch with a heavy burden of laws that brought them into bondage. My People were oppressed by their enemies on every side and there was no mercy for them. I brought them hope, and they wanted to cling to Me. They wanted to walk everywhere I went to be close to Me. I brought them hope, because they thought if I were the Messiah that I would be their King and deliver them from their enemies. I had to overcome death and bring deliverance from death to My People first. They did not understand My Mission and lost hope in Me. Do you have hope in Me? My Mission is still the same. I will come to deliver you and bring you back to My Kingdom. Rejoice and be glad and praise Me every day for all I do for you.

Matthew 21:18-22

My Beloved, as I walked along with My Disciples I became hungry. I saw a fig tree, but it was barren without fruit. The tree was taking up space, because it was not baring fruit. It was sick and diseased, so I cursed it. The tree shrunk up and soon died to make room for another seedling that wanted to come up and bear fruit. I am the Supreme Gardener, and I prune the world. I know what is best for the planet and how to groom it properly. My Disciples were amazed at what happened before their eyes. I wanted them to know that if they had faith in Me and did not doubt that they could do the same things. All they had to do was ask Me in prayer, and I would do it for them. The level of your faith increases the power of your prayers. If you have no faith, then your prayers will not be heard. If you go to a man of faith and he prays for you, then your requests will be heard and I will act on them. Do you have faith to believe that I will hear your prayers? You must trust Me to do what is best for everyone around you. You must not look at the flesh or the natural world, but you must look at the spiritual realm around you and know that your power comes from a spiritual realm. If you want to please your flesh all the time, then you will have no faith. You must want to deny your flesh and walk in My Ways, and then you can walk in faith. If you fast and pray, then you will be able to draw close to Me. I will lift you up, so you can hear Me. I will show you the way to go. You will never be alone, and you should never be afraid. I AM always beside you.

Matthew 21:23-32

My Beloved, the religious leaders came to Me and asked Me by what authority did I perform miracles and teach from the Scriptures. I knew they wanted to trap Me and bring the people against Me. I asked them a question, "By what authority did John come proclaiming My Words?" They knew it was a trick question. Either way they would be trapped, so they refused to answer. Therefore I did not answer their question. They were furious with My answer. They wanted to find some reason to criticize Me in front of My People. I gave them no such chance. I asked them another question, because they liked to show others how smart they were. I asked them a question, so they would look foolish in front of My People. I wanted to show the religious leaders that the lowest of people would go before them into My Kingdom. Those who they looked down on, because they trusted in Me would enter My Kingdom. The religious leaders would not enter My Kingdom, because they rejected Me and My Ways. Are you rejecting Me and My Ways? Are you rejecting what I AM telling you to do? Open your eyes and see clearly. I want you to do as I tell you to do and not as the world tells you to do.

Be obedient, and I will bless you.

Matthew 21:33-46

My Beloved, the religious leaders came to Me and asked Me many questions. All the people listened to them ask Me questions, and I answered them wisely. The religious leaders tried to trap Me by asking questions that may cause harm to Me. They wanted to twist My Words for the people to hear. All day long the people were in My Presence listening to My Words. The religious leaders could see that the crowds were larger every day. They had to stop Me or lose some of those who followed after them and their ways. They said that they maintained My Temple and cared for My People. They said that they taught My People the Truth. Yet when Truth came to the religious leaders, they did not recognize Me. They wanted to kill Me and get rid of Me just like they did to My Prophets. They wrote My Prophets' words in a book, and then they killed My Prophets. Later they found out that their words came to pass, and then they believed in their words. The religious leaders were lost and had no vision. Could they not see that I would destroy the Temple and scatter My People just like the Prophets said? When I told the people stories, the religious leaders knew that I was talking about them and they were furious. They knew that I despised what they were doing to My People. After they killed Me they realized that they had killed a good man, but never did they accept Me for who I AM. Have you accepted Me as your Messiah? You must believe that I AM who I AM. You must believe that I AM Creator Almighty, Ruler of the Universe. There is no one above Me. I AM the Eternal One. I create and give life, and I take away life. Worship Me for who I AM- the only One worthy of praise and adoration, and you will rejoice with Me in My Kingdom.

Matthew 22:1-14

My Beloved, I talked to the people in stories. I told them about My Kingdom. I told them that I wanted to have a great feast for the marriage of My Son. I told them that I invited all the respectable people in the kingdom, but they would not come. They rejected My Son and his wedding to His Bride. They treated My Servants shamefully and even killed them. I sent My Soldiers and killed all of them that harmed My Servants. I chose those who were not worthy and called them to the wedding, and they came joyfully. They were rejoicing to be invited. There were some who were invited to come that did not wash themselves and wear the proper attire to the wedding, and they were cast out of My Kingdom. Only those who cleansed themselves and came in wedding attire were received into My Kingdom and celebrated with Me. All the others were cast into outer darkness. My Slaves are those of My Servants who obey Me and do as I tell them to do. My Soldiers are My Angels. Those who rejected Me are the people who would not accept My Son. How can you enter the wedding feast? Be cleansed from the world and walk in oneness with Me. If you love Me, you will listen to My Voice and be obedient. You will walk hand in hand with Me and rejoice.

Matthew 22:15-22

My Beloved, the crowds that followed Me grew larger every day. The religious leaders wanted to trap Me with My Words to bring up contentions within the people. The religious leaders wanted the people to turn against Me. They wanted to stop Me from teaching the Truth. Some of the religious leaders sent their disciples and some of Herod's party to trick Me. I knew their hearts. I knew their evil intent. They asked Me a question, but I could see that they were evil. I answered it in a way that they could find no fault with Me. They asked Me if a person should pay his money to the Temple or to the Romans. The people hated the Romans, because they made them pay taxes. The Temple also made My People pay taxes. I told them to pay taxes to those to whom they are due. This made some of the rebels against the Romans mad. Most of the people understood My Words. They could not fight against these foreign invaders. Only I could redeem them from the Romans. They were looking to Me to be their King and rule over them. They wanted Me to stand up against the Romans and destroy them. The time had not come for Me to stand up and fight for My People. This time is still in the future, but I am starting to call My People back to My Land. I am revealing the hidden Truth to My People, so they can walk in My Ways and find favor in My Sight. Are you ready to hear My Call? Look up and see Me. Look up and know that I can do all things, and rest in My Arms.

Matthew 22:23-32

My Beloved, My People had many questions. They wanted someone to tell them how to live their lives, but they wanted to live the way they wanted to live. They wanted wise teachers to guide them, but they wanted them to say what they wanted to hear. Many men asked Me questions, and the religious leaders listened to every one of their questions. They hoped to find some way to criticize Me in front of the people and turn the crowds away from Me. Every day they sent some of their disciples to listen to My Words, so they could find a way to trap Me and cause Me harm. There was a group of men who came and wanted sincerely to know the answer to a question. Their reasoning was flawed, because they did not understand what My Words said. They did not realize that no one could be married in heaven. They did not realize that they would not have children in heaven or have fleshly needs. They did not realize that they would be like the angels who do not have fleshly needs. I settled their question, but the religious leaders were furious that they gave me the authority to answer the question and accept it. They looked to Me as a great teacher of the Torah, but the religious leaders looked to Me as a threat and wanted to kill Me. How do you look at Me? Do you see Me as a threat to you, because you cannot do as you please? Do you see Me as your Savior, your Husband, your Beloved, your Father? How do you see Me? However you see Me is how I will present Myself to you and love you in that way. Draw closer to Me and I will reveal Myself to you.

Matthew 22:33-45

My Beloved, the religious leaders came to Me daily to try to trap Me with their questions. They wanted to find some fault in Me, but there was none. They wanted to criticize Me and belittle Me in front of My People, but they could not find any error in My Ways. One of the Torah experts asked Me what the greatest commandment was. I told Him to love Me with all his heart, soul, mind, and strength. All the other commandments hang on this commandment. If you do not love Me, you will not want to keep all the commandments. If you love Me, you will also love others. You will be compassionate and merciful. You will want to help your neighbor and do good things for him. You will want to see that he has all he needs. The religious leaders could not argue with this like they loved to do. They had nothing to say. I asked them a question, and they could not answer it. This made them look inferior in front of the people. They were ashamed and did not ask Me any more questions after this. In their efforts to humiliate Me, they only humiliated themselves. Even though it was apparent that I had Wisdom from heaven, they still wanted to kill Me because I was leading the people away from them. I was teaching the commandments in a way that the people could understand. The Torah teachers wanted to make their lives complicated with many laws, but I pointed them back to the laws of Moses. Do you make your life too complicated with too many laws? I told My People to keep only the laws of Moses, so they could rejoice and be set free. Focus only on what My Scriptures tell you to do, and keep it simple. Do not follow man-made traditions. Follow My Ways, and you will be greatly blessed.

Matthew 23:1-12

My Beloved, the religious leaders liked to have power and authority and wanted all the people to submit to them. They liked to do things in public to show the people that they were superior to them and more righteous than they were. They wanted to judge the people harshly. They wanted to tie heavy loads around their necks. Where was their compassion and kindness? They only wanted to have the people under their feet as servants, so I judged them and I removed their seat of authority. I destroyed the Temple in Jerusalem and removed their place of worship. I told My People to keep the laws of Moses, but do not act like the religious leaders. I wanted My People to be humble and walk in kindness and be compassionate. I wanted My People to be My Hands and Feet and help those around them. I wanted My People to become one with Me and walk hand in hand with Me. The religious leaders wanted to reign over the masses. They did not want to teach the masses how to know Me and walk with Me, because they did not know Me or walk with Me. I told My People to call no one Father or Teacher, but only call Me Father and Teacher. Do you look to one man for guidance? Do you seek Me for the answers to your questions? Torah teachers are given to you to help you learn the Truth in My Words. They are not to be worshipped or thought to be better than others. They are servants just like you. Seek Me for all the answers to your questions, and I will tell you. Do not seek a man to help you find the answers to your questions. One man does not have all the answers, but I have all the answers. Seek Me first and I will guide you.

Matthew 23:13-22

My Beloved, I told My People not to look at the religious leaders and what they do, but look at Me and what I do. The religious leaders wanted to put a heavy burden of laws on My People and keep them from becoming one with Me. My People were so worried about keeping all the laws that they had no time to spend with Me. The religious leaders would go to other nations to get disciples to follow them. The more followers they had the greater they looked. I did not pay for followers, but My People heard My Voice and wanted to follow after Me. My People were looking for ways to please Me. They were not like the blind guides that wanted the people to follow them blindly. They were concerned about their image and not My People learning to grow spiritually strong in Me. They thought the Temple will be around forever, and they would be leaders forever. They could not see the future how they would be cast down and considered as worthless. I told My People not to swear concerning the things of the Temple. Do you swear or make promises that you will do things? I do not want My People to swear at all. Let your yes remain yes and do not bend to circumstances. Nothing in the Temple is worth more than you. You are My unique treasure. I want you to remain faithful to Me. Lift your eyes up to Me and follow in My Ways. Be My Disciples and I will bring you great riches to your house.

Matthew 23:23-26

My Beloved, the religious leaders and Torah teachers were very careful to tithe every little thing that they grew even down to the herbs in their garden, yet they had no mercy and did not walk in justice. They did not care for My People, but they poured heavy burdens on their backs to keep all their rules and regulations. They did not teach My People to have love and compassion. They only wanted to rule over them and be harsh to them to show their superiority over them. They were cruel leaders and poor examples of how to live your life. They were not an example for My People to follow. The leaders must be upright for the people to stand up and be righteous. If the leaders are corrupt, then the people will also be corrupt. The leaders did not wash the inside of their soul, but they were careful to keep every law about washing dishes and cups. My Laws were meant to be guidelines to live a life of loving-kindness and tender mercy towards all men, no matter if the men are cruel to you or not. A righteous leader would stand firm and not give into bribes or any form of injustice. Already the religious leaders had been tainted with corruption and used the office of priest to acquire more from My People than they were supposed to receive. They had bent the laws to fit their pocketbook. They were getting richer every day at the cost of My People. Are you an example for those around you? Do you walk in righteousness? Someone that walks in the things of Me should be a servant to all. They should be loving and kind and forgiving knowing that no man is perfect and all men make mistakes. A wise man looks at the heart and knows what kind of man is before him. If you desire to please Me, you will walk humbly before Me and give love to others everywhere you go. You will feel My Presence on you to touch others, and you will be a blessing wherever you go.

Matthew 23:27-39

My Beloved, I sent My Prophets to your ancestors, and they killed them. They did not like what My Prophets were saying to them, yet they wrote down every word that each prophet said. When they saw that the words of the prophet came to pass, then they called them My Words and the man who said them was hailed as a prophet. They could not discern the times. They did not want to hear that they were in sin. They thought they were righteous in all their ways. They were greatly deceived! They were swept away to another land and suffered much under the hand of their enemies. In the time that I walked on earth, the religious leaders were arrogant and harsh with the people. They did not want to hear that they were like white washed tombs. They had no compassion. They were cruel and money hungry. They used the places of authority to make money and rule over My People. They did not teach My People to be kind and caring. I came to earth to look into what they were doing, and I was extremely angry with them. My heart was filled with compassion for My People. My People were without a leader. They had no shepherd. They were lost and in conflict with those around them. They had no peace. Do you have peace today? I came to earth to bring peace to My People. I gave them My Spirit-the Comforter. I gave My People a great gift. I taught My People to rely on Me and not religious men. Call on My Name, and I will answer all your questions. I will guide you down the path to eternal life and give you peace.

Matthew 24:1-14

My Beloved, My Disciples were pointing out to Me how beautiful the Temple was and all the surrounding buildings. I told them that all they see will be destroyed. They wanted to know the time that all this will happen. They knew that I would become King of all the earth, but they did not know when this would be. I told them that first I had to be a Servant and lay down My Life for My People, so I could take away all their sins. They did not understand this and did not want to accept it. They believed that I would come back very soon and take over My Kingdom. It has been hundreds of years since I walked on this planet. I set an example for My People, but man has refused to accept My Example of love and compassion for others. Are you prepared for My Return? I want you to be righteous in all your ways. Stay away from the world and do not sin against Me. It will be hard when all those around you are not following My Ways. You will have to remain steadfast and walk in what you know is good. I will return, but I am looking for a virgin bride. I am looking for a people who have not fornicated with the world and want to serve only Me. I will help you at every corner to guide you. If you are persecuted in a city, then move to another place. I will guide you. If you listen to My Voice, I will guide you out of the city before you fall into the hand of cruelty. Listen to Me, because I AM with you. I love you.

Matthew 24:15-22

My Beloved, I told My People to watch for the fulfillment of Daniel's prophecy. When this time arrives I wanted My People to flee from Judah and go to a safe place. I will open the door for My People to escape. I will show My People the great sacrilege that is happening in My Temple, and they will see clearly and know that I am showing them to leave quickly and not be caught up in the sudden destruction of Jerusalem. I will show My People a way out, so they will not be harmed. They will flee, and My Hand will cover them. This will happen after all My Children return to My Land and are dwelling in peace. This abomination will arise suddenly without notice, and only the faithful will be able to see what is happening. There will be much secrecy, and the evil one will reveal himself in a time when only the righteous will be able to see the Truth and flee. Are you faithful to hear My Voice and obey? You must be on guard, or you will be caught up in the destruction and be killed instantly. You must be watching and listening for My Call. I will tell My People in advance what will happen. Only those who are faithful will be obedient and leave. The others will not be so fortunate. This time in the history of the world will be the worst because of the extreme deception. Even the faithful will be swept up in the deception unless I cut the time short, because his power will be great to bring deception to all men. I will shield My People from his lies. They will see how he uses technology to cause the deception and warps the minds of many. Stand firm and listen. I will tell you exactly what to do. Listen!

Matthew 24:23-31

My Beloved, I told My People not to listen to others when they say that the Messiah has returned, because everyone will know when I have come. I will light up the whole sky when I return. All will know that I have come to gather My People back to Me. My Angels will gather My People from all over the earth and gather them to Me, so we can rejoice together. It will be a great celebration, because you have endured until the end and proven yourself faithful. You will hear of false messiahs, because many will say that they are the one. Even the evil one will try to come and deceive My People and say that he is the one that you have been waiting for. Will you be deceived by the evil one? The elect will see the signs and know that he brings only deception. Only the elect will know that he is not the Messiah. He will deceive many and say that he will bring peace to all the earth, but he has only come to entrap the world and hold captive those who love Me. You will see his evil plan and flee to a place where he cannot touch you. Listen, because the time is near. The earth will be shaken. The sun will grow dark and the moon will be hidden. There will be great confusion and chaos on the earth. There will be people wanting to die from fear. There will be many who love Me who are hidden under My Hand of protection. All will seek protection, but only My Children will be kept safe. You must be prepared and ready to listen and obey. You must know the season, and watch for the time. You must know that the evil one will try to deceive you so beware. You must know that I love you and will care for you even in the most troublesome times.

Matthew 24:32-35

My Beloved, just as you see the signs that flowers are beginning to bloom, then you know spring is coming. The coldness of winter is past and the warm days of spring are coming. When you see the signs that the great deceiver has come, you know My Appearance is near. You will see the evil one impersonating Me in the Temple saying that he is the one who the Chosen Ones have been waiting for to restore peace to the world. The evil one will try to kill all of My Beloved Children. He will command his elect soldiers to exterminate the world of all those who believe in Me saying they are trying to stop world peace. My Chosen Ones will run to safety as guided by My Hand. They will live in seclusion. They will have to be fed by Me by My Hand. They will not be able to roam the earth as they once did, but they will need to stay close to each other and be covered with My Hand. I will shelter My Children as I did in the Wilderness. I will care for them and keep them from harm. If anyone comes to harm them, they will be destroyed. Are you listening intently to My Voice? You must keep your ears open for the days are coming when you will have to do what I tell you to do. I will always be beside you. My Angels will surround you and fight for you and no one can harm you. You do not have to ever be afraid. You must trust Me to care for you. Watch for the signs. You will know the season. Already the time is at the door for darkness to cover the world and deceive many. Only the elect will be able to see in the darkness. Draw close to Me, so you can see clearly.

Matthew 24:36-44

My Beloved, you do not know when I will return, but I have promised My People that I will let them know the season and the season is soon. The darkness is growing over the earth. Many are turning to the evil one and want to walk in his ways. The time is soon for My Return. The world will continue like in the days of Noah. People will continue with their lives marrying and divorcing. They will be celebrating their successes and grieving over their losses. The earth will continue on until I return, but just like in the days of Noah the people will be very wicked. Only My Chosen Ones will be able to overcome and stand up in spite of all the wickedness around them. They will remain the pure seed. They will remain faithful until the end. They are the ones who love Me and want to serve Me. They are My Beloved. Are you afraid of what the future will bring? You must be careful to listen during this time and not be afraid. The evil one thrives on fear. He wants to enter into people who are fearful and exaggerate their fear within their minds until it is monumental. You will see more fearful people than ever before. You will see people seeking medical help for their fears and anxieties. They will be lost with no one to help them unless they call on My Name and allow Me to bring them peace. I will heal all their wounds and correct their faulty thinking and restore them and make them whole. You must not ever fear. You must only trust Me to help you at all times. You must love Me with all your heart, and then you will know that I will help you at every corner with every decision. You are My Beloved. I will hold you in My Arms of love all day.

Matthew 24:45-51

My Beloved, are you a faithful servant? Are you doing well the task that I have put before you? Are you working to the best of your ability? Are you complaining about what I have given you to do? Are you giving love and compassion along the way? Have you decided not to do your best? Have you decided to get away with as much as you can? Have you decided to hurt others, because they have hurt you? Are you an example of righteousness to those around you? Are you the one who leads others to do what is right? Have you done all that you can do for others that have come across your path with needs? Do not forsake your brothers of the faith. Do not try to close your eyes to their needs. I will bless you greatly for all you do for Me. If you continue to serve Me with all your heart, then I will reward you when I return. I will give you special gifts to fill your house. You will reign with Me and be blessed by Me. You do not have to be afraid of anything in this life. I will give you all you need. I will do everything for you, so you can complete the tasks that I have given you to do. I will help you by bringing others along your path to light your path and show you the way to go. They will strengthen and encourage you and bring Truth to you. Arise and lift up your head. Look into My Eyes and listen for My Voice, and then you will be a faithful servant. You will have a special place in My Household. You will be lifted up and become My Child of Authority reigning with Me forever.

Matthew 25:1-13

My Beloved, are you ready for Me to return? You must be ready and prepared to meet Me. You must not be like the foolish virgins who were not ready. All the virgins had promised to cling to Me and remain loyal to the Bridegroom in the engagement period even though He was away for a long time. As the years went by some of the virgins became slack and were not ready to meet the Bridegroom. They began to slip into the things of the world. They were filled with the oil of the Spirit in the beginning and they were ready, but they did not continue to remain alert and fell asleep. The righteous virgins continued to trim their lamps and remain full of Light. They were waiting eagerly for My Coming. They were filled with the oil of My Spirit and listening to My Voice. Even though both began in righteousness, only some of the virgins continued in My Ways. You must not allow the world to tarnish your Light. You must not give in to the things of the world. It is very easy to take your eyes off Me. It is very easy to be caught up in fleshly pleasures. Every day I see so many get lost into what they want and not what I want. If you are not sacrificing your flesh daily, then you can be tempted to fall away. You must be vigilant and not grow weary. I will help you if you call on My Name. I will show you the way to walk along side of Me, so you can stay in the path that I have for you. Many want to run ahead of Me. Many more fall behind Me. Only the faithful will walk hand in hand with Me and trust Me in all I tell them to do. I will make the pathway straight, and the Way will be clear.

Matthew 25:14-30

My Beloved, I came to tell My People what would happen in the future, if they followed Me and did not turn back to the world. I told My People that they were My Servants and I was their Master. I will give them commands while they are on earth, and they will obey knowing that I would only ask them to do things that would benefit My Kingdom on Earth. My Servants are humble and want only to serve Me. They are not self-seeking, but they are seeking Me. They want to know My Ways and follow close to Me. They want to hold My Hand and walk hand in hand with Me. They want to love others and be kind and understanding. I have given each man certain abilities. Are you using the abilities that I have given you? Each man must use what I have given him in the best way that he can. He must see how he can help others with the gifts I have given him. If he tries to be compassionate with all men, his gifts will come shining through. He will grow strong and mighty. If he allows fear to dominate him and he does not trust Me to help him, then he will be like the man who dug a hole and buried his talent. He will have nothing when I return to show for how he served Me. You must be bold and brave and allow Me to shine through you. I will bless you with what I have given you. If you trust Me, I will take you to great places. You will soar above the others. You will see ahead and never fear. You will be mighty and hold firm. You will be greatly rewarded in My Kingdom.

Matthew 25:31-46

My Beloved, at the end of this age I will return. I will come with all My Angels. I will sit on My Throne and bring all the peoples to Me. I will judge them according to their works. If they loved Me and served Me and only wanted to please Me, then I will reward them greatly. If they only served themselves, then there will be no reward. They will be sent away from Me into eternal punishment. They will be utterly consumed in the flames of death and totally destroyed. There will be no trace of them and no memory of them. They will be as if they did not ever exist. They had their own way on earth and did as they pleased, so they will be punished in the end for their selfishness. They will be punished, because they did not love others or give freely to others. If you love yourself, how good are you? If you love others, then you give and give and give. My People are the ones who continue to love and be kind to all around them. My People never hurt others and do not want any harm to come to anyone. They only want Me to judge the wicked fairly and do what is just. Are you loving others and walking in righteousness? Look at your life and examine yourself very carefully. Do you need to change the way you live your life? Call on My Name, and I will help you see clearly. You will be able to walk in the way of righteousness. Knowing Me is knowing Truth.

Matthew 26:1-5

My Beloved, I told My Disciples everything that was going to happen to Me, but they did not understand why it had to happen. I told them that in two days I would be handed over to their enemies and crucified. They could not bear the thought of Me having to sacrifice Myself in such a way. They expected Me to begin My Kingdom on earth. They did not understand that I would have to pay for their sins by shedding My Blood for them. They wanted to rule with Me on earth. They would have to wait until the end of this age on earth was over, and I returned to claim My Throne. They could not see ahead as I saw ahead. They were blinded by their own ambitions. They did not want to suffer persecution any longer under the hand of their enemies. All the people that followed Me and came to hear Me teach were looking for a Messiah to deliver them. The message that I gave them was too hard. They did not want to pick up their execution stake and sacrifice themselves and follow Me. Are you ready to put aside all that you want to do and follow Me? Are you sacrificing yourself daily? Are you giving Me time for your morning and evening sacrifice when you spend time with Me and worship Me and commune with Me? Do you set aside time in the day to be at one with Me, so I can guide you and tell you what will happen in the future? Do not be afraid of anything, but trust only Me. I will show you the way to go, so you will be safe and complete in Me.

Matthew 26:6-13

My Beloved, there was a woman who came to Me and covered Me with an expensive oil. She was led by My Spirit. She was preparing Me for burial that would happen very shortly. She was grieving knowing that she would lose Me soon. She could see that I was a great treasure. Those around her criticized Me for allowing her to anoint Me with oil. They thought I should sell the oil and give the money to the poor. They were always trying to find fault with Me. They did not want to accept My teachings. They did not want to accept the Truth. They wanted to continue in their wicked ways being blinded and greedy. I came to them to try to show them the Light, but they rejected the Light and would not receive Me. I had come to die for the sins of many, but even My Disciples could not accept this. They wanted Me to deliver them from the oppression of their enemies. They knew I AM the One. They would follow Me to the end. They were devoted to Me, yet they had their own fleshly desires and could not see the big picture. They were tired of being oppressed by their enemies, but they had not suffered enough for their sins. They would even see their Temple destroyed and be scattered to all parts of the earth. They wanted victory over their enemies, but instead I gave them victory over death and the grave. They would live with Me eternally and reign with Me in My Heavenly Kingdom. They were given a greater gift than they could imagine. They were adopted as My Children, and they will be given My Authority. Rejoice and be glad. Are you being oppressed by your enemies today? Be strong. Be brave. The time is short. I AM coming soon.

Matthew 26:14-16

My Beloved, I told My Disciples to go out and tell all the peoples about Me. They all wanted to go and expand My Kingdom except Judas. He wanted Me to stand up and show My Authority. He wanted Me to show My Power. He wanted Me to overcome their enemies that oppressed them. He wanted Me to release them from bondage, but the time was not ready for this. He did not want to wait. He wanted for Me to do something now. He became very angry with Me, and he wanted to push Me to stand up and exert My power. He thought if he went to the High Priest and turned Me over to the Jewish authorities that I would stand up for Myself and prove Myself to be King. He did not realize what he was doing. He was selfish and self-centered wanting his own goals to be met and not accepting what I was doing for My People. He did not see the plan to save My People from their sins. He did not care about others, but only himself. He was part of a group of men who wanted to overthrow their enemies. He would use violence for the greater good. He would even sacrifice Me, if I did not do as he desired. He saw too late that I had a different plan, and I would be true to that plan even to give up My Own Life. Judas could not see what I saw. He could only see what he wanted to see. Are you following your own selfish ambitions? Do you want to do what you want to do? If you really love Me, you will want to obey Me and walk in My Ways of love and compassion. You will want to give up what you want, and do what I want you to do. You will know that whatever I ask from you will be the best for you. You will rejoice in how I lead your life. You will want to be close to Me and hear My Voice and know the way to go. Do not try to do what you think is best, but seek Me in every decision you make. Judas betrayed Me. You will turn your back on Me too, if you do not lay down your own selfish ambitions and turn your eyes to Me. I can guide you into the only way that will bring you growth and prosper you. You will be filled with joy over submitting to Me at last.

Matthew 6:17-25

My Beloved, I told My disciples to go prepare the Passover Seder for Me. I told them where to go to ask for a place to eat the Seder. I had already prepared the owner of the house to open his doors for Me. My Disciples bought all they needed for the Seder. We all sat at the table to begin our meal together. This would be my last meal with them. I was sad to leave them, but I knew that if I did not go away that My Children would not be filled with My Spirit. I wanted them to be able to feel My Presence always. I wanted them to never feel alone. I wanted My Children to hear My Voice clearly and know the way to go. In the midst of My Disciples there was a dark one. He was constantly a source of grief for Me. I knew from the beginning who he was. I knew that he would betray Me. I loved him in spite of what he was going to do. Yet he was there in the midst of My Love, and he did not turn towards Me. He wanted to see his own goals come to pass and not what I wanted for My Children. I tried to warn him many times that My Way would bring life, but he was angry that I did not do something about the situation of My People. "How could I continue to allow them to be oppressed by their enemies?" he argued. He could only see the present and not the future. Do you trust Me when you cannot see the future, but only know what is happening in the present? I know what is best for you at all times. I know what you need for your future. Do not be like Judas and want you own way, but trust Me to guide you into eternal life. He lost his entry into My Kingdom, and he lost his life eternal.

Matthew 26:26-29

My Beloved, I sat with My Disciples and held them close to Me. I knew this was the last time I would be with them in the flesh. I wanted to tell them many things and prepare them for the days ahead. They would be sheep without their Shepherd for awhile. They would need Me to stand close to them and bring My Spirit to fill them, so they could hear My voice. I blessed the bread at the Seder. I told them to eat because this was My Flesh that would be broken for them, so they could live with Me eternally. I blessed the wine. I told them that this was the blood that I would shed for them to pay for their sins, so they could be cleansed and begin a new life with Me. They did not understand any of what I was saying. This was a spiritual idea that they could not understand until I brought My Spirit to dwell in them. My Disciples were sad and grieved over My Words. They knew that one of them would betray Me to their enemies. They could not bear the thought of Me being betrayed. They never thought that any of them would betray Me or any of My inner circle of disciples would betray each other. Their world was shaken, and I could see the pain in their eyes. I knew they would have to be strong and stand firm. It would not be easy. All they knew would disappear, and they would have to make a new life for themselves. They would have to hide from religious authorities. They would have to face being jailed for what they believed. They would be beaten and put in prison. Those that they loved would be taken from them. I told many of them to flee the city and go to another place to live. I wanted the believers to spread out across the earth and tell all people the Good News of what I had done for them. Those that would not leave the city were driven out by their enemies until those who believed in Me were like salt spread across the earth. Are you telling others the Good News about Me? You are My Salt and Light. You are My Hands and Feet. Stand up My People and walk in what I have for you. Be strong and brave. I AM with you.

Matthew 26:30-35

My Beloved, I sat with My Disciples and ate my last meal with them. My heart was heavy for them. I knew they would lose faith in Me. They looked at Me like their future king. They wanted Me to release them from their enemies. Now they would see Me nailed to a stake and executed. "If I was a king, I would stand up and call on My Angels and they would come to My Side and fight for Me", they thought. Their faith in Me vanished, and they were heartbroken. They wept for the loss of their vision. They wanted to stay close to Me, but they were afraid of their enemies. They knew how cruel they were. Peter told Me that he would never reject Me or lose faith in Me, but when confronted his fear overtook him and he did reject Me. He grieved over what he had done for many days. In his mind he should have died with Me and stood next to Me. He wanted to make things right with Me, but there was no way to talk with Me. He saw Me die and his sorrow was great. All My Disciples had lost their Shepherd. They had lost the One who they believed in. They lost Me only for a moment in time, but then they received My Spirit and their wounds were healed. They were given a great gift of My Spirit. Have you received My Spirit? Have you become one with Me? You can accomplish great things if you cling to Me, and do not lose sight of Me. I AM your Shepherd. I AM the One who guides you at all times.

Matthew 26:36-45

My Beloved, after our last meal together I took My Disciples to a place to pray. My heart was very heavy. I knew My Disciples would be lost and alone without Me. I was grieved for them, and I wanted them to pray that they would be strong enough to stand firm and not fall under a heavy test of their faith. I wanted them to be able to pray with Me before I entered My Fiery Test. I knew what I would have to endure, and the pain would be great. I cried out for the deliverance of My Flesh, but I knew that My Flesh had to be sacrificed for the sake of My People. I wanted My People to become at one with Me and be able to talk with Me. The task ahead was difficult, but it was temporary and brief as compared to the time I would have with My Children. You must realize that I did live in flesh and felt all its pain and sadness just as you feel daily. I understand the burden you carry daily. I know how the flesh weighs you down and hinders your walk with Me. You may be tired or hungry or in pain, and your flesh rises up and wants to be satisfied. This is when you must allow your spirit to rise up and stand firm and take charge of your flesh. Do you allow your flesh to rule you? You rule over your flesh. Sometimes you will be very angry or sad, and the emotions will wash over you and overcome you. Even in the midst of these strong emotions, you must keep your eyes set on Me and know that I will help you and lift you above the situation. If you hold fast to Me, I will give you the strength you need to carry you through these difficult times. I will hold you close to Me, and you will be comforted. Sometimes you do not understand why certain things happen, but I have a plan through all of it. I have a plan for your life, and if you trust Me and accept what comes your way, then I will bless you greatly.

Matthew 26:46-56

My Beloved, Judas came to Me to betray Me. He brought men with weapons to force Me to come with him. He came to Me and kissed Me and showed the men when to arrest Me. I knew My Time had come to lay down My Life for My People. I was grieved that I must leave My Disciples. I knew it would be a very dark time for them. I knew that they would run in all directions, because their Master was taken from them. They looked to Me for everything for years and now all their hope in Me would vanish. They wanted to fight back and save Me from the mob of pursuers, but I stopped them. I told them that I had to do this to fulfill all the prophecy about Me in the Scriptures. They did not understand any of these things until later when they searched the Scriptures and found how I fulfilled all the prophecy and brought to pass the living Word. I gave them a firm foundation, but still they were scared and fearful. They did not understand what was happening to Me. I told them that I would call My Angels down to help Me, if I wanted them to come. The heavenly realm watched in awe as I laid down My life for My Children. They were ready to fight on behalf of Me. They were ready to lift Me up and carry Me to My Kingdom, but I never told them to come. They were amazed at what was happening. They did not know or understand what I was doing either. They knew I had to lay down My Life, but I did not tell them the complete meaning because I did not want the evil one to change his plan. He thought if he killed Me that he would stop My Mission on earth. He did not know that he had started or put in motion exactly what I wanted to happen. Do you understand why I had to die for you? I had to shed My Blood to cover the sins of My Children, so they could dwell with Me forever in My Kingdom. I did this for you, so we could always be together. I did this for your children and the children after you. I did this so you could be heirs to My Kingdom, and I could give you My Authority. You are My Beloved, and I did this all for you.

Matthew 26:59-67

My Beloved, I was taken to the religious leaders, so they could find fault with Me. They wanted to get rid of Me like all their ancestors did with the prophets who came to tell them the Truth. They tried to make Me guilty. Finally they chose to call Me a blasphemer, so they could put Me to death. I knew what My Fate was, so I accepted it and did not try to argue with them or even state My Case. I could have given arguments that would overrule them. They would not have been able to find fault with Me, but that was not what I came to do. Every day they heard Me teach in the Temple, and they knew that the people followed Me and wanted to hear My Words. There were many who followed Me, and the number of people was growing larger every day. They had to stop Me. They had to kill Me. They gave Me a guilty verdict, and they hit Me and spit on Me and mocked Me. They were putting a guilty verdict on themselves. They would have the death verdict placed on them, and they would no longer have eternal life in My Kingdom. They wanted to be superior to Me and not allow Me to pull the people away from them. They were blinded, because they were proud and arrogant. They thought they had victory over Me, but they only brought Me power and life. They gave Me victory, and with it I defeated all such people like them. I overcame death and led a host of captives free. I gave you life eternal, and all they gave Me were a few bruises. I gave up Myself for you. I sacrificed Myself for you. Will you also sacrifice yourself for Me?

Matthew 26:57-58, 69-75

My Beloved, My Disciples were scattered after I was taken from them. They ran in all directions. Only Peter followed Me to see what would happen to Me. He loved Me deeply, but he was also afraid. He knew how cruel his enemies could be. They were known for their torture and cruel punishment. They kept all My People in fear. He tried to hear what was happening to Me, but instead he had onlookers accuse him of knowing Me. He knew that they would turn him over to the authorities if he was associated with Me, so in fear he denied that he knew Me. I already told him that he would deny Me, but he swore that he never would deny that he knew Me. He never expected for Me to be taken from him, and that he would have to go through all the suffering that he would have to endure. When he heard the rooster crow he remembered My Words, and he went away and wept bitterly. He was so grieved that he was not bolder. He was grieved that I knew that he would deny that he even knew Me. He knew how much it would hurt Me, and he could barely think about the pain he had caused Me. He could not stop grieving. He hid himself from everyone and cried painfully. He cried out for Me to forgive him. I heard his prayers and forgave him. I knew he loved Me and would endure much to see My Kingdom established on earth. He gave up his life for Me and surrendered all he had for Me. Will you do the same? You may have rejected Me in the past, but I will forgive you. You may have lived a sinful life, and you are ashamed of yourself. Peter was also ashamed of himself, but I forgave him. I will forgive you and redeem you and set you free from your sins. I will make you My Own. I will take you into My Arms and love you tenderly. Surrender and come to Me.

Matthew 27:1-10

My Beloved, I was taken away by the religious leaders, and I was given to the Roman soldiers. The religious leaders made up a false accusation about Me, so that the Roman leaders would hand me over to be put to death. My People rejected Me and gave Me up to My Enemies. This was spoken of by the prophet. I knew that this would happen. I told My People many years ago that I would be put to death to cover the sins of the guilty. I would be lifted up and brought into My Kingdom of Light, so I could live with My People forever. Judas saw that his plan had failed. When Judas saw that I was condemned to death, and I had not tried to argue My Case and claim My Kingdom, he was extremely grieved. He was so devastated that he could not live with himself, and he killed himself. The weight of his sins was on his head, and he died in his sins. He betrayed Me and turned his face against Me. He would have to pay a high price for his sins and not live with Me eternally in My Kingdom. He wanted to rule with Me, and then he chose to betray Me for 30 pieces of silver. He could not bear his sin, because he knew that he could not do anything to help Me. I had been turned over to the Romans, and he knew what My Fate would be. He knew that I would be crucified. He could not stand to be the one that caused My Death Sentence. Judas did not realize that I would have to fulfill the prophecy that was written in My Scriptures. He did not realize that My Kingdom would begin on earth with My People, and I would come again to redeem them. Thirty pieces of silver were thrown all over the Temple floor by Judas, but this did not pay for his sin against Me. No one who betrays Me or rejects Me can be redeemed from his sins. Judas' fate was sealed. Has your fate been sealed? Your fate is not sealed. You can still repent from your sins and come to Me and receive Me. You can still be My humble servant and obey Me in all I ask you to do. Come to Me today. My arms are open for you.

Matthew 27:11-26

My Beloved, I was taken to stand in front of Pilate. He was a wise man and knew that I was brought to him out of jealousy. He knew that the crowds were growing larger for Me every day. He knew the people looked to Me as their Savior and their King. He knew that the religious leaders were losing control of the crowds of people. The religious leaders set up a mob of people to stand before Pilate. They paid them well to shout out to have Me crucified, and that I was a liar. They shouted all sorts of blasphemies. They drew the rest of the people around them into the mob and had them all shouting to crucify Me. Their religious leaders were well pleased at the outcome. They knew that I would be executed. The people were lost and without a leader. They were pulled by every man. They needed a Savior. They needed Me to guide them. Pilate could see that the crowd was becoming unruly and he needed to disperse them. He knew I was innocent, so he washed his hands of the sentence. He let the people decide My Sentence, and they chose to kill Me. My Blood was on their hands. Everyone that was in that crowd that shouted out to kill Me was cursed at that moment. All of their children were cursed. They were doomed. They had pronounced a death sentence on an innocent man without any evidence. I have forgiven My People for their sins, but those who pronounced Me guilty had to pay heavily for this sin. It was so heavy that it was placed on many generations of their children. Think before you pass judgment on yourself. Do you consider your words before you speak? Be wise. You are responsible for every word that you say. You will pay the price for your words.

Matthew 27:27-31

My Beloved, I was turned over to the Roman soldiers. They wanted to make a mockery of Me. They thought it was so funny that I was considered King of the Jews. The Jews had rejected Me as their King, and only those who really loved Me wanted to serve Me. The soldiers spit on Me and beat Me and tormented Me with their lies and sarcasm. They wanted to hurt Me. They beat Me down, and then they dragged Me out to be executed. These Roman soldiers were a product of a violent army who did not care about human life. They are arrogant and fierce. They hated My People and hated that they were in a foreign country away from their home. They looked at all other people as inferior to them. Roman soldiers had to be born within the area of Rome. They had to go through grueling training to produce violent warriors who thrived on punishing My People. They were trained to be heartless and serve only Rome. They were an abomination to Me, so I cut them down by their enemies. Rome who thought no one could conquer them was conquered. I brought up an army to hate them and treat them cruelly like they had treated My People. These Roman soldiers paid for their crimes against Me and My People. They lost their children and most of them were wiped off the earth without a trace. My People have been preserved through the ages. I have kept My Hand on them and provided for them even in the darkest of days. Even when their enemies were trying to wipe them out, I have upheld them and covered them and led them to safe places. Do you listen to My Voice? I will guide you to safe places. Only those who hear My Voice and call on My Name will be saved in these Last Days. Soon I will come back again to gather My People back to Me. Be strong and brave. Be ready for My return, and I will bless you greatly.

Matthew 27:32-37

My Beloved, after the soldiers mocked Me and beat Me they took Me outside, so I could drag my execution stake to the hill. My flesh was weak and I fell under the load of the stake. The soldiers made another man carry the stake for Me to the hill. They stripped Me of all My clothes and humiliated Me in front of My People. They divided My clothes among them and laughed over who got the robe of the King of the Jews. They nailed Me to the stake and made Me drink wine made bitter with vinegar. They hoisted Me up for all the people to see. I stood above all of them and saw the sins of My People fall upon Me. The darkness was much too heavy to bear. The weight of it was tremendous. My Innocent Blood fell on the ground as others looked on. The Roman soldiers were stationed to guard Me. They knew that the crowds would come to look at Me hoping that I would arise and overcome the Roman rule. The soldiers mocked Me in front of My People, "This is your king. Why doesn't he save you?" My People felt sad and lost. They did not understand that I was giving them eternal life by shedding My Blood and laying My Life down for them. I was the slain Lamb without spot or defect that was offered as a sacrifice during the Passover, so I would pass over your sins and not kill you, but give you eternal life with Me in My Kingdom. This was an act of righteousness, but My People could not understand. Some people came to mock Me and others came to grieve over Me. I wanted to comfort them, but I knew that I would comfort them later when My Spirit came to them and filled them and made them new inside. I wanted to reach out to them and let them know that I would rise again and bring strength to our covenant. My People were lost and dying. They were without hope being persecuted by wicked violent enemies daily. Their life was miserable, but I would bring them new life very soon. Hope was on the horizon, but in this moment there was only darkness. Do you feel that you are without hope? I hear your prayers. Repent of your sins and draw close to Me, and I will bring new life to you. I will cover you with My Arms and bring Light and Truth to your eyes. Rejoice that I love you so much.

Matthew 27:38-44

My Beloved, I was placed between two robbers who wanted to do harm to others, yet I was innocent and did not want to harm anyone. Everyone passing by mocked Me and insulted Me, "Who are you? If you are who you say you are you would be able to save yourself and come off this stake. Who are you anyway?" They did not understand the price I was paying for your sins. My Innocent Blood fell on the ground, and the earth received it and began to quake. All of heaven stood in awe at My extreme act of love. I laid down My Life for a people who rejected Me. They will not know that their children would cling to Me as their King. The religious leaders would die and what they stood for would crumble. My People would be driven far away from their Land and suffer much under the hand of their enemies. Eventually they would see their sin and turn to Me. They would be redeemed at last. Do you suffer under darkness and cannot find the way to go? A great Light will come to My People and the scales will fall off their eyes. An outpouring of My Spirit will break the darkness and bring the Light. You will see this happen before you. My People who have rejected Me for so long will open their eyes and see Me clearly before them. Rejoice that this day will come soon, and you will see a great redemption.

Matthew 27:45-50

My Beloved, I called out in agony, because all I could see was darkness around Me. There was no Light, because the sins of the earth covered Me. I felt forsaken and alone. I looked up, and there was no Light. I was terrified that this darkness had covered Me so completely. I had never been in sin, so I had not seen this darkness before. When I took on the sins of My People, I took on the separation from the Light also. I cried out to be delivered from this darkness. My Spirit was released from My Body, and I was free at last of My Mission on earth. I looked to see those that I left behind, and My Heart grieved for them. They needed Me, and I knew they were hurting. I knew they were alone and afraid. They felt that isolation that I felt, and My heart grieved for them. I knew that soon My Spirit would come to them and fill them and comfort them once again. If you love Me, you will want to be close to Me and reach out towards Me and receive the Light. The Light will cast itself on all your hidden sins and reveal them to you, so you can repent and walk in oneness with Me. Do you have to live a perfect life to serve Me? You do not have to live a perfect life, but your heart must want to serve Me. You will have moments when the flesh overcomes you, and then you will control your flesh and seek repentance from your sins. You will be free to make your own choices, but you will want to please Me and walk in My Ways. Lift up your head and know Me and find Me, and you will do well. I will always be beside you, and you will never be alone. Lift up your heard and stand firm in the faith, so no one can deceive you.

Matthew 27:51-56

My Beloved, I gave up My Fleshly Body and My Spirit was released. As My Innocent Blood fell on the ground the earth shook and broke open in horror, because My Blood was spilled. My Blood seeped into the earth and touched the graves of many of the righteous ones, and they were redeemed and set free from death. They sprang forth with new life. They arose and went into the city proclaiming the Truth about Me. I died and set them free. The people who saw them were fearful, and they ran in terror. Even their loved ones did not know what to do. They were very afraid. The curtain in the Temple that divides the temple area from the most holy place was ripped into two pieces revealing the place where the Ark of the Covenant was supposed to be but had not been in years. The priests had been deceiving the people and saying that they were making atonement for them, but this was a lie. The new Temple had been constructed without the Ark of the Covenant, and only the High Priest knew that it was not there. Only the resemblance of the Ark was there. The original Ark had been hidden away, because My People were afraid that one of their enemies would take it away. They lived in fear that their most holy pieces would be stolen from them, and this was exactly what happened. Their enemies came in and stole all that was precious to them. Now they are without a temple or any of their artifacts. They are grieving over the loss of the Temple. They are preparing for the new Temple that will be constructed. They are waiting for this day. They do not realize that I paid a great price to shed blood for them, so they could be redeemed from their sins. If only they could see clearly, they would see in a different way. Soon My Spirit will overtake them, and they will see the Light of My Presence. They will repent of their sins and turn to Me, and we will be at one again. We will walk hand in hand and rejoice over their homecoming. Do you see clearly? Do you see the Light of My Presence? Repent and come to Me.

Matthew 27:57-61

My Beloved, a very wealthy man named Joseph came to Pilate and asked him for My Body. He was one of My Followers, and he did not want Me to hang on the execution stake anymore and be humiliated. Pilate gave My Body to Joseph and told his guards to go with him. He knew the Jews were very upset over My Execution. Many were happy to see that I had died, and others were angry that Rome could allow such a thing to happen. The guards went with the man to the tomb where I was laid. Joseph laid Me in his tomb, since another one was not available at such short notice. I had not prepared a place for My Body to rest, because I knew that it was temporary. I was wrapped in linen very quickly and not prepared for burial like most believers. Mary and Mary came to see where I was laid to rest. They watched as they laid Me in the tomb and rolled a large stone to cover the entrance. They wondered how they would be able to come back and anoint Me for burial, but they knew that Joseph was a good man and maybe he would allow them to come back to the burial site. The two women mourned over Me not understanding what had happened. They were confused and scared. Their Master had left them, and they were so alone and afraid. Joseph left the burial site in extreme grief. His teacher who was so wise and had so much insight had been murdered before his eyes. The grief for his country was overwhelming. I left many who loved Me in much confusion and sadness. Do you see why I had to die for you? Rejoice that I have given you so much Truth. Rejoice that I love you so much!!!

Matthew 27:62-66

My Beloved, I was laid in the grave, and the stone was rolled over the entrance. My Body was there, but I had left the flesh. I went to Abraham's bosom where My People waited for Me. I brought them out of the bondage of the evil one into a place of rest. My People were released from captivity and brought into My Arms of Love. They were no longer held in the bondage of death, but now they were in the Light of Life. Do you fear death? I created a beautiful place for all My Children to go, so they can be in the Light of My Presence. This is where you will rest after you die, but you will not realize how long you have slept. The next thing you will see is My Coming, and you will rejoice in it. You will go from death to resurrection in a moment. You will not know the years you have slept in My Presence. You will not be alone or afraid. You will be at peace in your sleep, so do not fear death. Rejoice that you love Me and know Me and are close to Me, so you can be worthy to enter My Kingdom of Light. You must know who I AM and cling to Me daily always calling on My Name for counsel and advice. I will help you with all the answers to your questions. I will tell you the direction to go. Now is the time to make major changes in your life, so you can walk in righteousness. You need to be able to hear My Voice, and listen to what I say and do it quickly. I will help you with what I tell you to do. I will help you even though the path ahead may be difficult. I may ask you to leave your home and all your family and go to a place that you have not been before. I AM creating a place for My Children, so they will be safe in these Last Days. I want them to rest in My Presence and not be tormented by the evil one. I will bring you to a safe place and care for you tenderly. Listen to My Voice, and do what I tell you to do and all will go well with you.

Matthew 28:1-10

My Beloved, the women went early Sunday morning to the place where they laid Me. They wanted to prepare Me for burial. They wanted to see if the guards would allow them to come near Me. As they approached an angel appeared to them. The earth shook as he appeared. He rolled away the stone for them and gave them a message from Me. The angel told them that I had been raised from the dead, and I would meet them in Galilee. They were terrified, but the angel told them not to be afraid. The angel showed them where I had laid and now I was gone. They were horrified that I was not in the tomb. They were confused. As they ran away from the tomb, I came to comfort them. They grabbed My Feet and wept. I told them to go tell the others to come to Me in Galilee and not to be afraid. They left Me rejoicing that I had risen again. These were brave women who loved Me and would give up their life for Me. They were brave enough to come back to the tomb and ask the soldiers for help to come near Me. These women wanted only to serve Me even after their world had been shattered after My Death. The guards were the terrified ones. When the earth shook and the angel appeared to them they fainted and lay motionless on the ground, so the angel could talk only with the women. Are you in a trying situation that you do not understand? I always make a path for those who love Me. I bring blessings to their door. I cover them with My Hand. I make sure they have all they need. Rejoice that I love you so much. Rejoice and be glad even when things come upon you to change and mold you into My Image. I AM your Creator and I AM still creating you as you are molded in your cocoon of flesh. When you emerge you will be a glorious creature!!

Matthew 28:11-15

My Beloved, I arose from the dead, and I left the tomb where they laid me. Those who came to see Me could not find Me. I sent an angel to comfort them and tell them that I had risen and was no longer there, but I would return to them in Galilee. The soldiers passed out from the shock of what happened. They fled to tell the religious leaders what had happened. The leaders were very afraid that the people would know that I had risen just as I had said. They paid the soldiers a large sum of money to tell the people that My Disciples took My Body away, so it would look like I had not risen from the grave. The soldiers told all My People the lie, and many believed it. The soldiers were very careful that the governor did not know about their lie, so they would not get in trouble. They guarded over their secret very carefully. The women had seen the place where I was laid. They heard the message from the angel, and they knew that I had overcome death. The women tried to convince the men that I had risen from the grave, but the faith of the men was weak. The men did not believe the women until I made myself known to them. Do you question some of the things that others tell you about their faith? You may question their faith. You may think that I operate in a different way. Whatever you believe, you should search My Words and stay open to find out actually what is the Truth. Then you will never be deceived and will always walk in Truth. Beware! Stay on guard against deception from all men.

Matthew 28:16-19

My Beloved, I told My Disciples to meet Me on a certain hill in Galilee. All My disciples came to see Me, but some were afraid. They prostrated themselves before Me recognizing Me as the Creator, the Eternal One, and the Most High. They understood that I had risen from death, but they did not understand what this meant for them. They were confused, but were rejoicing over My Resurrection. They wanted Me to come back with them again, but I had to leave them. I left them a mission. I gave them authority over all things, and I told them to walk in My Ways and do as I did. I wanted them to teach others what they had learned from Me. I wanted them to go all over the world and share the Good News with all men no matter who they were or where they lived. I encouraged them to move forward, but some were afraid. They were afraid of their enemies, so I told them to leave the area and begin a new life in other places. Some listened to My Voice, but others didn't. The ones who stayed in Jerusalem and the surrounding areas were driven out by their enemies. I dissolved the state of Israel for many years to keep My Children out of My Land due to their sins. I also wanted them to be salt and a light and tell others about Me wherever they were. What is your mission in this life? It does not matter where you live today. You still have the same mission to go out and tell others about Me. If you are not being a light to others, then you are not fulfilling your mission for this life. You need to be loving and kind to others and give generously to them. You need to tell others that the only solution to their problems is to turn to Me. If you will point others in the right direction, I will bless you for your good works. I will prosper you at every corner. I will open My Hands to you. Be brave and strong. Open your mouth and I will fill it with the words I want you to speak to others. Rise up! I AM always with you. I will never leave you or desert you.

John 1:1-5

My Beloved, I existed in the beginning when I was creating this world. I AM everlasting and eternal. I know all things. I create and I give life. I hold life in My Hands. I give and I take away. I allow you to live in the flesh for a very short time. You are here to be tested and tried to see if you are worthy to enter My Kingdom of Light. If you sacrifice your flesh and do My Will, then you will prosper and have life eternal with Me. If you do what you want to do and do not care about My Laws but want to seek your own pleasure, then you will suffer destruction. You will go to the Lake of Fire and burn and be no more. Your life will be taken away from you. You will no longer exist. The memory of you will be lost to everyone. Your name will be erased, and no one will think of you. In My Presence is great joy and you will rejoice in Me daily. You will worship Me and cling to Me and want to know My Ways. Have you found the pathway that leads to Me? If you cannot find the pathway to Life, then repent of your sins and turn to Me and I will help you find your way back to Me. I want you to be at one with Me. Are you allowing something to keep you from coming back from Me?

Repent and turn away from your sins.

John 1:6-14

My Beloved, I created the world and all that is in it. I created you in My Image. I created you to be My Child. I want you to walk in My Ways and be an example of Me. I want you to look to Me all day long and love Me and serve Me. You are My Beloved, My First Born. You are the one who will rule with Me. You must walk in one accord with Me. You must be keeping My Laws and doing as you hear My Voice telling you to do. Do you want to go your own way? You will have My Hand on you correcting you until you turn to Me once again. I will not give up on you, but I will continue to form you into My Image, so you can be counted worthy to enter into My Kingdom of Light. I AM Light. I see and know all things. No man can look on Me, because I would consume him. If you want to draw close to Me, then you must be under the covering of the Blood of the Covenant. You will be able to hear My Voice and know exactly what I want you to do. Many are turning away from Me in these Last Days. Many want to do what they want to do. I bought you with a price. I gave you a precious gift. You must be humble before Me and walk in My Ways. I will take whatever you give Me and begin there and work with you until you can give generously of yourself to Me. I will bless you greatly for surrendering your all to Me. I will adopt you as My Own, and you will rule in My Kingdom with Me.

John 1:15-28

My Beloved, I sent John ahead of Me to proclaim My Coming. The religious leaders sent messengers to him to ask him who he was. He told them that he was not the one they were looking for, but the One who existed before him was coming. This One would bring Truth to the world and set the world free from sin. Even John did not really know what I was going to do. John knew what his mission was. He knew that he was preparing the path for Me. John went to the river and began to baptize those who wanted to repent of their sins and be cleansed. Many came to be baptized. John told them about Me and how I would soon come and walk in their midst. "Who is this person?" the people would ask John. They wanted a savior to come save them from their enemies. They were treated cruelly by their enemies. They were carrying a heavy burden on their shoulders. They cried out to Me under their oppression. I did not come to overthrow their enemies, but I wanted to give them a way to eternal life. I wanted My People to be redeemed from their sins. I wanted My People to know Me and serve Me and walk hand in hand with Me. I wanted My People to be at one with Me and commune with Me as a father with his child. Will you take Me by the hand? I will guide you while you are here on earth. I will show you the way to walk. Take My Hand and follow along with Me.

John 1:29-34

My Beloved, I sent John ahead of Me to tell My People that I was coming. I told him to go to the water and begin to immerse the people who wanted to repent of their sins and get ready for the Messiah to come. Many came to humble themselves and be baptized. Many came to watch not knowing what was happening. John continued to tell the people that I was coming, and I was in their midst. He knew that the One who came to him to be baptized and My Spirit rested on him was the One. He would be the One who would take away the sins of the world. He would lay His Life down like an innocent Lamb and make a sacrifice for the people. John was watching daily for Me to come. My Spirit was on him and it burned inside of him to see Me. When he saw Me coming towards him he could see the Light on Me. My Spirit manifested in the form of a dove and rested on Me. John knew that I was the one that My People had been waiting for. My People were looking for a savior to deliver them from their enemies. They wanted a king to arise. I came only to deliver them from eternal death, so they could live with Me forever. I come to you and bring you gifts, but it may not be the gifts that you want. I want you to be changed into My Image and formed into a child of Light, so you can immerse from your fleshly robe as a glorious creature formed to serve only Me. You will be counted worthy to enter My Kingdom of Light and live eternally with Me. Do you think that your life is difficult here? Having a difficult life is a blessing for you. The testing will produce a strong faith and prepare you for the days ahead. Be strong and overcome. I will give you all you need.

John 1:35-42

My Beloved, John saw Me as I passed by, and he said to his disciples that I was the Lamb that would be sacrificed for their sins. One of his disciples, Andrew, left John to follow Me and find out if I was the Messiah. Andrew decided to stay with Me and learn from Me. Andrew went to his brother Simon and told him all about Me. Andrew was so excited to find Me, because he knew that I was the Messiah, the Anointed One, sent to My People as their Savior. Simon and Andrew vowed to stand beside Me and follow Me and be My Disciple. I changed Simon's name to Peter meaning "the rock". He would be the foundation for many. He would be the one that many leaned on to have faith in the trying days that My Disciples had to endure after I was taken from them. Peter was the one that wanted to be strong and bold and courageous. He was the one who wanted to have no fear. He was a rough man. He had been through many difficult and trying situations already. He was a fisherman and he lived from day to day from what he caught. He had little. He had a strong love for Me and wanted to serve Me all the days of his life. He was totally dedicated to Me. When I walked on earth it was those who had little that clung to Me and wanted to follow Me. Those who had authority and riches did not want to give up what they had to follow Me. Being My Disciple was not a popular decision. Many hated Me and wanted to kill Me. Even today following Me in spirit and truth is not a popular idea. Do you say that you know Me and follow Me? Many men say that they know Me, but they do not know Me. They are deceived. They only want to serve themselves. If you love Me, you will be listening for My Voice and following close to Me. Listen and you will find Me.

John 1:43-51

My Beloved, I saw Philip and called to him to follow Me. He knew that I was the One that he had been waiting for. He knew that I AM and there is no other. He knew that he would lay down everything and follow Me. That was the man that I was looking for. This was a man that I could leave in charge of My Flock after I had to leave this earth. Philip went to his friend Nathaniel and told him to come see Me, the Messiah, the One that Moses spoke about. Nathaniel did not believe that I could be the Messiah, "Could anyone of importance come from Nazareth? Could this man have not been noticed until now? Why didn't one of the prophets let the people know that He had arrived? Who was this man that Philip was so excited to find?" Nathaniel came to see Me only because Philip insisted that he come. Once he saw Me he knew that I was the One. I knew him, because I created him. I knew that Nathaniel was a true believer and followed My Ways and My Laws. He was brought up as a child to follow the ways that Moses had given My People. Now I would bring My People a clearer version of the Truth and not tainted by man through the ages. I told Nathaniel that I saw him while he was still under the fig tree talking to Philip before he ever came to see Me. Nathaniel believed in Me, because I could see all things. He was yet to see the miracles that I would perform for My People. I did not call Nathaniel to be one of My Twelve disciples, because he would not leave his home to follow Me. He was a man of responsibilities to his family. He had a mission to tell others about Me where he lived. What mission do you have? You have that same mission to tell others about Me while you live in exile. You must speak Truth to those around you and love others around you. You will then be walking in My Ways of Life.

John 2:1-12

My Beloved, I went to a wedding with My Mother and family and disciples. While we were there the wine ran out, and the family could not afford more. My Mother did not want to have the family embarrassed, so she asked Me to help them. I did not want to come forward at this point and begin My Ministry, but I had compassion on the family and made more wine. I knew My Mother's heart and how she wanted to help them have a joyous celebration. I could not turn My Back on these people, since it was within My Power to help them. My Disciples knew that I turned the water into wine, and they were impressed that I could do something so wonderful. They rejoiced that I could help others in need, even if it were to make wine. My Disciples had more faith in Me after the wedding. If you have the power to help someone, then help them. You must always look at someone with compassion and kindness. Do you love those around you? I want you to be My Hands and Feet. You will spread My Love to others. You should tell others how I saved you from sin and redeemed you, so they can have eternal life with Me. Do not think that the world can give you good gifts. Only I can give you good gifts. I know exactly what gift to give you to humble you or correct you or bring you to repentance. I know what you need to mold you into the glorious creature that will immerge from your flesh and be heir to My Kingdom. You must be ready to listen. You must be ready to hear. You must be ready!!

John 2:13-22

My Beloved, I went to Jerusalem for Passover in keeping with My Laws, but what I saw was disgusting. The money changers and merchants had turned My Feast Day into a time to make money from My People. They were setting up their wares like it was a market when no man should buy, sell, or trade on My Feast Day. My People had been brought low by their enemies, and now the merchants and money changers were also taking advantage of My People. Everywhere that My People turned, someone was taking from them. I was disgusted by the spirit of My Feast Day. Where was the joy? Where was the praise to Me? My People were burdened down with extra laws and things they had to do to worship Me, but this was not My Way. My Way is easy, and My Burden is light. Just read My Words and do only what is written within My Words. Man has added so many laws that he cannot keep up with all the laws he has to obey. Do you obey only My Laws? If you obey only My Laws and listen to My Voice, I will bring Truth to your house. My Feast Days will be joyous instead of burdened by a heavy load. You will be able to walk in the Truth and stand strong. Man waivers, because he does not see the Truth in all the man-made laws. He should question all things until he finds Truth. Look towards Me, and I will enlighten your eyes, so you can see clearly. I do not want you entangled in a web of man's traditions that are alien to Me. Man-made traditions only leave you empty and without hope. Come to Me, and I will give you rest and hope and purpose in this life.

John 2:23-25

My Beloved, I went to Jerusalem to celebrate the Passover as is commanded by My Laws. I did many miracles for My People during this time. Many of My People believed in Me that I was the Messiah, the King that they had been looking for. They believed in Me for what they saw, but their heart was far from Me. I knew the heart of every man and whether he wanted to walk in covenant with Me or not. These people were under a heavy burden of oppression, and they were looking for hope. I brought them hope. The People knew that the Messiah would come healing the sick and blind, and delivering them from demons. They knew that I would set them free from bondage and destroy all their enemies. They were looking for a savior to deliver them from their enemies, but I came to deliver them from their sins, so they could live with Me eternally. My People came forward when they saw Me, and they wanted to follow Me. My People are few and scattered. Do you do what I ask you to do? Do you hear My Voice and follow Me? Only My True Children know My Voice and follow close to Me. If you really love Me, you will follow Me and do My Will. Do not be as other believers and not keep the words of My Scriptures. Arise! Wake up! Get up and move forward. Do not allow the world to pull you away from Me any longer. I will reward you for your faithfulness to Me.

John 3:1-15

My Beloved, there was a leader of the Jews who came to Me by night. He was afraid to come in the day time, because he was afraid of what the elders would say to him. He had many questions for Me, but I had many questions for him. He did not understand who I was. I told him that I was his Savior, and I came to die for him so he could live. I told him that he must be born of the spirit and not the flesh. I wanted him to be born anew with the spirit. I said to share the Truth with others, and tell them about Me and how they could be joined with Me. Many came to Me and united with Me, even the man who came by night. Some people rejected Me, and suffered loss. They were wiped away by their oppressors. Those who listened to the Truth and came to Me and joined with Me, I held in My Hand and kept them from their enemies. Only My People who call on My Name will know My Voice and walk with Me. Do you trust Me with all your heart and lean not on your understanding? The world is in turmoil, so you will have to look to Me for peace. Take My Hand, and I will guide you along the path. I will be your Right Hand. The man who came at night came fearfully, but you will come boldly to Me and bring deliverance for many. Rejoice that you love Me so much. Rejoice that I have given you so much!!

John 3:16-18

My Beloved, do you know why I came into the world? I wanted to save My Children who were bound under the sins of Adam and his sons. I came to My Children to save them from eternal destruction in the Lake of Fire. I came to save My Children and give them eternal life. Those who trust in Me will be saved, but those who do not trust in Me will be destroyed. You must believe that I AM the only Eternal One, and there is no other. Many men will say, "I am the Messiah", but there is only one Messiah or Savior. There is only One who can die and be completely innocent. There is only One who can shed innocent blood, so that the sins of many will be covered. I came to die for you, so you would not have to die, but you could dwell with Me eternally. You are My Children, and I love you deeply. I made a great sacrifice to humble Myself as a man and walk among you and teach you, but I wanted you to know the Truth. I wanted you to know how much I loved you. There are many that say they will lay down their life for you, but only One is the true Savior. Only One can save man from his sins. Draw near to Me, and I will draw near to you. I want you close to Me. Rejoice that I love you so much.

John 3:19-21

My Beloved, I came to the world as the Light from above. I brought judgment to the world. The people of the world have to decide if they want to follow Me and draw closer to the Light, or if they want to remain in their sins and stay in the darkness. My People chosen by Me came to The Light and wanted to learn from Me. The wicked people of the earth wanted to stay in the darkness and remain in their sins. They wanted to see the world and not My Spiritual Kingdom. They could not turn from their lusts and carnal desires. They wanted to live selfishly and not a life of love. They wanted to stay in the darkness, so their sins will not be exposed and they would be naked before Me. My People want to draw close to Me and be delivered from darkness. My People will walk away from sins and into the Light. Have you purified your life? Do you live according to My Words? Do you struggle in darkness? Do not struggle any longer, but emerge and know you are My Child and have been given authority over the evil one and all his followers. I will bring Light at every corner of your life. I will listen to what you say and help you at every turn. Do you think that you cannot overcome? You need to turn completely to Me and acknowledge Me for every decision. If you will stay turned towards Me, then you will walk in the Light. I will make the path ahead bright, and you will know the way to go. The world will be burned and all that reject Me will be burned in the Lake of Fire. If you love Me and want to serve Me, you will dwell in the Light and the world will not be appealing to you. You will see it as wicked and not want to be close to the people of the world. Come and cling to Me and I will hold you close, and you will always be in the Light.

John 3:22-30

My Beloved, many were coming to be baptized in water. They wanted to repent and turn from their wickedness and come into the Kingdom of Heaven. John was also continuing to baptize any that wanted to change their lives. Many were eager to see the Kingdom of Heaven come to earth. Many wanted to have the oppression lifted from them and be free of the bondage of their enemies. They were oppressed daily, and they wanted the Messiah to come and redeem them. Some men came to John and asked him if I was the Messiah. John told them, "I never said that I was the Messiah, but I am preparing the way for the Messiah". John told them that I was the Messiah, and they should follow Me. He told his disciples that they should follow Me, and not him. This upset many of his disciples, but John continued to point the way to Me. He continued to tell others that I would be the One that would take away the sins of the world. Many did not understand what John was saying. Many did not know what I was saying that the Kingdom of Heaven was close to them. When the Truth came to the surface, and I laid down My life for them, then they understood what I was saying to them. They received My Spirit, and became one with Me. Do you lack understanding today? Come to Me and I will help you understand the way to go. I will help you at every turn. I will give you the ability to stand firm and be bold and walk in the way of righteousness. Keep your eyes on Me, and you will overcome.

John 3:31-36

My Beloved, I came from above down to earth to show My Children a better way to live. I came to give them life eternal, but first I had to release them from the bondage of death. I tried to tell everyone what I could do for them, but most of them rejected Me, and thought that I lied to them. They could not understand what I was saying to them. They were blinded and their hearts were hard. They loved themselves and the things of the world. They were not interested in spiritual things. They only wanted what they could see. They only wanted to have power and authority and wealth. Many did see what I was saying, and they accepted Me and sealed themselves to receive eternal life and live in My Kingdom forever. There is nothing more beautiful than My Kingdom filled with Light. There are things there that you could not even imagine, like colors you could not even imagine and complete peace and rest. You would be heirs to My Kingdom and be placed above all things and subject only to Me. The others in My Kingdom try to look into these things and understand it, but they are lacking. They do not see what you will become. You are being transformed into My Image, and you will emerge as a glorious being after you are released from your flesh. Does your flesh wear on you daily? Fight against it and become strong. Soon you will be victorious over your flesh and walk in My spirit. You will become at one with Me. You will be able to hear My Voice clearly and know Me intimately. You are My Beloved, and you are My Bride. We will wed and become one. We will be together forever. Do you become discouraged in this life with all its difficulties? You must continue to trust in Me and know that I will take care of you. Be strong. Be brave. I will help you overcome!!

John 4:1-30, 39-42

My Beloved, when the religious leaders saw that I was baptizing more people than John, I left the area and went to Samaria. My People had been taught by their religious leaders not to associate with the Samarians, because they worship in Samaria and not in Jerusalem. When I came to earth, I came for all My People, even the lost tribes of Israel. When I sat at the well, a lady came to Me with her water bucket to draw water. I asked her for water, and she questioned why I was speaking to her. I spoke to her with love and compassion, because I knew that she would hear the Truth and want to adhere to Me. I told her about Myself and that I AM the Living Water. If you come to Me, I will fill you with the Living Water that comes from on high, and you will draw close to Me and live with Me eternally. She did not understand that I could give her eternal life, if she repented of her sins and turned to Me and accepted Me as her Savior. I told her about her past, and then she knew I was a prophet. What she did not know was that I was the Messiah. When I told her, "I AM the Messiah", she believed Me and ran to the town, and told everyone to come see Me. This lady was in sin. She had lived a life of sin. Yet when she heard the Truth, she received it and was delivered from her sins. Are you living a sinful life today? You can hear the Truth and be delivered from your sins. Arise! Look up and see My Eyes. I AM looking at you. I want you to repent and turn from your sins and walk in the way of Truth and Light. Arise! Be strong. Be brave. I will help you overcome.

John 4:31-38

My Beloved, I waited by the well for My Disciples to return with food for Me to eat. As I was waiting a lady came to get water. I told her about Me, and she was filled with joy. She ran into town to tell everyone she knew that she had found the Messiah. As I was waiting for her to return My Disciples returned with the food. They wanted Me to eat with them, but I was too overjoyed that I could bring the Truth to a whole town. This town was filled with My Children from the lost tribes of Israel. These were the tribes that separated from My Children in Jerusalem and set up their own temple in which to worship Me. They knew all My Laws and walked in My Ways, yet they were shunned by their brothers who lived in Jerusalem, because they did not worship in Jerusalem. These people received Me gladly, and yet My People in Jerusalem rejected Me. Which of these people loved Me more? Do not be deceived by whether a person goes to church and follows its traditions. Look at the heart of the man, and see if he will receive the Truth, and then you will know if he wants to follow Me or not. My Disciples did not see what had transpired before they came. They did not know that a whole town would receive Me. They did not know all things. They only knew what they could see. You are the same way. You do not know all things. You know only what you can see. Look with My Eyes and see that many desire to be told the Truth, and many will receive it. It will then be up to them to walk in it. The way is difficult, and few can walk the path of righteousness. Few can trust Me to guide them. Do you really want to please Me? You must be listening to Me at all times and obey My Voice. I will then be able to use you greatly for My Kingdom.

John 4:43-53

My Beloved, after I left Samaria, I went to Galilee to see the people who wanted to hear My Words and accept the Truth. I told My Disciples that a prophet is usually not accepted in his home country. The people of Galilee received Me gladly, because they had been to the festival in Jerusalem and had seen Me there. They knew that I had turned the water into wine at the wedding in Canaan. They had heard about the miracles that I had done. They were anxious to learn more about Me. I wanted to tell them about Me, and what I could do for them. While I was there a man in the military came to Me and asked Me to heal his son who was at the point of death. Since he came to Me believing that I could heal his son, I healed his son the very moment that he asked Me to heal him. When the soldier returned home he asked when his son was healed, and it was the same time that I told him that his son was healed. The man and his entire household believed in Me and never deserted the faith. Many times I do miracles for people, and they do not recognize that I have healed them. Many times I do miracles for people, and they know that I did the miracle, but they soon forget about it. A few times I do a miracle for someone, and he remembers what I have done for him and it changes his life. Do you remember the things I do for you? Are you thankful everyday that I love you so much to heal you and protect you and provide everything that you need? Always remember what I have done for you. Always remember how much I love you. Always remember that I am changing you into My Image. Be strong and brave. You will overcome, if you cling to Me and allow Me to guide you through the dark days ahead.

John 5:1-13

My Beloved, I went to Jerusalem and there was a man who wanted to be healed. He had been sick for 38 years and he could not walk. He was weak and had almost lost all hope. He laid by the pool hoping that an angel would stir the water, and he could be healed. He hoped that someone would have mercy on him and put him into the water. He looked to the water for his healing. I came by him and looked into his eyes. I saw his great sadness and had compassion on him. He wanted so much to be healed. He wanted to be a whole man again, and be able to take care of his family. His heart was grieved as he looked into My Eyes. I asked him if he wanted to be healed, and he said, "yes". I told him to get up and walk and take his mat with him. He found hope in My Eyes, and he believed. He saw the Light and Life within Me. No one encouraged him to believe in Me. He could see that I was someone special. He got up and his faith made him whole. He carried his mat towards his house, but the religious leaders saw him carrying his mat and told him that he was breaking a law of the Sabbath. The man told him that the One who healed him told him to carry his mat. The religious leaders were furious, because I told him to carry his mat knowing that it was Sabbath and against their laws. Sabbath is a day for man to rest. Sabbath is a day to draw closer to Me and enjoy My Presence. Sabbath is not a day to be burdened with laws and be afraid that you may break one of them and displease Me. As long as you rest and do not work or make money, then you are obeying Sabbath. How do you keep the Sabbath? How you keep Sabbath is between you and Me and not the rules of the religious leaders. I will guide you as you begin to keep Sabbath. I will show you a way to walk uprightly as you keep Sabbath. You will enjoy you day and enjoy My Presence.

John 5:14-16

My Beloved, I healed a man on Sabbath. I told him to get up and walk and carry his mat. He believed in Me and took up his mat and walked, even though he knew that there was a law not to carry your mat on Sabbath. The religious leaders questioned him harshly about why he was carrying his mat. He did not know who I was. He knew that he trusted in Me, and he was healed. When I saw the man again, I told him to stop sinning or something worse would happen to him. He had been sick for 38 years. He knew what it was like to walk, and then he could not walk. He knew that his sins were upon him. He knew that he had been forgiven and healed by Me. The man told the religious leaders who I was, and what I told him to do. The religious leaders hated Me, because I told the man to pick up his mat on Sabbath. They began to question Me and harass Me by saying, "This is the man who told that man to break the laws of Sabbath by carrying his mat". The religious leaders tried to harm Me by their words and belittle Me in front of the people. I saw what the religious leaders were doing, and I always put them in the wrong in front of the people by My Answers to their questions. When you are in sin, you are blinded and cannot see. These leaders could not see, because they were lost in tradition and not in Truth. When I told them the Truth, they mocked Me. They did not want to hear the Truth, because they would have to change their ways of tradition. They were lost in the sins of their ancestors. Are you searching for Truth but lost in the sins of your ancestors? If you reject the Truth, then sickness will come to your body, and you will be punished for your rebellion. Open your eyes and see clearly. Open your eyes and receive the Truth and be free at last.

John 5:17-30

My Beloved, the religious leaders did not like for Me to say that I AM the Eternal One, and there is no way except through Me. I came to earth to tell My People to receive Me and trust in Me, and I would give them eternal life. If they rejected Me, then they would be bound for judgment. Each man who does not receive Me will have to stand before Me, and I will judge him according to his deeds. He can never reach eternal life through his deeds, because he is a sinful man. He has to have My Innocent Blood to cover him, so he can have eternal life. Man is nothing by himself, but if he receives Me and wants to walk with Me, then I will draw close to him and we will become one. We will walk in the same path and be of one mind. If a man does not know Me, then he is blinded and cannot see the path ahead of him. If he comes to the Light of My Presence, I will guide his path. No man comes to Me except through the Son. If a man turns to Me, then I will uphold him and care for Me. I will watch over him, and he will stand close to My Shadow. He will be My Hands and Feet. Are you foolish? The foolish man will try to fight against Me and will be judged harshly. Are you wise? The wise man will listen to My Voice and obey Me whether he desires to or not. Ask Me to change your heart, so you can be obedient. Be wise. Be strong. Be brave. I am always with you.

John 5:31-40

My Beloved, I came to you to tell you the Truth. I came to you bringing a message from above. I came to you to bring you understanding into who I AM. I wanted My People to know Me and believe in Me and walk in My Ways. My People received Me gladly. I told them I had a witness to testify with Me about the Truth. My Law says to believe in the message only if there are two are more witnesses. John and I were the witnesses bearing the Truth. We came to open the eyes of My People, so they could walk hand in hand with Me. Do you understand who I am? If you do not understand who I AM, then call on My Name and I will show you. I will take you by the hand and lead you into all Truth. I will show you the hidden things. I will take you to places that you have never known. You will be able to walk in total peace and trust and faith. You will have no fear. You will be able to handle anything that comes your way, because you will know that only good things come to you. Only good things will be sent your way. Do life events appear to be bad at times? The end result will be good, because I only bring good gifts to My Children. What is a good gift that I give you? If whatever comes to you builds your faith or makes you have compassion on others, then this is a good gift. Many times you have to experience the low places in this life to appreciate My Love for you to bring you to a high place in Me. You will always have Me by your side even if you fall. You will be able to rejoice that I pick you up and put you back on the Rock of your salvation. Rejoice and be glad that I love you so much.

John 5:41-47

My Beloved, I came to tell My People who I AM. They could not believe that I was the One they were waiting for. They could not see, because they were blinded. They wanted their own way. I came to tell them the Truth, but they did not believe the Truth. They wanted to continue in the ways of their ancestors. They wanted to follow the written laws that were handed down by men. The religious leaders had so many laws for the people to keep that they were burdened down by man-made laws. I told My People to forget about all these laws and only follow the laws given to them by Moses. My People received these words and were glad, but the religious leaders were angry, because I was trying to change their traditions. They were blinded and wanted to remain in the dark. They were greedy men who wanted the praise of men and were not concerned about serving Me. Are you walking in the traditions of men? Are you searching My Words to find Truth? Are you looking for the laws written in My Words? These are the laws that you should obey. There are the laws that I gave you, so you could walk in oneness with Me. Do not listen to what men tell you to do. Who are you trying to please? If you want to please Me, then you will be listening for My Voice and walking in My Ways of love and compassion. If you are following the path I have for you, then you will want to be led by Me. Do not be concerned about what men think of you. Do not be concerned if you lose friends, because you are following Me. I never said that you would be taking the popular choice. The world will hate you, because they hate Me. Rejoice that I love you so much and have called you out of the world. Rejoice that you are free from the traditions of men, and you only walk in My Laws. My Way is easy and simple, but the ways of men are difficult. Men want the favor of men, but My People want My Favor. Are you seeking My Favor or the favor of men? If you seek only Me, then I will give you all that you need, and you will never need for men to give you anything. You will be satisfied in Me.

John 6:1-15

My Beloved, I took My Disciples to the hills to be alone and teach them more about Me. We noticed that a great crowd followed us into the hills. They had seen the miracles I had done to heal the sick, and they wanted to be near Me. They wanted to see what I would do next. This group was so large that there were five thousand men not counting women and children. I sat them down on the grass growing on the hills, so they could hear My Words for them. Philip was amazed at all the people who came to hear My Words. I decided to test him and see if he trusted Me to do great things for My People. I asked him, "How can we get food to feed all these people? They all came to hear My Words. They have traveled a long way. They are hungry. They must be fed." Philip could not even conceive of feeding all these people. He turned to another disciple and asked him how to feed them. The disciple gave him a few fish and a few loaves, but what was that with so many people. I looked at them both as they tried to reason what to do. I took the bread and fish and blessed it, and they multiplied. The people were amazed that the bread continued to grow as they passed it around, and the fish also was multiplied. The people knew I was the Prophet that had come to rule on earth. They wanted to take Me and make Me their king, but I slipped away from My Disciples and went inside the hills to be away from them. The people slowly left to go home. My Disciples did not know where I had gone. I wanted to stay with them, but the people wanted to make Me their king. So many days have passed since then, but My People still want Me to come to earth to rule. Do you long for Me daily to come back? The time is short now when I will return. I will come back for My Chosen. I will be their Deliverer.

John 6:16-21

My Beloved, I left My Disciples and went to the hills to escape from the crowd. The crowd was so excited about Me feeding such a large group of people that they were convinced that I was the One they had been waiting for to become their King. I escaped to be alone, so My Disciples left in a boat late at night not knowing where I was. They had waited as long as they could and did not want to be in the boat at night. The wind began blowing, and a storm arose. I was testing My Disciples to see if they would call out to Me. The storm grew intense, so I walked out on the water towards them. They were terrified to see Me on the water. They thought I was a ghost. They did not know if I had died and was coming back as a ghost to tell them what had happened. They were very afraid. I called out to them not to be afraid. They were like children. They did not understand much. They did not know what to think of Me walking on the water. I got into the boat, and I stilled the waters. They were amazed at what I could do. They still did not know that I was the Creator of all things. They did not understand that I held all things in My Hand. They did not know who I really was. They could only see a man, but I wanted them to see that I was much more than a man or any prophet. I AM and I AM. How do you see Me? Am I your Creator? Do you know who I AM? Do you trust Me to care for you? Do you know I will protect you and keep you safe? Do you know that I will only give you good things? Rejoice and be glad that I love you so much.

John 6:22-33

My Beloved, My Disciples and I went to the other side of the lake to rest for the night. The crowd that I had fed the day before was waiting for Me to return to them. When I did not return, they got in boats and went to the other side of the lake to find Me. They did not come to hear My Words, but to be fed and satisfied. They did not desire food from heaven, but earthly food that would fill their stomachs and take away their hunger. I came from above, and I wanted to teach them about Me and show them the way to have eternal life. I told them that they needed to desire the food that would take away all their hunger and satisfy them eternally. They did not understand what I meant. They asked Me where this bread was, and I told them that I AM the Bread of Life. They could not understand this. They were blinded to the Truth. They were fleshly and desired only to satisfy their flesh. I told them to desire the things of heaven, and they asked Me what these things were. I told them to believe in Me and trust Me to care for them. They only trusted in themselves. They could not trust in Me. They could not see or understand. If you love Me, you will want to know Me and walk with Me. You will be satisfied. Are you satisfied with the things of the spirit and not the things of the world? If you love Me, you will be satisfied and not desire earthly things. You will grow numb to the things of the world and crave the things of the spirit. You will long to leave the place where you are in exile and come to the Promised Land. You must be ready to do as I tell you to do at all times. Listen! I AM speaking to you. Open your ears, so you can hear. I will tell you what to do, so you can walk hand in hand with Me.

John 6:34-40

My Beloved, I told the People that I AM the Bread of Life. They could not understand what I was saying. I told them that if they ate of Me that they would live eternally. They did not understand that I AM the Eternal One. They did not understand that I AM the Creator. They did not understand that I came down from heaven to be with My Children and teach them My Ways. I came down to die for them, so if they believed in Me that they would be filled with My Spirit and dwell with Me forever. They did not understand, because they did not have a heart to understand. Their heart was hard and stubborn. They wanted to go their own way and not follow after Me. They desired the things that satisfied their flesh. They did not long for the things of the spirit. They were people who were lost in tradition. I had to drive them out of their Land and make them forget all their traditions, so they could actually look at Me and try to understand Me. They suffered much, so they could be humbled and look up to Me and see Me. They wanted to be a superior people, but they could not be a superior people unless they were humble before Me and served Me with all their hearts. Those who are My Servants and listen to My Voice and want to follow Me will be the ones that I raise up on the Last Day. They will spring back to life and join Me in My Kingdom. Now they sleep and rest as they wait for the Last Day of Judgment when all will stand before Me and be judged according to their deeds. Do you love those around you? Do you want your own way? Do you help those in need? If you love Me, you love those around you. I love all men no matter who they are. I want you to love the man and hate the sin. Your love will change those around you and make your world a better place. You will rejoice that I love you so much, and you will want to share that love with others.

John 6:41-59

My Beloved, I told those around Me that they must eat of Me and drink My Blood for them to receive Me and live with Me eternally. They did not understand what I was saying, but they knew that you only eat the flesh and drink the blood of the gods to live forever. They knew that I was saying that I AM the Eternal One the Creator and yet here I AM in fleshly form. They knew who My Parents were and they were not gods. Gods are supposed to come from gods. They thought I was blaspheming the god they served by setting Myself up as a god. They wanted to kill Me. They were blinded and could not understand that I loved them so much. I came down from heaven to walk among them and teach them My Ways, so they could live with Me forever. They did not know how to receive Me. Only My Children are drawn to Me and can understand Me and want to know Me. Only My Children will serve Me. Only those who can see who I AM are My Children. You have been chosen as My Own and I guard over you tenderly. I make sure that you stay close to Me. If you begin to drift away, I draw you back to Me. I want all My Children to walk in the path of righteousness. I want all My Children to know Me and serve Me. Are you walking in the path of righteousness? Come close to Me and walk in the things of Me. Do you desire the things of the world? Desire the things of the spirit, so you can hear My Voice and know the way to walk. You will rejoice in My Presence and always be in My Will!

John 6:60-71

My Beloved, I knew who would trust Me and who would betray Me. I could see the hearts of men and the shadows within. When I told those around Me that they must eat My Flesh and drink My Blood and become one with Me, some of My disciples turned back. They did not see Me as the Eternal One, the Most High, the Creator. They saw me as a good man, a prophet, a healer. They did not think that I was the Messiah that came to save His People and free them from sin. If they agreed that I was the Messiah, then they would have to drink from the same cup as Me and be persecuted by the elders. They knew that as long as they thought of Me as a teacher, then they would be spared. As soon as they decided to drink the cup of the Covenant and become one with Me, they would become enemies of those who controlled the synagogues. Many were afraid to give this up. Others knew that I was the Messiah and wanted to share the same cup with Me no matter what path they had to take. Many died confessing My Name as the Messiah. Many escaped persecution. Many were not brave enough to confess Me aloud and went around in secret worshipping Me and praising Me. They eventually had to leave and worship Me in another place, so they would not have to live in fear. You must be brave and strong and confess Me to others. You must let them know who I AM. If you will listen to My voice, I will guide you. I will show you the way to go. What does it mean to drink of the blood of My Covenant and become one with Me? This means that our blood becomes one, and you are joined to Me and you will live with Me eternally. Stand up and be strong. Be an overcomer. I will return shortly for My Bride. Cleanse yourself and be clean when I return.

John 7:1-13

My Beloved, I stayed away from Judah, because the Judeans wanted to kill Me. They hated what I was teaching. I told them that they should drink My Blood and be in Covenant with Me, and they hated Me for this. They knew that I was saying that I was the Only One, the Eternal One, the Creator. They thought that I was blaspheming. They hated Me, because they could not see clearly. They were threatened by My Teaching, because many of the people believed in Me and wanted to receive Me as their Redeemer. They were all watching Me and hoping that I was the Messiah who could redeem them and set them free from the oppression of their enemies. My Brothers came to Me and asked Me to go up to Jerusalem with them for the festival as a family. My Brothers wanted Me to perform miracles and let everyone see who I AM. They did not understand who I AM. They did not trust in Me. They saw Me only as their brother and not as the Messiah. I told them to go ahead and go without Me, so they would not draw attention to Me. I went by Myself, because I knew what was ahead of Me. I knew My Fate was at the hand of My Enemies. I could only walk this path alone. Do you feel like you have to walk alone? You have Me beside you all the time. Just call on Me, and I will be there for you. Do not be afraid. I will help you through all your troubles and bring Light to your path, so you will know just what to do.

John 7:14-24

My Beloved, I came to the festival late, so that I would not come with My Family. I wanted to come in quietly, but My Heart was bent on teaching My People. I had compassion for them, because they did not have a teacher. They had no one to teach them the laws that I gave Moses. My People were burdened with man-made laws. I told the religious leaders that they were not keeping the Torah that Moses gave them. They were angry with Me for teaching something different from what their fathers had taught them. They did not want to go back to the Scriptures and see what Moses taught them. They wanted their own way. I told them that they wanted to kill Me, because I healed a man on Sabbath. Yet they circumcise their male children on the eighth day even if it is on Sabbath, so they will not break a commandment. I did a good thing on Sabbath. Yet they wanted to kill Me, because I said that I did not break a commandment on Sabbath. The man picked up his mat and walked away praising Me. The religious leaders wanted to cause him harm, because he carried his mat and broke one of their commandments, instead of rejoicing with the man who was now whole again. They were amazed by My Teaching, and yet they could not believe in Me. They wondered how I learned so much about the Scriptures. I was only a carpenter's son. I told them that My Wisdom came from above. I did not want praise from men like most men do. I wanted men to believe in Me and the One who sent Me. I wanted them to know that only through Me is eternal life. They saw what they wanted to see. They never tried to seek Me and find the answer to their questions. They were blinded, so they were sent into exile and persecuted until their children could see clearly and come to Me. Only those who accept Me as their Savior will be enlightened and can see the Truth. Are you hindered by man-made doctrine?

Open your eyes and search for the Truth, so you can know Me.

John 7:25-36

My Beloved, I was teaching in the Temple and not one of the religious leaders tried to stop Me, even though they hated Me. They were afraid of the people and what they would do if I were arrested. The people began to question why the religious leaders allowed Me to continue to speak openly. Maybe the religious leaders knew that I was the Messiah. "Doesn't the scripture say that no one will know when the Messiah comes?" they said. I told them not to look at My fleshly body, but to know who sent Me. My People needed a teacher. The religious leaders were not teaching them how to worship Me and obey Me and serve Me. The religious leaders did not know Me, so they stumbled about like blind men. I wanted My People to not be blinded, but see clearly. I wanted My People to not be deceived by the religious leaders any longer. I wanted them to think clearly and hear My Voice. My People would rise from the ashes and walk in oneness with Me. My People did not want to hear what the religious leaders had to say, because they had heard it all before. They wanted the Truth. The religious leaders wanted to arrest Me, but now was not the time. I hid Myself from them and continued on My Way. I told My People that I would bring Truth to meet them. Many believed in Me and this made the religious leaders furious. They trusted Me to redeem them and save them. They wanted a Savior, so I came to the world just for them. I told them that I was going to a place where they could not go. They did not understand what I meant by this. They wanted to go with Me, but they had to stay until I returned. They had to stay and tell the world the Truth. Do you believe that I was sent from above to show you the way to walk? Take My Hand and I will guide you.

John 7:37-50

My Beloved, I went to the Temple to speak during the festival and all the people were amazed at My Words. No one had taught them the way that I taught them. I explained the Scriptures, and they could see the Truth. They could understand, because I allowed them to see. They came searching, and they found the Truth. Many said I was a prophet, but many said I was the Messiah. They were divided about what was the Truth. They knew what the Scriptures said about the Messiah, but they could not put all the pieces together. They needed someone to guide them. Once I died for My People, I sent My Spirit to guide them. I told them to receive Me, and I would give them rivers of Living Water. I gave them My Spirit and life flowed through them like water from above. I gave them My Spirit, and they were transformed into My Image. The religious leaders sent their guards to follow Me and report to them what they heard and saw. The guards told them about how I taught the Scriptures. The religious leaders were furious to think that the guards had been also deceived by Me. Instead the guards were receiving life from Me, and they wanted to know more about Me. They wanted to come close to Me, but the religious leaders were keeping them from Me. The pull of the religious leaders on the people was strong. Just like today, the pull on the church is strong on many of My People. They cannot break man-made traditions, so they cannot worship Me in spirit and truth. Are you afraid of what men will say to you? Are you afraid to break man-made traditions? Do not be afraid to leave all you have ever known and draw close to Me, so you can really know who I AM. I AM not your father's god. I AM who I AM. Come close to Me and know Me for who I really am. Come close to Me, and I will guide you and direct you and fill you with peace.

John 8:1-11

My Beloved, many nights I spent praying in the olive garden. Many nights I cried out in agony. My flesh was weak, but My Spirit was strong. I AM one with the Father. I was sent to earth of the same spirit. We are one, but I AM wrapped in flesh. I know it is hard for you to understand who I AM. I will give you a revelation of who I AM, so you can understand and know Me. We must be one as My Father and I are one. We are of the same spirit. You and I must be of the same spirit, so we can commune with each other. You must spend many hours in prayer talking with Me to know Me and understand Me. Do you read the Scriptures to find out who I AM? The more you read the scriptures your eyes will be opened to the many facets of Me. I have many dimensions, and I want you to know all of them. I came to the Temple Court at sunrise to teach. The people were waiting for Me. They were hungry to hear the Truth. The religious leaders were furious and tried to trap Me and make Me look foolish in front of the people, so they would not believe in Me. The religious leaders brought a woman who had been caught in adultery to Me and asked Me what to do with her. I knew the woman was guilty, but where was the man who was also guilty? They wanted Me to say that they should stone the woman, but I knew their plan. I did not speak. I asked them a question, "Are any of you without sin, then you cast the first stone?" All have sinned. No one is perfect. No one was able to pick up a stone, so they left. They were furious that once again I was not caught in their trap. I told the woman to repent and turn from her sins and walk in the way of righteousness. She joyfully repented and went home cleansed. She saw the error of her ways. Do you see your errors? Do you see your sin? Turn from your sins and be cleansed by My spirit. I will lift you up and help you overcome. You are My Beloved, and I will hold you close to Me. Arise!

John 8:12-20

My Beloved, I AM the Light. Are you walking in the Light? If you walk in the Light, you will be able to see clearly. You will be able to see the path ahead, because I will show you the way to walk. If you come to Me, I will give you life eternal. You will no longer have to see death looming before you, but you will see life with Me. You will see that I overcame death for you, so you could live with Me forever. If you know Me, then you can see the Light. If you do not know Me, then you walk in darkness and you cannot see. You live in deception. You live in a world of lies. You cannot trust anyone who walks in darkness. You can only trust those who walk in the Light. Some men say that they are of the Light, but if you do not see love in their life, then they are not of the Light. Those of the Light are loving and kind and do not seek their own pleasure. They want to bring joy and happiness to others. They want to see people filled with Light and Truth. They grieve over those who are lost and cannot find their way. They grieve over those who have rejected Me. I came to tell others about Me, and many rejected Me. They are not of My Seed. They hold no seeds of righteousness. They are not covenant people from the line of Abraham, Isaac, and Jacob. I have grafted some into My Line, but most prefer to walk in darkness. Do you want to serve Me today? You must know that I AM one with the Father. We are One-the Eternal One- and there is no other. You should rejoice in this that the Maker of the Universe-the Creator of all things-loves you and wants you to be His Own and rule with Him forever. No greater gift has been given than this. Rejoice this day, and let there be no sadness in your heart.

John 8:21-29

My Beloved, I told the people that where I was going they could not come unless they believed in Me. They did not believe in Me, so I told them that they would die in their sins and not enter the Kingdom of Light. They would die in darkness never knowing Me and My Love. Some of the people believed in Me, but many more did not believe in Me. Do you believe in Me? Do you reject My Love for you? I told the people that My Father sent Me, and we are one. I speak only what My Father told Me to speak. I did only what My Father told Me to do. My Father was well pleased with what I did on earth. I was in a fleshly suit, but I was part of the spirit of the living Eternal one. We are one now that I have died and risen and dwell in heaven. There is only One who rules all things. I AM the Creator. I AM the King of the universe. I know all things and control all things. You are made of dirt, but you are emerging into a glorious creature of Light. You will be bright as the sun. You will have no darkness in you. You will pierce the darkness and destroy it. You will be brighter than any living being. You will be able to see clearly into the hearts of men. You will have compassion on them and know how difficult it is to dwell in the flesh. You will teach them the way to walk, so they will be lifted up and become one with Me. Rejoice that I have given you so much.

Rejoice that I love you so much.

John 8:30-38

My Beloved, many of the people in Judea believed in Me, and they wanted to follow Me and be My Disciples. I told them that if they wanted to be My Disciple that they must obey Me and trust in Me to guide them. They would be free, if they believed the Truth. They could not understand, because they were free men and not slaves already. How could they be set free? I told them that sin puts them in bondage, and they become a slave to the sin that holds them captive. Once you see the Truth and receive it, then you become free. Only if you accept the Son will you be free indeed. They still did not understand, "We are from the seed of Abraham. We have never been slaves." Even if you are from the seed of Abraham and you reject the Truth, then you are lost to your father the Devil. Satan tries to deceive all men. Only those who receive the Truth and want to walk in it will be set free from sin and will no longer be in bondage to the evil one. Be careful, because the evil one will try to seduce you gradually by showing you some truth and some deception. Do you want to go your own way? You will gradually turn following the deception, and before you know it you will be blinded and cannot see. Stay close to My Words. Meditate on them, so you know them. Commune with Me and you will not lose your way. I will keep you on the right path, and you will grow stronger day after day. You will know that I AM the Eternal One, and you will gain strength from calling on My Name and seeing how I answer your calls. We will be as one. We will walk hand in hand every day. You will rejoice in your life with Me. You will rejoice forever more.

John 8:39-47

My beloved, My People wanted to be My Disciples, but the religious leaders only wanted to cause disputes. They loved to argue whether it was about the Scriptures or another matter. They argued often with Me trying to find fault in Me. I told them that if they loved Me that they would believe in Me. They said that they only had one Father and that was Abraham. I asked them why they did not act like Abraham. Abraham believed in Me. I came out of My Father. I am one with Him. When I walked on earth My Spirit was wrapped in flesh, so I knew what My Father wanted Me to do. He had already given Me the message, because we are one. You may not understand this, but I looked at it in this way. The Father is the Creator and he made all things. He made a wrapping for His Spirit and placed part of His Spirit in the wrapping. His Spirit was a projection of the Father-like an arm. His Spirit understands all things just like the Father. His Spirit wrapped in Flesh was like a Son. His Spirit came from Him and was a part of Him-like a son is part of his father. Do not separate the Father and the Son. They are one and know all things. When I walked on earth many hated Me, but I knew who hated Me and who loved Me. Those who hated Me loved the evil one and wanted to serve him. The evil one is a deceiver. There is no Truth in him. He has tried to deceive all My People by filling them with lies. Can you discern lies? My Children know Truth and turn away from darkness. Open your eyes, My Children, and beware of the evil one. He will come quickly and steal all you have. Turn your back on him and walk away from him, and you will be greatly blessed.

John 8:48-59

My Beloved, I told the people that if they believed in Me that they would not see death. They did not understand this, so they said that I had a demon and that I was a liar. They thought I was deceived, but they were deceived. They could not believe that if they believed in Me that I would give them eternal life. Their flesh would die, but their spirit would live forever with Me. I told them that Abraham believed in Me and found eternal life. They wanted to know how I could know Abraham when I was such a young man. They laughed at Me, but I told them that I was alive before Abraham, because I AM the One who made him. They wanted to stone Me for saying that I AM the Creator of all things. They did not understand that the same spirit in Me was the same spirit in My Father who sent Me. I have the same spirit as the Creator, Father of all things. I had Abraham in My Mind before I ever created him. I had you in My Mind before I ever created you. I formed you with a certain purpose in mind to fulfill a certain task. Do you know the purpose I have for you? I want you to walk in My Love. You touch people every day and you do not even know it. You should look at who you touch, and the words you say to others. Do you say loving and kind words to others? Do you give your love to others? Do you know that My Spirit inside of you is a loving kind spirit that will flow through you, if you allow Me to move through you? Many times the people wanted to kill Me even though I spoke to them in love. This may happen to you. Even if your love is not received, I will bless you for giving your love to others. I will give you favor and help you walk in My Way by telling you the way to go and prospering you along the way. Keep your eyes on Me, and you will do well.

John 9:1-12

My Beloved, I saw a man on the road that was blind from birth. He had never seen daylight. He lived in constant darkness. My Disciples asked Me why the man was blind. I told them that he was made just for this day, so he could bring glory to My Name. I spit in the ground and made mud. I put the mud on the man's eyes and told the man to go to the pool and wash himself clean, and then he could see. The man found his way to the pool and washed himself and he could see. He was so joyful that he told all he knew what happened. Eventually the religious leaders saw the man and wanted to know how he could see. He told them that I healed him. They wanted to know where I was, so they could come find Me. The man did not know where I was, so the religious leaders began to search for Me. I healed the man, and he could see light. He saw light as the world gives you, but he was touched by the Light of the world. The man was given sight by the One who created the eye. The man was confused about all the religious leaders wanting to accuse Me. Couldn't they see that I had just healed him? The people around him saw what I did for him. He told everyone who had healed him. The people heard that I had healed them, and this added to what I had already done. They knew I was the Messiah. My People know who I AM. Those who do not know Me are lacking and without. Do you cling to Me? If you cling to Me, I will give you good gifts. I will shower you with blessings. Draw close to Me, and you will be greatly blessed.

John 9:13-34

My Beloved, I healed a man that was born blind on Sabbath. The religious leaders were furious that I had healed him on Sabbath. They were more concerned about Me breaking a law than the miracle that I had done. They took the man to the synagogue and questioned him before the leaders. They tried to find out if the man was really born blind and who really healed him. They even told his parents to come testify that this man was born blind. His parents were afraid of being banned from the synagogue, so they told the leaders to ask the man because he was old enough to answer for himself. The man I had healed was very angry with these leaders, because they kept questioning him and tried to get him to change his answers to the questions. They did not want the man to be healed, because they would have to explain to the people why the man was healed and who healed him. The man said that I was a prophet, because he healed him. The leaders said that I was a sinner, because I healed on Sabbath. The man told them that I did not hear the prayers of sinners unless they repent, but I hear the prayers of those who are obedient and want to keep My Laws. I will hear the prayers of those who love Me and want to serve Me. The leaders became so angry with the man that they threw him out of the synagogue. The man was not concerned, because he had found Me and we would be My Disciple and follow Me. Who else could heal the blind eyes and make men see? The man was not concerned about being disgraced, because he had been blind and humbled by his situation. You should not be concerned about what others say about you, if you speak the Truth about Me. Do you tell others about Me and all the wonderful things I do for you? I bring good things to you every day, and I want you to see that it is My Hand that sends these things to you. Open your eyes! Do you have blind eyes? Allow Me to let you see the Truth. Call on My Name, and I will come to you, and remove the darkness from your eyes.

John 9:35-41

My Beloved, I found the man who I healed. I knew he had been banned from the synagogue. I asked him if he believed in Me, and he said, "yes". I asked him to follow Me, and he did. He became one of My Disciples. He loved and cherished Me and did not care that he was banned from the synagogue. My People were beginning to realize that those who were in charge of the synagogue walked in darkness. They were blind and could not see. The religious leaders heard Me tell the man I had healed that those who did not believe in Me were blind. They confronted Me as they always liked to do. "So you say we are blind?" I told them that if they continued to reject Me that they were blind. I AM the Light and those who close out the Light are blind. Do you reject Me? Do you hear Me speaking to you? What am I saying to you? Listen. Do not be like the stiff necked religious leaders of old who thought they knew the Truth and didn't. They were blind and walking in darkness. They were trying to follow My Laws, but their hearts were cold and dark. They wanted their own way. They were trying to steal and lie and deceive others to get what they wanted. They were corrupt and harsh with My People. They had taken up the ways of their enemies who oppressed them. They had become like the people they hated. Do not allow those around you that oppress you to bring you down to a place that you become like them. Rise above them. Walk in love and compassion. It will not be easy to give love when others are harsh. Rise above them and fill yourself with love for Me, and I will give you all you need to love them. Your love will break the darkness. Your love will overcome those around you. I came to judge the world. Those who say they walk in righteousness are blind. Are you humble before Me and know you need My Help every day? You are My Child who loves Me and wants to please Me. Arise My People, and call on My Name, and I will help you overcome.

John 10:1-10

My Beloved, I told My People that they must enter into the Kingdom of Light only through Me. Many men will come to you saying, "I am the one", but do not listen to them. They will bring a new way of doing things. I want you to trust in the Words that I have given you a long time ago through Moses. These words have been preserved through the ages for My People. My Words have survived, because I have made them survive. Many documents have been lost thorough time and disasters, but I have kept My Words alive and safe from all destruction. Lean on what My Words say, and they will speak to you, and you will gain life from them. Do you listen to men tell you how to serve Me? Men will deceive you. They will even take My Words and change their meaning to suit them. I AM the Good Shepherd. I care for My People and keep them safe from destruction. My Sheep hear My Voice and follow Me. They will not respond to the voice of another. They listen only to Me. When I tell them to come, they will come. When I tell them to stay in this place, they will stay in that place. I will keep them safe even in the darkest of days. Are you afraid of what will happen tomorrow? I will provide all you need. You need to be afraid, if you are in sin. You need to repent, and I will hear your cry and redeem you. Walk in righteousness and never be moved.

John 10:11-16

My Beloved, I AM the Good Shepherd. I take care of My Own. I care for those who have been given to Me. I have a place where I protect My People. All those who turn to Me and want to serve Me are My Own. They draw close to Me and want to obey Me, because they love Me. I take care of all those who are part of My Flock. You are My Sheep and you hear My Voice. You know My Voice and listen for My Call. You are only interested in what I tell you to do. You do not listen to man and his voice. Man wants to change My Laws and throw them away. My Children know My Laws and cling to them and are righteous before Me. They want to obey all My Laws and hold firm to them, because they know that they bring them Life and Liberty. Those who turn away from Me will not enter My Kingdom of Light. They will stay in darkness and never know Me and what I can give them. I laid down My Life for My People. I laid down My Life, so you could be delivered from your sins and live with Me eternally. Do you struggle with your flesh? Draw close to Me, and you will be strengthened by Me. Do you hear My Voice and know what to do? Many voices are calling you to come to them, but only My Voice will bring you life. The other voices of the world will only bring you death. I want to unite all My Children and bring them all back to My Land and unite them in Me. Now they are scattered across the nations, but soon I will call them all home. Only those who are listening will hear My Call and come to Me. You will give up all you know to come to My Land. It will be an act of faith, but the rewards will be great. You will have protection from all your enemies. You will have all you need to survive while others will die of starvation and thirst. They will suffer loss, but you will be greatly blessed, because you have obeyed Me to come when I called.

John 10:17-21

My beloved, I came to earth to lay down My Life, so you can gain life. You do not know what I suffered in the flesh to carry out My Mission. I came for one reason and that was to free you from sin. Adam and Eve sinned in the garden and broke covenant with Me. I established a new covenant with Abraham, Isaac, and Jacob. I watched carefully over their children and protected them, so not one tribe was lost. I kept a remnant even after they sinned against Me. When I made the covenant with Abraham, he slept and I came between the meats and established the covenant. Abraham was not capable of fulfilling the covenant, because he was just flesh. I came in the flesh to fulfill the covenant. Even if he sinned against Me, I would still fulfill the covenant. Abraham brought his son Isaac to sacrifice on the mountain, but I stopped his hand and said that I would lay down My Life for My People. I would be the only Son that was sacrificed. Abraham trusted Me to raise Isaac back up, because I promised him that through Isaac would be the promises of the covenant. Abraham trusted Me, and I counted it as righteousness. I came to lay down My Life to fulfill what I spoke to Abraham. I laid down My Life, and I spilled My Blood on the ground. The ground shook, and the graves opened and the dead came to life. Do you know that the earth has been changed? It is no longer under a curse of death but a blessing of life. I have done this for you, and you probably do not understand it. I have opened My Arms of Love for you to enter and be free from all oppressors. Rejoice that I love you so much. I have given you a great gift, so praise Me for all My wondrous works.

John 10:22-29

My Beloved, I went to the Temple during Hanukkah or the Feast of Dedication. I came to the feast to see My People and teach them My Words. The religious leaders surrounded Me and demanded Me to tell them if I was the Messiah. I was not ready to tell them who I AM. They would reject Me no matter what I said. They were not My Children. They were wicked and wanted their own way. They searched the Scriptures for verses that would tell them who the Messiah was when he came. I came, and they could not see that I fulfilled all the verses. John even prepared the way for Me to come and testified on behalf of Me. The religious leaders would not listen to what I was saying, because they wanted their own way. When I told them that I was one with the Father or that I AM the Eternal One, they wanted to pick up stones and kill Me. I passed through them, because it was not My Time to die. I would lay down My Life. No one would take it from Me. These wicked religious leaders were not My Children, yet they were pressing down My Children with numerous laws. The only law they should ever keep is to love Me with all their heart, soul, mind, and strength. Do you love only Me? If you love only Me, then you will want to obey all the laws that I gave Moses, because through them you will be able to prosper and be in good health here. Blessed are those who follow Me. They will never be put to shame.

John 10:30-42

My Beloved, I tried to explain to the people that I AM the Creator, the King of the Universe, the Eternal One, but they wanted to stone Me. I told them I AM the only One through which they will receive eternal life, but they rejected My Words. They saw the form of a man and could not discern who I AM. They looked at My Flesh and were too blind to see the Truth standing before them. Many received the Truth and were delivered from darkness. John baptized many who believed in Me every day. They came to him wanting to repent of their sins and have eternal life with Me. John told them that I was the One that they should cling to. John told them I would do miracles-heal the sick, raise the dead, deliver those oppressed by demons, open the eyes of the blind. The people saw Me do these things, and they believed in Me because John told them that I was coming. He pointed Me out when I arrived. John was a Light in the darkness, and he shone brightly. No man testified of Me like he did. No man prepared the path for Me but him. He knew Me and loved Me. He gave up his life for Me. He is greatly loved by Me. Those who were not blinded by the religious leaders could see the Light and not be deceived. Are you blinded by the religious leaders? Do you listen to what they teach you and believe what they tell you? Do you search the Scriptures for the Truth and find Me? Only if you search for Me with all your heart will you find Me. Search this day and you will see clearly. Put aside all man-made laws and doctrines. Find Truth in My Scriptures, and I will set you free.

John 11:1-16

My Beloved, Mary and Martha sent a messenger telling Me that Lazarus was sick, and I needed to come quickly. I knew that Lazarus's death would bring glory to My Name, so I waited until he died before I came to see him. Lazarus lived in Judea where the Jews hated Me and wanted to kill Me. The last time I was there, they wanted to stone Me, because I said that I AM the Eternal One. My Disciples did not want to go back there. They were concerned that this time the Judeans would kill Me. They did not understand that no one would harm Me unless I allowed them to harm Me. They did not understand that I controlled all things. Even the evil one does not understand these things, or he would change his actions. He should know that no matter what he does the end result will be the same, because I have ordained it so. I told My Disciples that we must bring Light to the world and not be afraid of the people. Some people will receive Me, and they will receive you. Some will not receive Me, and they will not receive you. You must accept that not all men will accept you, because you love Me. Be strong and be mighty. Stand firm. The way is not easy. Have you stumbled and fallen in your sin? Do not wallow in your sins and self-pity. Get up quickly and repent, and go on your way. I will strengthen your legs, so you stand firm and walk steadfastly.

John 11:17-31

My Beloved, I delayed coming to see Mary and Martha, so that Lazarus their brother would die. I wanted to bring glory to My Name. I got to their house four days after he had already died. Many were gathered around Mary and Martha to comfort them. When Martha heard I was coming she ran out to meet Me. She said that she wished I had been there, because I would have healed her brother. She had a strong faith, because she knew that even now whatever I asked for would be done. I told her that her brother would rise again, but she thought I meant in the last resurrection. I AM the Resurrection and the Life. I give Life, and I take it away. I resurrect, and I diminish. I AM the One who decides who will live and who will die. Martha believed that I AM the Messiah, so she knew that I had power to do whatever I wanted to do. Martha ran to get Mary, because she knew that she would want to see Me. They were both comforted that I had come to them at last. Their faith was in Me, and I would not disappoint them. I acted on their faith, and I brought their brother back to life. No man could do this. No man has the power of life and death. Men may try to bring life into the world, but they do not have power to create life. Only I AM the Creator. I AM the one who counts the days of every man. What is your choice? Do you want to live your allotted days for Me and be greatly rewarded in My Kingdom? Do you want to live for yourself and be thrown into the Lake of Fire and be no more? You will no longer exist and even the memory of you will fade away. You are only a breathe. Trust in the One who gives you breathe, and you will do well.

John 11:32-45

My Beloved, I came close to where Lazarus lived, and Martha came out to meet Me. I told her to trust in Me and she would see the Glory of God. Martha ran to get her sister Mary. Mary ran out to meet Me and rejoiced that I had finally come. She told Me that if I had come earlier that her brother would not have died. She was grieving over the loss of her brother along with the other Judeans that came to comfort her. I was also grieved that Mary and Martha had to suffer such loss. I wept for them knowing how much pain they were in. I told the men with them to remove the stone. I was told that he would smell, since he had already been dead for four days. I told them to roll away the stone, and they did. I called to Lazarus to come out. He heard My Voice and awoke from his sleep and walked out of the tomb with his burial clothes still on him. Everyone cried out in surprise. They could not believe that I had brought a dead man back to life. Mary and Martha rejoiced and wept over their brother. Lazarus had only been asleep. I took away his breath for four days, and then I gave him back his breath. I give life, and I take it away. I hold all things in My Hands, and no man can take anything away from Me. I made you with My Hands. I formed you for a certain task. You must listen to what I say for you to do. You must be obedient to My Voice. You must want to love Me with all your heart, so you can always be hearing what I tell you to do. Mary and Martha believed in Me and trusted Me, and they were greatly rewarded. Many believed in Me that very day. Others ran into town and told the religious leaders what I had done. They were blinded and could not see that I had done a miracle in front of their eyes. Look around you, and see what I AM doing. Do you see that I am working miracles every day? I move on behalf of your everyday. Watch and see!

John 11:46-54

My Beloved, after I raised Lazarus from the dead, many believed in Me. Others ran to the religious leaders to tell them what I had done. All the religious leaders were upset. They called a meeting of all the leaders to discuss what to do with Me. If they continued to allow me to perform miracles, then all the people would follow Me. They thought this would mean the destruction of their nation. They thought that they would have no need for the Temple or synagogues. They thought the Roman government would support Me, since most of the people believed in Me and not in the present leaders. They imagined all sorts of things that could happen. The High Priest stood up and told them that it is best to have one man die to save the whole nation from destruction. I came to save the nation of Israel. I came to save My People in Judea and in all the areas of the world where they have fled to escape persecution. I came that you may be saved from destruction and live with Me eternally. You do not realize how much I love you. I died for you. I walked in flesh for you. I humbled Myself and took human form to teach you about Me and My Ways. If you love Me, you will want to know Me. You will seek Me with all your heart. You will not listen to false teachers who want you to only listen to them. How do you know if a man seeks Me? A man seeks Me if he wants to pray with you concerning your problem and waits to hear My Answer. If he tells you what to do without seeking Me, then you know you have come to the wrong person for advice. Listen for My Voice. I will show you the way.

John 11:55-12:11

My beloved, Passover was about to begin. According to the laws of Moses all men were supposed to come to Jerusalem for the Feast of Passover. I had not come to the festival yet, so the people were wondering if I would come at all. They wondered if I would break one of the laws of Moses. The religious leaders had warned all the people to tell them when I arrived, so they could arrest Me. The people knew that they wanted to kill Me. They knew that I had done many miracles, and the religious leaders were saying that My Power came from the evil one. They were trying to trap My People and make them believe a lie. They even wanted to kill Lazarus, so the people would stop going to his house and hearing his story how I raised him from the dead. My people were afraid. They loved Me, and did not want harm to come to Me. They cautioned Me to stay away from Jerusalem, and celebrate My Passover a month later as the scripture allows. I came to Lazarus' house to eat with him and his sisters. Mary poured perfume on Me and the aroma filled the house. Judas was upset that Mary wasted the costly perfume on Me. Judas was a thief and stole from the common purse used to buy supplies for Me and My Disciples. Judas was wicked from the beginning. His heart was dark. He continued to sin against Me while he was My Disciple. I knew he would betray Me. I knew My Mission was to die for My People, and Judas was just an accessory to that plan. Are you walking in darkness? Arise and wash yourself, so you will not betray Me. Follow Me and be at one with Me. Arise!

John 12:12-19

My Beloved, many people in Judea believed in Me, because I raised Lazarus from the dead. They were going to Lazarus' house to hear his story of how he was raised from the dead. The religious leaders knew they would have to kill both Lazarus and Me to stop the people from believing in Me. When the people heard that I was coming into Jerusalem, they gathered palm branches and waved them before Me shouting to deliver them from their enemies and bring My Kingdom on earth. They knew I was the Messiah. They were looking for Me to take over the city. They did not realize that I was a humble servant. I had to lay down My Life, so they would live with Me eternally. I laid down My Life to cover the sins of many. My Blood covered the sins of the guilty. All have sinned and come short of My Glory. That is why you cannot pay the price for your sins. Only I can pay that price. The people were excited, because they thought redemption had come at last. They praised Me with their voices, and it was beautiful before Me. Their praises only made the religious leaders furious. Something had to be done immediately to remove Me and end this madness. As I entered Jerusalem I could see the hopeful faces that had turned to Me to save them from their oppression. I wish that I could help them be delivered, but they had to pay for their past sins. It would be many years before they would be brought back to Jerusalem singing and dancing. Until then I would be their comfort. Do you need comfort today? Do you need hope? I AM your Hope and Comfort. I dwell within you. Call on My Name. I will bring you home once again. I will deliver you from all who hate you. I will redeem you by My Blood. I will arise in your midst and teach you. I love you, My Children. Hold fast until the end.

John 12:20-26

My Beloved, I went to a hidden place in Jerusalem, so no one would bother Me. Some Greek speaking Jews came searching for Me. My Disciples came to Me to tell Me that they were there. I was in turmoil with My Flesh as I saw the end approaching. I knew how they would torment Me and kill Me. I struggled with the task before Me, but My Disciples did not know My Torment. As they came to Me asking Me to speak to these Jews, I gave them a message. I wanted them to know that I must die, so I could save many from destruction. If a piece of grain falls on the ground and does not die and take root, then it is worthless. If the piece of grain falls into fertile soil and dies and produces a new plant, then it will produce a great harvest. I had to die, so that I could harvest the many that were lost in sin. If you love Me, you will follow what I did on earth. I laid down My Life for others. I thought of others before Myself. Do you think of others before yourself? Are you selfish? If I was selfish I would have never laid down My Life for you. My Love for you was overwhelming. My Love for you overcame My Flesh and gave Me the ability to pour My Blood out for you. At any time I could have released Myself from My Flesh and took My Throne in Heaven. I watched as My Blood poured out on to the ground for you, and I was pleased that you could be redeemed. Rejoice that I love you so much!

John 12:27-36

My beloved, I was in turmoil with My Flesh, because I could see what I would have to endure in the coming hours. I called out to My Father to receive Me from this task, but then I conquered My Flesh and said that My Father's Name must be gloried. My Voice spoke from heaven that I would indeed glorify My Name through the act of My Son. Those around Me heard the voice as thunder. They thought it was the voice of an angel speaking to Me. Many around Me believed in Me. They knew I was the Messiah sent to rescue them. I called out for help to overcome My Flesh and proceed with the task at hand. I came to die for My People. I told those around Me that I would be lifted up and overcome the evil one. They did not understand what I meant by lifted up until after I died and was lifted up from the grave and returned to My Throne in Heaven. Many believed after I gave My Life for them. They searched the scriptures and saw that indeed I AM the Messiah. I AM the Light of the world. I told them to walk in the Light while I was among them. They should be drawn to the Light, because they are people of Light and will enter My Kingdom of Light. If they reject Me, then they reject the Light also. The Light exposes their sins and brings them to repentance. If they hate Me, then they do not want to repent of their sins. They want to live in darkness. If you want to draw close to Me, then you must repent of your sins and walk in righteousness. Are you willing to lay down your life and become My Servant? My Servant listens to My Voice and does what I say to do. My Servant is humble before Me not wanting his own way, but seeks to please Me. Are you
My humble servant?

John 12:37-50

My Beloved, even though I did many miracles many did not believe in Me, because I had blinded their eyes. They were under the oppression of their enemies, because of the sins of their ancestors who turned from Me and worshipped other gods. I told them that I would send them out of the Land into exile. They were blinded and could not see because of their sins. Some of the religious leaders believed in Me, but they did not speak about Me in front of the others for fear that they would be banned from the synagogue. They could not stand the thought of being humiliated in such a way. They wanted the praise of man and not to please Me. I told those around Me that they must walk in the Light. If they did not walk in the Light, they would die in their sins. They must be a humble servant and put aside what they wanted to do and do My Will. This means that they would have to proclaim that I AM the Messiah in front of the religious leaders and not be upset about being banned from the synagogue. You do not serve religious leaders, but you serve only Me. I will reward you for your sacrifices when you stand before Me on the Last Day. I did not come to judge the world, but to save the world. The world will be judged on the Judgment Day when all the accounts will be read. Only the righteous will be found worthy to enter My Kingdom of Light. Do you walk in the Light all day long? If you seek Me daily, you will be found worthy to enter My Kingdom and rule with Me. You will be allowed to eat from the Tree of Life and live eternally in My Presence.

John 13:1-17

My Beloved, the Passover was almost here. I knew that My Time had come. I loved being among My People. My heart was filled with love for them. I knew how difficult it was to walk in the flesh. I wanted to stay and teach My Children, but I knew it was time to leave and go back to My Kingdom. I could see that the evil one had already put in Judas' heart to betray Me. He would tell the religious leaders where I was, so they could arrest Me. It was hard to believe that a man I had been with everyday for years wanted to betray Me to those who hated Me. He thought that he knew what was best, but he was deceived by the enemy. Do you think you see clearly the path ahead of you? You must come to Me and allow Me to help you see what the Truth is. Sometimes the enemy deceives you, and you are blinded. Pray to Me that you will not be deceived and will see clearly. I will destroy the darkness from you, and you will be able to see the Light. As I gathered My Disciples in the room to eat the meal, I wanted to show them how to humble themselves and wash each other's feet. This was the job of the lowest of servants, and yet I took this job to show My Disciples that it was better to humble yourself and show love to others. I want you to also humble yourself and put others before yourself. You may not wash their feet, because it is not your custom. It is My Custom to love each person tenderly. Think of their needs and love them in a way that would heal their heart. If you do this, you are My Servant, and I will greatly bless you.

John 13:18-30

My Beloved, as I gathered with My Disciples in the room to eat our Passover together. I knew this was the last meal I would have with them. I was grieved to leave them. I wanted to stay and teach them more about Me. I knew that I had to go, so My Spirit could come and make My People stronger. I wanted My People to be strong to stand against the enemy. If I left and returned to My Kingdom, then My Spirit would be able to come to those who loved Me. I told them that one of them would betray Me. They were shocked, "Who would betray the Master? It certainly is not one of us!" They looked at each other and wondered what I meant. Judas was the only one who knew what I meant. Once he knew that I knew about his plan, he left quickly. He did not want to stay with Me, if I knew his plot to turn Me over to the men who hated Me. This was a man who had seen Me do miracles. He had heard Me teach My People every day. He had seen many believe in Me, yet he was blinded and could not see. He wanted Me to proclaim My Kingdom on earth and drive those who oppressed My People out of their country. He wanted to push Me into this position where I had to stand up and proclaim My Kingdom or die. He did not realize that I wanted to lay down My Life for My People, so they could be released from the bondage of sin. Are you deceived like Judas? Are you accepting what I give you in your life? Do not push to make something happen that is not in My Plan for you. Accept what I bring to you, and you will do well.

John 13:31-38

My Beloved, as soon as Judas left I knew that My Time had come. I knew that the evil one had completed his plan in Judas, and soon I would be arrested. I told My Disciples goodbye, but they did not understand. I told them that I was going away, and where I was going they could not come. Peter wanted to come with Me. He said that he would lay down his life for Me. I knew the struggles he would have with his flesh in the next few hours. He would wonder what would happen to Me. Would I overcome or allow the Romans to torture and kill Me? He did not understand that I must lay down My Life, so he could be saved from eternal darkness. Peter loved Me and he wanted to serve Me, but when he saw Me taken away, his life was shattered. He was in confusion and did not know what would happen to Me. He wanted to stand firm, but he was afraid of the Roman soldiers and what they would do to him. These enemies were very wicked and heartless. They treated My People with no mercy. They tortured and killed My People all the time. My People lived in terror. My Disciples had found comfort in Me and felt safe. Now I was taken from them, and they were again filled with fear. Are you filled with fear about what will happen in your life? Sometimes you cannot see the road ahead. You must trust Me that I will do what is best for you. You may suffer disappointment, but this will keep you humble, and you will grow and prosper from what you have learned. You will see all sorts of things come your way. Some events will make you rejoice, and some events will make you cry. This is all part of life. Take the bad with the good, and use all of it to perfect you into the person I want you to become. You are to love others as I loved others when I walked on this earth. The people around you will know you by your love. They will see your good works, and it will bring glory to My Name. Bring glory to My Name, and you will be rewarded greatly.

John 14:1-14

My Beloved, I told My Disciples that I would be leaving, and they could not go with Me. They were upset and wanted to know where I was going. I told them that one day I would come back to get them and take them to My Kingdom. I left to prepare a place for My Children. It is a beautiful place filled with many treasures just for you. I will make a special room just for you, so you may dwell with Me eternally. My Disciples did not understand where I was going or why I was leaving. I had to go, so My Spirit would come and teach you My Ways. I wanted My People to walk in righteousness, but I knew they needed My Spirit within them to help them. Philip said to show him the Father, but I AM the same as the Father. We are one. I was an extension of Him wrapped in flesh. Now I have been delivered from the flesh, and I sit on My Throne and care for My Children. Many hate you and want to take you away from Me. I will care for you, and no one can touch you. I AM the Truth and the Way. You must come through Me, so I can wash you clean and save you from eternal darkness. Many men will miss the narrow door and will not be able to pass through. Many men will allow riches and power to keep them from searching for the open door. Are you searching for Me with all your heart? If you search for Me with all your heart, you will find Me. I will give you whatever you ask, if you ask in My Name. Call on Me, and I will answer you. I will give you good gifts, and you will be greatly blessed.

John 14:15-21

My Beloved, if you love Me, you will keep My Commandments. I gave My Commandments to Moses, and he taught them to your ancestors. They have carefully been written down and kept perfect through the ages, so you could have My Words. I have not allowed anyone to destroy them. I have not allowed anyone to alter them. I have kept them so my Children can have them and learn from them. My Children look for Me and find Me. They want to serve Me. They want to please Me. They search the scriptures for My Ways. I guide them by My Spirit. If they come to Me seeking, I will give them the answers. Many say they know Me, but they do not come to Me and seek Me. They want to go their own way, but they say they know Me and love Me. A man must come to Me seeking before he can be considered My Own. If he comes to Me, I will not reject him. I will hold him close to Me tenderly and teach him My Way. Do you want to show Me how much you love Me? Keep My Commandments and walk in My Way. How do you walk in My Way? My Way is being loving and kind to others. If you love others, you are loving Me. Give to others, and you are giving to Me. You are one with Me, if you walk in My Will. Walk in My Ways, and you will see Me.

John 14:22-31

My Beloved, I told My Disciples that if they loved Me they would do what I have told them to do. I told them that I would send them My Spirit to dwell within them and comfort them and counsel them and remind them of the words that I spoke to them. They could not understand these words. The only thing that they could think about was that I was leaving. They knew that I said that I was going back to My Father, but they did not know where this would be. They were confused and afraid. They did not want to lose Me. They did not realize that they would not lose Me, but I would come live within them and fill them with My Spirit. They knew that I would never leave them, but they did not understand how I would always be with them if I was going away. They would learn in the days ahead what a gift I had given them. I told them that the ruler of this world was coming to get Me soon. He was using his vessel Judas to take Me to My enemies. Judas was deceived by the enemy and could not see the Truth. He had ignored all My Words and wanted his own plan to work. I told My Disciples that the ruler of this earth has no power over Me. I lay down My Life for My Children, because they love Me. I did the will of the One who sent Me. I was obedient until the end. I overcame the flesh, and I gave salvation to all those who believe in Me. I told My Disciples to be on guard. The evil one would come to them and try to make them doubt who I AM. Do you think that the evil one cannot deceive you? He will come to you and try to deceive you. He will come and trap you with his words. He will come to you and steal the Truth from you. Beware! Be on guard.

Do not be deceived.

John 15:1-8

My Beloved, I AM the Vine and you are the branches. If you do not receive My Spirit and walk in My Ways, then you will wither up and die just like a branch that does not receive water from the vine. If you love Me, you will cling to Me. You will be united in marriage to Me. You will want only to please Me. You will be at one with Me and do whatever I ask you to do. If you love Me, you will obey My Commandments. You will want to love others and be kind and gentle never speaking harsh words. You will want to let your love radiate from Me to those around you. Are you bearing fruit from the Vine? You will bear much fruit, if you are receiving the living water from the Vine. You will bear the fruit of love, kindness, patience, long suffering. You will be joyful and praise Me in all I do for you knowing that I only bring good things to those who love Me. If you ask Me in My Name, I will give you whatever you ask, because you are united to Me. You are My Beloved, and I will give to you generously. You will be at one with Me and rejoice in all I do for you daily.

John 15:9-17

My Beloved, if you love Me, you will keep My Commandments. If you keep My Commandments, then you will stay in My Love and rejoice in Me. Your joy will be complete as I rejoice over you. I will shower you with blessings, because you stay in My Love and keep My Commandments. If you love Me, you will walk hand in hand with Me. I will teach you secret things. I will teach you hidden things that only those children who are close to Me will know. I do not tell the world My Ways. I choose those children that I want as My Own. They do not choose Me. I choose them. I know your heart. I know how you will love Me. I know how you will love others. I know if you will be obedient to Me or fall into rebellion. You are no longer slaves in Egypt. I brought you out of Egypt and made you My Own. I have drawn you close to Me and My Spirit abides in you. Only My Children have My Spirit abiding within them. I do not live in alien people. I only unite with My Own. Are you confused over some things that are happening in your life? If you call on My Name and search for Me, I will tell you what you need to know and you will have peace. You may not know Me very well right now, but I will show you My Ways. Do you feel alone at times? I AM always with you. I AM always by your side. Call on My Name, and you will find Me. You will get the answer to your question. It may not be immediate, but wait on Me and keep on asking and the answer will come. It may not be the answer that you want, but you will receive the answer I have designed for you. Trust Me, because I know what is best for you. I will bring only good things to your door.

John 15:18-27

My Beloved, the world will hate you, because they hate Me. If they persecuted Me, then they will persecute you. It is only a matter of time before the whole world will hate you. Today there are some who tolerate you under the guidelines of religious freedom. This religious freedom will come to an end. They will want you to worship as they worship, and they will not be worshipping Me. They will have one religion for the sake of peace. Everyone must abide in this religion, or they will be accused of not wanting to walk in peace. I AM the only One who can give peace. Do not believe anyone else who comes in My Name and says that he will give you peace. There is no peace except in Me. The world will hate you, because you know Me and want only to serve Me. You will want to keep My Commandments, and they will not allow you to keep them. They will count you as enemies of the state. They will want to arrest you and kill you. They will call you rebels. They will attack you and hate you for no reason like they hated Me for no reason. I will shelter you, if you listen to My Voice. I will take you to a place where you will be safe just like I did for My Children in the desert. Do you call on My Name for what you need? I will provide for you. You will cling to the Counselor. He will bring you the Spirit of Truth who comes down from the Father of Lights. The Comforter will give you peace when the world is in torment. I will be faithful to those who are faithful to Me.

John 16:1-11

My Beloved, I came to bring Truth to My People who love Me. Many said they loved Me, but when persecution came they turned away. Only the righteous stood firm and did not move even in the midst of persecution. I told My People to leave Jerusalem and go to the surrounding areas, but then even the surrounding areas were not suitable to live. The Romans were harsh people and wanted to torment My People. They became harsher as they saw their enemies breaking down the edges of their empire. The once mighty Roman Empire came to an end. They were no longer a world power who could crush their enemies. A stronger people came to fight them and defeated them. I sent a stronger people to crush them. I enjoyed their victory over the Romans who had punished My People so many times. The Romans were a harsh task master. They were brutal, but a brutal people had victory over them, and they suffered extreme loss. They no longer had wealth and power, but they were humiliated in defeat time after time until they were destroyed. They no longer held vast territory, but they held only a few corners of the world. Now you still have the Romans who want to torment you. They have invaded the religious system, and they want to tell you what to do. They want to lead you astray. Do you cling to men and false doctrine? Listen to My Voice and I will guide you. I will teach you the way to go, so you will never be led astray. Lift up your head! See My Face and I will hear your voice, and do whatever you ask Me to do. Do you say that you love Me? Prove that you love Me by keeping My Commandments. Rejoice that you love Me and obey My Voice.

John 16:12-22

My Beloved, I told My Disciples that I would leave them and would not see them for awhile. They were grieved that I was leaving them. They did not know what to do without Me. I had to leave, so I could send My Spirit to dwell within them. They needed to learn how to be led by My Spirit. They had to learn to listen to My Voice and be obedient. My People who are called by My Name are humble people. They walk in humility. They want to do My Will, and they do not long to do their will. Are you able to give up what you want to do and do My Will? You can be used by Me, if you can do My Will and not yours. You must realize that you have to yield to Me and allow Me to mold you into My image. You will have many people try to lead you away from the Truth. Hold fast to the Truth, and do not depart from My Ways. If you know Me, then you will want to cling to Me. I told My Disciples that I must go away, but I would let them know what the future holds. I told My Son John about the future events that My People must be prepared for. Men have read the revelation that I gave John and have tried to see what will happen in the future. Only My Children will be given the ability to interpret the future. I will show them the signs along the way. I will show them when to turn aside from their enemies, so they will be safe. Are you listening to My Voice? As long as you listen and follow what I tell you to do, then you will be safe and protected by My Right Hand. Cling to Me and allow Me to show you hidden things. I will give you sound counsel, and you will walk hand in hand with Me.

John 16:23-33

My Beloved, I told My Disciples that I was leaving this world and going to My Father. I told them that I would not see them for awhile. I told them that they must receive My Spirit and listen to what My Spirit tells them. I told them to call on My Name, and I would give them whatever they needed. I would not leave them alone in the world. I would always be with them. Do you think that I have left you alone in this world? I left those who hated Me, but I draw near to you and tell you secret things. I have seen the men of this world hate you and want to kill you, but I will not allow anyone to harm you. I will keep you close to Me. You will be free to walk in peace. I told My Disciples what would happen in the days ahead, so they would not be afraid but have peace. I wanted them to trust Me and believe in Me. I wanted them to know Me and hear My Voice. I came to teach you My Ways. I came to bring Salvation to you, so you could live with Me eternally. I came, so you could be intimate with Me. Now you see Me from a distance, but soon you will see Me face to face. The evil one wants to destroy you like he wanted to destroy Me. I have overcome the world. I will give you peace to walk in the world, and trust Me in all things. The world will have tribulation, but I will give you joy, because I have already overcome the world. You can rejoice that your name is written in the Book of Life. You can rejoice that I love you so much!

John 17:1-8

My Beloved, I came to this world to tell you about Me and how to serve Me and how to be obedient to My Commandments. I came to earth to deliver you from the bondage of sin and suffering. I know you have endured much already at the hands of your enemies. I have given you a way out. I have opened a door for you, so you can be delivered from those who oppress you daily. I AM the Way. Have you walked through the door to eternal life? You must walk with Me daily, so you will not be oppressed by the world. You will be free to rejoice in Me. You may not have anyone around you to rejoice with you, but you can rejoice in Me. I will send you joy and fill you with gladness. I came to glorify My Name. I AM and I AM. I AM from the beginning. I AM One. There is no other but Me. I came wrapped in flesh to die for you. I saw how you suffered in flesh, and I had mercy on you. My Heart yearns for you to come home to My Heavenly Kingdom. I know the time is not right. You must be molded into My Image. You must change from glory to glory. You must emerge a glorious being ready to serve Me and take your place next to Me as My Heir to the throne. You do not understand these things now, but soon you will. The angels and other heavenly hosts look on in wonder at what you will become. You will be a fiery creature filled with love and compassion, but will not bend to anyone. You will be fierce and strong in battle, but loving and kind to others. I came to deliver you and bring you back to Me. You are now free from the hands of the evil one. You are now Mine. I love you deeply and will continue My process to change you and make you My own.

John 17:9-19

My Beloved, before I left My Disciples I prayed for them. I asked My Father to protect them and keep them safe from the evil one. I knew what they would suffer when I left. They would miss Me and grieve for Me. They would have questions and no answers. They would have to learn to hear My Voice and be guided by My Spirit. When I walked on this earth they did whatever I told them to do. Now they will have to learn to walk in the direction of My Spirit. They also struggled with the Romans who invaded their country and oppressed them daily. They would be hunted down by the religious leaders and persecuted, because they loved Me and wanted to serve Me. They would flee to unknown lands to escape their oppression. This was My Way for them. I wanted them to tell all the people in other lands about Me and My Ways. My Light and Love would be brought to all peoples as they spread to other nations. Do you cling to Me and love Me? Only those with My Righteous Seed will see the Light and run to the Light and rejoice in My Coming. The others would run from the Light and hide, so their sins would not be uncovered. My Hands are on you to help you. Call on My Name, and I will lift you up from every harmful situation. I will hold you consistently in My Arms.

John 17:20-26

My Beloved, I prayed for My Disciples before I left, but I also prayed for you. I prayed that those that My Disciples told about Me would receive Me and would unite together and stand firm against the evil one. I have seen the evil one gradually take My Children away from the faith and the One who chose them. I have My Hand on them, but they are wandering around and do not see. They are blinded and need someone to tell them how to find their Way. Arise, My People, who love Me and tell these lost ones how to find their way home. They will hear the Truth and receive it gladly. They have been searching for the Truth and cannot find it, because no one has brought the Truth to them. You must be sensitive to My Spirit. When I tell you to tell others about Me realize that they are searching for Me and have not been able to find Me. Trust Me that I will give you the Truth to say to them, so they can receive Me gladly. I prayed for you before I left that you would all dwell in peace together and support each other. Now you are all separated by doctrine. You are at war with each other over what is Truth. Unite together. Pray and fast and Truth will come to your door. Do you fight with your brother over what is Truth? One man does not have all the truth. Each man is in error in some things. Only I know truth. I AM Truth. Do you long to worship Me in a way that pleases Me? Worship together as one without fighting over what is Truth. I will lead you into all Truth. Be at peace with each other and love each other. I will reward you for your acts of kindness to your brothers.

John 18:1-11

My Beloved, I took my Disciples to one of my usual places to pray. This was a quiet place surrounded by olive trees. We prayed there often, and I talked to My Disciples about the things that they needed to learn for the days to come. Judas knew of this place. He knew I would take My Disciples there after we had our Passover meal. He told the temple guards where I would be, so he could betray Me. The other disciples were surprised by Judas leading the guards to Me, but I knew what he was about to do. I could see the future and knew what suffering I was facing. My Disciples did not know the future, but they trusted in Me to care for them. When the guards and soldiers came for Me I told them to let the others go, and I would go with them. I went with them peaceably. I went not because I was forced to go, but because I was obedient to the task again. I came to lay down My Life for My Children who love Me. I came to deliver them from the bondage of sin. I came to show them a better way to live their life. I taught them My Commandments and how to obey them. They were lost, but I took them in and gave them hope and life. I can do the same for you. Peter tried to stop what I came to do by pulling a weapon out to fight on My Behalf, but I rebuked him and told him to stop. Do you fight against what I want for you? Submit yourself to Me. You may be like Peter and not understand what I want you to do. You may not see the future. Trust in Me. I will guide you, and whatever I ask you to do I will give you the ability to do it. I will bring you help. I will give you all you need.

John 18:12-27

My Beloved, the Temple guards and the Roman soldiers took Me away like a criminal. They treated Me like I was a violent offender of the law. I never hurt anyone in My Life. I was always kind and loving to all men, even if they were mean to Me. I was totally innocent, and they took Me away and treated Me shamefully. They took Me to the father-in-law of the High Priest that year. He wanted to hear the charges against Me. He asked Me what I was saying to the people. I taught publicly in the synagogue for everyone to hear Me. I never tried to hide My Words from others. I wanted all to hear the Truth and walk in it. I told them that My Words were free for all to hear. They heard Me speak and never arrested Me. They could not find fault in My Words, because they were Truth. They did not like the miracles I did, because more of the people believed in Me as their Messiah. The religious leaders saw Me drawing the people away from them, and they were afraid of losing their power over them. One of the Temple Guards did not like My response and hit Me across the face. It hurt My Flesh, but I only felt pity for him. He was lost and dying in his sins. He would not enter My Kingdom, but he would be thrown into the Lake of Fire. I looked at all the others there. They were all filled with darkness, and yet they called themselves the spiritual leaders of My People. It was time for a change. I would bring them change that day, and a new life would emerge for My People. Is it time for a change in your life? I AM your Savior. I AM the only Way to Life.

John 18:28-40

My Beloved, I was led from the father-in-law's house to Pilate's chambers. The religious leaders did not want to become defiled for Passover, so they brought Me to Pilate so he would kill Me. If they killed or condemned Me to death, then they would be unclean for Passover. They had to ask Pilate to kill Me, since he was a foreigner, an alien, a pagan. They did not even use their own court system to judge Me, because they knew there was no fault in Me. If the religious leaders judged Me, then My People would be outraged. Pilate was a harsh man who ruled over Jerusalem. He tried to get the area under control, but there were groups that would rise up against the Romans from time to time. He did not like living in Jerusalem. He wanted to go back to Rome instead of living with people he hated. He looked at Me and knew that I was the One that they hated. He had heard of the miracles that I had done, and he knew their jealousy. He knew that I had not done anything worthy of death. He wanted to release Me like it was his custom to release one prisoner before Passover. There were many men in prison who fought to overtake the Romans. The release of one of them would make the people happy. He was not concerned about any of these men, because his forces were overpowering. He looked at Me and wondered who I was. He asked Me if I was King of the Jews. I told him that My Kingdom was not of this world. I was not a threat to his kingdom, but only through Me could all men have eternal life. He had no understanding of these things, but he knew I was not a threat to his rulership. He decided to satisfy the religious leaders and sent Me to My Death. Could Pilate have stopped My Death? Pilate was guilty for how harshly he dealt with My People, so I used him as an instrument to kill Me. My Innocent Blood fell on him and the Romans and the religious leaders. They had to suffer the consequences for My Death, and they still suffer to this day. They are blinded and dying without the Truth. Only My Children will see the Light.

John 19:1-16

My Beloved, Pilate looked at Me and knew that I was innocent. He did not want to kill Me, but I had to die so you could come live with Me eternally. That was a far greater reward for Me to lay down My Life for you. Pilate asked Me who I was. When he found out that I was King of a spiritual realm, then he called Me King of the Jews. Pilate thought that if he ordered Me to be flogged that this would satisfy the religious leaders. The soldiers took Me away and whipped Me. They mocked Me and put a crown of thorns on My Head and a purple robe on My flesh torn back. They hit Me and insulted Me. I was surrounded by pagans who wanted to harm Me. They laughed and joked among themselves. They were lost and dying, and they thought they had power over Me. Pilate again called Me to him and questioned Me. He wanted to have no part in My Death. He took Me before the people. The High Priest and his Temple Guards shouted to have Me put to death. Pilate could get no one to stand up for Me. He knew that I was innocent. He could see something in Me that the others could not see. He said that he could not kill their King. The people said they had no king but the emperor. If he refused to kill Me, then he would allow the people to place charges against him for not stopping opposing enemies of the Roman Government. He handed Me over to be killed. My Blood was then on his hands and all those who said to kill Me. Do you have innocent blood on your hands? Have you repented from the sins of your ancestors? You may still have curses on you from the sins of your ancestors. One of your ancestors may have been in that crowd cursing Me. Ask Me to remove all curses from your family. If you are walking in righteousness, I can do this for you. Just call on My Name.

John 19:17-30

My Beloved, I was taken to the stake where I laid down My Life for you. They pierced My Hands and Feet with nails. They hung Me up for everyone to see like I was a criminal. I was humiliated in front of all those going by. I was placed between two men who were worthy of paying for their crimes. I was innocent and paid for the whole nation's sins. I was looked upon with contempt by those who hated Me. They mocked Me and insulted Me. They came to look upon My Nakedness and humiliate Me. Even My Mother and those who loved Me came to look upon Me. I cried out to My Mother to be cared for by My Disciple who loved Me. He took My Mother and cared for her for the rest of her life. She grieved for Me deeply, but she knew that I had a greater purpose. She did not understand at the time what was happening, but she trusted Me to bring it to pass. The soldiers around Me mocked Me and divided My Clothes among them. They placed a sign over My Head saying that I was King of the Jews. The High Priest was furious and went to Pilate to remove it, but Pilate refused to change it. To him I was superior to the religious leaders and should rule over them. He was captivated by Me. He could see the good inside of Me, but he had to go forward with killing Me. It was the plan I had given Myself, and no one could change it. I had to shed My Innocent Blood, so you could once again be in covenant with Me. Now you can be married to Me. We can be intimate together and live eternally together. You are My Bride. Are you keeping yourself pure for Me as My Bride? I will reward you greatly in My Kingdom for your righteousness.

John 19:31-42

My Beloved, I came to give My Life for you. I laid down My Life, so that you would have eternal salvation. I came to teach My People My Ways to walk in love and compassion. I came to see My People released from the slavery of sin. Many people did not understand all that I taught, but they wanted to please Me. They wanted to do My Will, so I will gradually teach them about Me. My People do not understand even today all that happened by the shedding of My Blood. My Blood kept the nation of Israel from destruction completely. I kept a remnant of My People close to Me, so I could teach them My Ways. I wanted them to be a Light to the world. I gave up My Life freely. After My Task was finished I said, "It is finished". I left this earth and went to My Throne Room in heaven. I once again filled My throne. I took My Position in Heaven as all looked on in amazement. My Disciple, who came to Me in secret for fear of the religious leaders, came to Pilate to ask for My Body and prepared Me for burial. I was buried in his tomb in a garden. My Disciple did not know that I would be there only temporally. No one knew that I would rise from the grave. No one knew that I would have victory over death. The evil one did not understand My Plan or he would have stopped it. Do you understand all that I have done for you? Rejoice that I have given you victory over death.

John 20:1-18

My Beloved, I laid down My Life for you, but I lifted Myself up again. I had victory over death, and I ascended into My Throne Room. I sat in the presence of My Angels and all the other heavenly beings. They rejoiced with Me in My Victory. They still did not fully understand how you would come to My Kingdom of Light. They trusted in Me just as you trust in Me when you do not fully understand. The women went to find Me as soon as it was light on the first day of the week. I was not there and the stone had been rolled away. The women were afraid and ran to tell Peter what had happened. Peter and John ran to the tomb and no one was there. They saw My Burial Clothes lying inside the tomb. They thought that the soldiers had done something evil with My Body. They did not understand what had happened. They ran back to tell the others. Only Mary remained behind weeping over Me. I came to comfort her, but she did not know it was Me. She did not recognize Me until I called her name. She looked upon My Face and tried to hold Me, but I told her not to touch Me. I was no longer in earthly form, but in a resurrected form that she could not touch. I told her to go to the others and tell them that I would come to them. She ran away filled with joy. She thought I would stay with them, but I was only here to comfort them and tell them what I wanted them to do while I was gone. Do you long for My Return? I will return to you, and you will be once again filled with joy. All your suffering will be over, and you will once again be able to hold Me.

John 20:19-31

My Beloved, I came to My Disciples that same day at night to see them. They were afraid and locked in a room. They thought the religious leaders were looking for them and would kill them also. I appeared to them in the room, and they rejoiced over Me. They saw where I was pierced, and they wept over Me. They did not understand everything that happened. I tried to explain to them that now they must go tell everyone about Me and My Love for them. I wanted them to tell everyone that I laid down My Life, so they could be delivered from their sins. I paid the price for their crimes. I was innocent and I laid down My Life, so they could live with Me eternally. I laid down My Life, so they could enter into My Kingdom of Light. All those who listen and receive Me are chosen by Me. They hear the call to come to Me, and they obey. They are humble servants who want to please Me. They want to obey Me and do what is right. They love others and want to help them. They are filled with compassion for others. How will you know if someone loves Me? You will know those who love Me by their love and kindness towards others. If you see others who love Me, then help them if they are in need. I provided for My Disciples. Provide for your brothers around you. Thomas doubted that I came to see My Disciples. I came back the next week for him, so he could believe in Me. He had to see where I was pierced, but you believe in Me and you have never seen Me. You will be greatly rewarded for your faith. I breathed My Spirit on My Disciples and gave them guidance. I have also imparted My Spirit to you. I will guide you and direct you, because I love you.

Listen to My Voice and obey Me, and I will bless you greatly.

John 21:1-14

My Beloved, I came to My Disciples again. They were disappointed, because they had not caught any fish all night. They were sad, because they felt like they had no purpose for living once I had left. They talked among themselves about Me. They wondered if I would return and what I would say. They longed for Me to come to them. I came to comfort them and restore them. It was so difficult to be without Me. I stood on the shore and asked them if they caught any fish. They replied to Me that they had been unsuccessful. I told them to try on the starboard. When they brought in their net they caught so many fish that they could barely bring in the net. John knew at once that it was Me on the shore. Peter swam to shore to see Me. They were all so happy to see Me once again. I cooked fish for them for breakfast. We ate together as we had done so many times before. They were comforted in My Presence. Are you ever disappointed because you have not been successful? Have you been disappointed by others? Have you lost purpose in your life? Call on Me, and I will meet you at the shore. Draw close to Me, and we can commune together, and you will be comforted. All My Children need comforting at times. This is a difficult time to be wrapped in flesh. You are pulled by the flesh and your spirit tries to keep you stable. Only if you stand on the Rock will you win the battle. Stand firm! I AM with you.

John 21:15-25

My Beloved, Peter was grieved, because he had denied Me three times. I gave him three chances to declare his love for Me, so he would be healed. He was hurt that I asked him three times if he loved Me. Later he realized that I was giving him a chance to make restitution to Me for the three times he denied Me. I wanted his last memories of Me to be by the fire exclaiming his love for Me. I want all My Children to be forgiven for their sins and to make restitution. You will never be healed until you make restitution to others. You may not know what to say, but I will give you the words. Forgive yourself, and call on My Name. I will guide you to a place where you can make restitution to them. Do you hold unforgiveness in your heart? Forgive all men, and extend your hand to them. Let them know you have forgiven them. Let them know that you want to love them in spite of their sins. This will bring healing to them. I brought healing to Peter, because I extended My Hand to him. I cooked him breakfast and allowed him to declare his love for Me. You must do the same for others who you know have wronged you. Go to them and allow them the chance to make amends to you. You will be comforted also once you heal what is broken between you. Are some of the people around you not getting along? Try to help them resolve their differences. I want all My Children to live in peace with each other. The world will never live in peace, but My Children should always live in peace. Call on My Name, if you are striving for peace and cannot find it. I will come to you and bring you peace.

Luke 1:1-25

My Beloved, I chose John to go before Me to prepare the way for My People to receive Me when I came. John told them about Me and called them to repentance. He was chosen from birth to be My Servant. He was from Aaron's (Moses' brother) blood line. The seed of righteousness was strong in both his mother and father. I withheld a child from Elizabeth and Zachariah until they were old even though they were righteous before Me. I heard their prayers, but I wanted them to be prepared to receive My Message. I sent My Angel Gabriel to Zachariah to tell him that I was going to send him a child. He did not believe My Message and asked Me for a sign. I gave him a sign by closing his mouth and making him silent, so he would believe in My Words. Gabriel gave him a message that I said to name his son John, and he would prepare the way for Me to come to My People. From the time he was conceived he would be filled with My Spirit. He would prophesy in My Name. He would take a Nazirite vow from the moment he was born. He would have no grapes or wine nor cut his hair. He would be totally dedicated to Me. Zachariah and Elizabeth understood how important it was to raise this child in My Ways. They did what was right in My Eyes, and they suffered greatly for being obedient. They raised John to be at one with Me and serve Me whole heartedly. Are you teaching your children to serve Me? Are you serving Me with all your heart? If you have received Me, then you have the same spirit that John had within him. You must be moved by My Spirit and not by your flesh. Rise up and serve Me today!

Luke 1:26-38

My Beloved, when Elizabeth was six months pregnant, Gabriel came to Mary to tell her to rejoice, because she was highly favored by Me. Mary was engaged to Joseph from the house of David. Mary was afraid when Gabriel came to her. Gabriel told her not be afraid, but rejoice because she had been chosen by Me to have a child. Mary did not understand what he meant, so he explained that she would have a child conceived by My Spirit. My Spirit would cover her and fill her and create within her a fleshly covering for Me. I was immediately a part of her and filled her. She was humble and willing to do whatever I asked of her. She could tell that a miracle had happened. She was filled with joy. She wanted to go tell her cousin Elizabeth. Gabriel had told her that Elizabeth was six months pregnant, and she wanted to go rejoice with her. Mary believed that there was nothing impossible with Me. I can do all things. All you must do is ask and believe in Me. Many people ask, but they do not believe. Do you believe in Me? Do you believe that I will heal you? Do you believe that I will deliver you from your circumstances? Do you believe that I can use you greatly for My Kingdom? Draw close to Me, and I will tell you how I can use you. Draw close to Me, and I will show you great things. Nothing is impossible with Me.

Luke 1:39-56

My Beloved, as soon as Gabriel came to Mary and told her the good news that she would have a son blessed by Me, she hurried to see her cousin Elizabeth. She wanted to see if Elizabeth was indeed pregnant with child. Elizabeth was past the child bearing years. She was scorned by others around her. They thought she was cursed, because her womb was barren. She could not give Zachariah a son to continue his linage, which was very important to My People. I wanted My People to be blessed and prosper in all ways, even blessed by the fruit of their wombs. This was a blessing sent from heaven. Anyone that did not receive this blessing was considered under the curse, because they were sinful and not walking in righteousness. Elizabeth had to walk under the judgment of others for years, and now she was free from their condemnation. As soon as Mary came close to Elizabeth John leaped for joy within her. John recognized Me even when I was yet unborn. Elizabeth called Mary blessed among women. Elizabeth knew that Mary was special, because she had been given the great gift of carrying My Spirit in the flesh. Both Elizabeth and Mary were righteous women who loved Me and were humble servants. Both women wanted to serve Me. They were given great rewards, but they had to suffer greatly because they carried these children brought forth by Me. They both saw their sons die before their time. They both felt persecution from the religious leaders and the enemies that lived in their country. Both of these women had to have great courage and strength in this life. Do you have courage and strength? I call you to stand firm even when others oppose you. I call you to do whatever I ask you to do. I will not ask you to carry a child of extreme purpose, but I may ask you to do something just as difficult. Remember that I AM always with you, and I will give you everything you need to complete the task that I give you. Just trust in Me.

Luke 1:57-80

My Beloved, the time came for Elizabeth to deliver her child. All her neighbors rejoiced with her. This was a miracle that one so old could conceive a child. When the child was eight days old they had the child circumcised as My Law had told them to do. The child was to be named on this day. Elizabeth said that the child should be named John, but no one in their family was named john. They asked Zachariah what the child's name should be. He wrote on a tablet that his name should be John. As this moment his voice returned and he praised Me and prophesied about John. He told those around him that John would prepare the Way for Me to come. This was a child that would be dedicated to Me from the moment of this birth under a Nazirite Vow. The child was raised in the wilderness away from those who hated him. There are those who did not want to hear what he had to say. He rose up to be strong and mighty. He was righteous before Me. He was anointed by Me to prepare the hearts of My People for repentance. Are you prepared for My Coming? Are you prepared for the days ahead? Rejoice that I love you so much. Rejoice and be glad that I will guide you and direct you and show you the way to go.

Luke 2:1-7

My Beloved, the Roman government ruled over My Land at the time of My Birth. The Roman soldiers filled the area and made life difficult for My People. My People were hated by their enemies. There was violence and bloodshed often in front of My People. My People lived in fear of these people who ruled over them. The emperor at the time decided to take a census of all the people in the area including My People. He wanted all the people to come to their place of birth and pay a tax to the Roman government. Joseph took Mary to the city of David, Bethlehem, to be counted in the census and pay their tax. Joseph was concerned about Mary taking such a difficult trip, but this was part of My Plan for them. When she began her labor she had no place to stay, so she was offered shelter among the animals. I was placed in the animals' feeding trough after I was born. This was a great night for all of mankind. I had come to the world to bring salvation to all who would receive Me. I was just a child, but I was King of the Universe. I was King of Heaven. I was King of all Mankind. I came to walk among you and tell you how to live your life, so you could please Me. I wanted you to be strong and mighty here, so you could emerge into a glorious being once you have been released from your fleshly body. When your flesh dies, this is just the beginning for you. You will begin a wonderful journey as My Child, Heir to My Throne. You will rule with Me over the entire universe. You will be an extreme blessing to all around you, because you will hold My Spirit within you. You will be able to funnel My Spirit to others and tell others My Words. Are you My Hands and Feet today? Do you walk as I walked on this earth? Rejoice that I love you so much and have given you such authority.

Luke 2:8-20

My Beloved, there were shepherds in the field guarding over their flocks. I made an announcement in the heavens that I was born. My Presence shone brightly on the shepherds as I proclaimed My Birth. The shepherds were terrified when My Angel told them to go to Bethlehem and find the child that was born. The angel told them that he would be found sleeping in a feeding trough. I was brought into the world in a lowly state, but I would rule all things. The shepherds wanted to go see this child and worship Him. They went to Bethlehem and found the child just as the angel had told them. They told Mary and Joseph that the angels had appeared to them and proclaimed My Birth. The shepherds rejoiced over finding Me, because they wanted to worship Me. Mary kept these things in her heart and did not speak of them to others. These were glorious things that others would not understand. She did not want to speak about them to unbelievers, because they would mock her. She treasured these words and waited for them to come to pass. She trusted Me that I would bring to pass all My Promises. Mary knew more of what was going to happen that anyone else, but she still did not understand what exactly would happen. She knew I would be the Savior of My People, but she did not realize how I would save them. My People were looking for someone to deliver them from their enemies. They wanted to be released from oppression, but they were still paying for the sins of their ancestors. They were still under a curse. You are not oppressed by your enemies like they were, so lift up your heads and rejoice that I love you so much. Can you see that I have put you in a good place? Rejoice that you are free to worship Me and love Me in the way you wish.

Luke 2:21-39

My Beloved, when I was eight days old I was taken to be circumcised. Once I was circumcised I was taken to the Temple to be dedicated. Joseph and Mary brought doves as an offering for their first born child. This was a very lowly offering, but this was all they had. As soon as they entered the Temple Simeon came to them and worshiped Me. He had asked Me to be able to see the Messiah who would save his people. I had promised him that he would see Me. He not only saw Me, but he held Me in his arms and blessed Me. Hannah a prophet also prophesied over Me and told everyone who I AM. Hannah and Simeon were dedicated to Me. They prayed and fasted and wanted peace to come to My People. They were grieved over the oppression of My People. They longed for the Messiah to come and save His People. They did not realize that I came to call My People to repentance and lay down My Life for them. They did not realize that I came to shed My Innocent Blood, so their sins could be forgiven. They did not realize that I would not take away their enemies, because the nation must pay for the sins of their ancestors. Have you ever longed for something and when you got it, the gift was not like what you had hoped? I only bring good gifts to you. Whatever you need to transform you into My image is what I bring to you.

Accept the gifts that I bring to you, and rejoice that I love you so much.

Luke 2:40-52

My Beloved, when I walked on the earth as a child I was obedient to My earthly parents-those who raised Me as an infant. I was filled from the womb with My Spirit, but I grew in the fleshly robe. It was difficult at times to focus on the world around Me, because I was focusing and communing with My Father in heaven. I would listen to his Wisdom and teaching. When I became older I would go with My Parents to the Feast Days in Jerusalem. I loved to come to Jerusalem and go to the Temple. I was at one with My Father there. The rabbis were discussing My Words, and I could hear them debating certain sections. They did not have all the answers, but they continued to search My Words for the answers. One Passover instead of returning with My Parents and those that I came with, I stayed with the rabbis and listened to their questions. I began to share with them some of My Wisdom. They were amazed at the insight that My Father had given Me. I AM the Father and the Son is an extension of the Father. I had all the Wisdom of My Father when I talked on earth. I shared with My People the Wisdom that I had, but few understood. Most people wanted to go their own way and do what they wanted to do. Do you have questions about My Words? If you really love Me, you will search My Words and find the answers to your questions. I will bring the answers to you if you search with all your heart. Call on My Name, and I will answer you. You may not understand what all My Words mean. but one thing you do understand is My Love for you. Trust in Me to guide you, and you will always be where you need to be at the time you need to be there.

Luke 3:1-20

My Beloved, I sent John before Me to prepare the hearts of My People to receive My Words. John was filled with My Spirit from the moment of his conception. He was anointed by Me to be My Servant. He was My cousin, and we played together as children. We were very close to each other. John went to reside at an early age in the desert for his safety from those who hated him. He lived among the desert animals, and he knew how to survive on little. He was a man that lived off the things of the Spirit and not the things of the world. He was called by Me to come out of the wilderness and tell My People that they needed to repent and be baptized and trust in Me. John prepared the path before Me, so My People were expecting the Messiah to come to them. The people wanted to make John the Messiah, but he would not accept that title. He pointed out the sins of the people. He pointed out Herod's sins and this cost him his life. I mourned his death, but I knew his rewards would be great in My Kingdom. Rejoice that I have blessed you so richly. Will you have great rewards in heaven for all the good things you have done for Me? All the good things that you do for Me while you are on earth will be recorded, and I will reward you in My Heavenly Kingdom for all your good works.

Luke 3:21-38

My Beloved, I saw John immersing My People in the wilderness. The people would come to him and repent of their sins and want to change their lives. They would ask him what they must do to be a better person. He could see the hearts of the people who came to him, and he told the people to be fair and honest in business. He told them to love others and be compassionate giving freely to others. I came to John when he was baptizing those wanting to repent. He saw Me from a distance and rejoiced that I had come to him. I wanted John to baptize Me, but he felt unworthy. John knew who I was. He knew that I had come to bring salvation to My People. I wanted him to baptize Me as an example to My People. When I came up out of the water after John baptized Me, My Father's Voice spoke to Me saying that He was very pleased with Me. He bore witness to Me that I was from Him. His Spirit ascended on Me in the form or likeness of a dove. Those around Me could see and hear his approval, and many believed in Me at that time. I arose and left this area and went into the desert to prepare for beginning My Ministry. I was 30 years old at the time. I was ready to enter the priesthood, so others would not say that I was too young to speak for Myself. I was placed in a lineage directly from Adam to Noah to David to a man of flesh who ascended from a long line of people who wanted to serve Me. These were part of the remnant who I kept close to Me. Do you have a strong desire to serve Me and obey Me? You are part of the remnant that I have kept close to Me.

Rejoice that I have chosen you to be My Own.

Luke 4:1-13

My Beloved, after I was baptized by John I went into the desert to prepare for My Ministry. The evil one came to Me to tempt Me hoping I would sin. I had been fasting for 40 days and 40 nights, and I was hungry. The evil one told Me to make the stones into bread, but I would not listen to anything that he said. He took Me to a high mountain and showed Me kingdoms that he would give Me if I worshipped him. I told him that I would only worship the One who sent Me- the Father of all things. The evil one again tempted Me by taking Me to a tall place and told Me to jump off, because My Angels would pick Me up and I would not be harmed. I told him that I would not test My Father who sent Me. The evil one began to realize that I was a stronger opponent than he was. He decided to oppose Me at every angle. He could see the religious leaders were jealous of Me, so he used their jealousy to trap them and use them to entangle and kill Me. The evil one thought if he ended My Life he would win the battle, but instead he completed My Plan for salvation perfectly. Do you face temptations? When the evil one tempts you, he is completing the plan I have for you. As you resist the temptation you will become stronger and powerful. Do you ever fail to resist the temptation? Get up and press onward. You will be wiser next time and resist the temptation. His efforts to destroy you are making you stronger every day, so rejoice in this.

Luke 4:14-30

My Beloved, after I fasted in the desert for 40 days and 40 nights, I was ready to start My Ministry. I started teaching in Galilee, and the people received Me gladly. They rejoiced over Me. When I came to My hometown of Nazareth the people looked at Me as Joseph's son. They could not see Me as Almighty sent in flesh to save them from their sins. They were blinded and could not see the Light. I went to the synagogue to teach and was given the book of Isaiah. I read the Scriptures that promised to send the Messiah to My People. I told them that I was that Messiah. They told Me to show some signs that I was the Messiah. I told them that their lack of belief in Me hindered them from receiving any signs. This made them very angry, so they called Me a fraud and dragged Me out of the city to the edge of a cliff. They wanted to throw Me off the cliff, but it was not My Time to die. I walked through the crowd making Myself invisible to them. They were confused and amazed that I disappeared before them. They were focusing on My earthly body and not looking for the Truth. Eventually after I died and rose again many from this town were saved from destruction by believing on Me. Are you looking at the messenger's flesh and missing the message I have for you? Do not look at the flesh, but take the message to heart. I will show you what to do and when to do it. Keep your ears open for My Messages. They come to you daily through people, situations, My Words, and dreams. Listen! Keep your ears open for My Words coming to you.

Luke 4:31-37

My Beloved, it was my custom to teach in the synagogues on Sabbaths. Everyone came to the synagogue to hear the Scriptures being read. Everyone did not have a copy of the Scriptures. Only the very rich were able to have a scroll written for them. Everyone discussed the Scriptures on Sabbath as they rested from their work. It was a place to pray and praise Me without going to the Temple in Jerusalem. I taught every Sabbath to those who wanted to listen. They asked Me questions, and I answered their questions. They were astounded by the authority and wisdom that I had. They were hungry and wanted to learn the Truth. There was man who came to Me one Sabbath who had a demon. The demon wanted to yell at Me and mock Me. The demon said that I came to destroy him, because I was the Son of God. I rebuked the demon, and the man was set free. The people were amazed that the man was totally delivered. The story about this incident was spread to many cities. My Name became known among the peoples, so that many came to hear Me teach. Soon so many came to hear Me teach that I had to teach on a mountain where everyone could hear Me. The synagogues became too small for the crowds. I looked into the eyes of these people and could see that they needed a Savior. Turning away from their religious system would be difficult for them. Life revolved around the synagogue. They would be totally rejected in society. Most of the believers banned together in certain places, so they could support each other. Are you without believers to stand with you in the place where you live? You are not alone. I AM with you. I will stand beside you. If I ask you to move to another location, then go quickly. Be obedient and I will take you to a safe place with other believers to comfort you.

Luke 4:38-44

My Beloved, I continued to teach in the synagogues on Sabbath, so My People could learn My Ways. They were hungry and needed to hear the Truth. They had been taught so many laws that were not from My Words. The religious leaders had added to My Laws and burdened My People with a heavy load. My People were burdened with laws and oppressed by their enemies, so they were lacking hope. I came to lift them up and bring them comfort. They received My Words gladly and rejoiced. After I finished teaching in the synagogue Simon asked Me to heal his mother-in-law. She had a high fever, and he was afraid that she would die. I came to his house and rebuked the fever and it left. She got up and was completely healed. Simon and his household rejoiced, because she was greatly loved by everyone. After the Sabbath Day was over the people began to bring their sick to Me. I healed all who came to Me. I told them to repent of their sins and once they repented, they were healed. I told them to go and sin no more. They left filled with joy. They looked to Me as their healer. They wanted Me to stay with them and live among them, but I had to go teach at other towns. I wanted all men to be able to hear My Words of truth and be set free from the bondage of sin. Do you have questions with no answers? You have My Words with you. Call on My Name to give you the answers to your questions. If you are sick, call on My Name and I will hear you and heal you. You must repent of your sins and believe in Me. Your faith in Me will restore you.

Luke 5:1-11

My Beloved, I was teaching My People on the Sea of Galilee. The people were pressing closer to Me to hear My Words, so I got into Simon's boat and began to teach the people. They were hungry to hear My Words. They wanted Me to heal their sick and provide them hope. I told them to repent of their sins and walk in My Ways of love. Many received My Message and repented and changed their lives. They wanted to become My Disciples and follow Me. When I finished teaching the people, Simon took Me to deeper water. I told him to cast his net and he would catch fish. Simon had been fishing all night and caught no fish, but since he was obedient to Me I rewarded him with a large catch. The catch was so large that he needed two boats to pull it in. He called to his partners to come help him pull up the fish. They were astonished at the catch and recognized that I was the One they had been waiting for. These fishermen had not been taught to be teachers of the Law, but they immediately knew that I was from God. They threw themselves at My Feet. They knew they were sinners and were unworthy to be in My Presence. I told them that they would now be fishers of men. They would tell men about Me and bring them to the Truth. These men were brave and strong. They had been fishermen for many years just like their fathers before them. They were not men of wealth, but I had just bestowed great riches on them. Are you sharing the Truth with those around you? You have given them the greatest gift they could receive. Give Truth to all those who will listen, and I will reward you for your faithfulness.

Luke 5:12-16

My Beloved, I went from town to town and village to village around the Sea of Galilee. Some of the towns already knew about Me and wanted to hear My Words. As I was teaching in one of the towns a man with a skin disease came to Me and wanted Me to heal him. He was an outcast among the people. He was supposed to stay away from people and shout "unclean, unclean", so that no one would come near him and contract his disease. He was not allowed in the Temple or synagogue. He was broken hearted and robbed of all his dignity. He came to Me desperate and pleading for Me to help him. I told him that I would heal him. I could see that he had faith in Me, so he was instantly healed. He was rejoicing and all those around him were rejoicing with him. I told him to go to the priest and show him that he was healed from his disease as the Law commanded him to do. He ran to the priest and showed him his skin. The priest pronounced him clean! He was free to go wherever he wanted to go without fear of being rebuked. He was no longer an outcast. He was a free man. I had liberated him and set him free from his sin. He told everyone about Me and what I had done for him. He told the Truth, and many believed in Me because of his testimony. Do you share your testimony with others? Tell others the Truth and set them free from their sins. The Truth you tell them will penetrate their hearts, and they will repent and turn to Me as their Savior. Rejoice that you have Truth to bring to them.

Luke 5:17-26

My Beloved, I continued to teach My People around the sea of Galilee where the people would bring their sick to Me to heal. Sometimes I would teach in homes, but this limited the number of people who could hear Me teach. One day as I was teaching in a house, a man wanted to be healed and his friends brought him to Me. They had carried him on his mattress, because he could not walk. When they got to the house so many people were outside the door that they knew they could not get in. The men were determined that the man would see Me, so they took the tiles off the roof of the house and lowered the man down through the roof. I had great compassion on them when I saw how determined they were to have their friend healed. I looked at the man and knew that for years he had lain on his mattress and could not walk. He was a desperate man who needed My Healing Touch. I told him that his sins were forgiven. The religious leaders who had come to hear Me teach were upset, because I told him that his sins were given. No man had authority to forgive sins. I knew their thoughts, so I addressed them, "What difference does it make if I tell him that his sins were forgiven or to get up and walk?" I could forgive sins and heal. I told the man to "Get up!" The man arose slowly and strength returned to his legs. He jumped around rejoicing. The people were astounded, "Who could heal like this? Who is his man? Is He the Messiah?" Many believed in Me, because of the miracles that I did. Many more mocked Me and said that I had a demon. Do you believe in miracles? Every day is a miracle. Nothing is ordinary around you. I created this world for you to live in. I give you every breath you take. You have life only because I allow you to live. I hold all things in My Hand. Look at all the miracles around you and rejoice.

Luke 5:27-39

My Beloved, I came to a tax collector named Levi. I looked into his heart and knew that he would believe in Me and follow Me. I said to him, "Come follow Me". He got up quickly and rejoiced that I asked him to follow Me. He hated his life and did not like his occupation. He was searching for some fulfillment in his life. His heart had been prepared to receive Me. He wanted to honor Me, so he gave Me a large banquet. He invited all his friends and other tax collectors. I was honored to sit among these men who desired to hear My Words. The religious leaders were outraged that I sat with the tax collectors. My People hated the tax collectors who worked for the Roman Government. My People hated paying taxes to their enemies. The tax collectors were looked down upon, because they not only took their taxes but cheated them as well. I told the religious leaders that the righteous do not need a doctor, but the sinners need a doctor to heal them. I had the opportunity to minister to those men who needed to turn from their sins and be honest with My People. The religious leaders wanted to find something wrong with Me. They asked Me why My Disciples did not fast like they should. Even John's disciples fasted. Did I think I was greater than John? They could not understand who I was. They could not see that I was the Bride Groom. I had come to prepare My Bride. Of course My Disciples would not fast as long as I was with them. They rejoiced to be in My Presence. Later they would fast and pray, because they would endure many days of trouble. Do you criticize how others worship Me? You fast and pray and seek Me, and do not be concerned about others. I will reward you for your faithfulness to Me.

Luke 6:1-5

My Beloved, some of My Followers ate some of the wheat as we passed by a wheat field. Some of the men who were with Me questioned Me about their behavior, "Aren't they breaking Sabbath? Isn't this work?" I could see that they did not understand the meaning of Sabbath. Men had made so many rules to keep Sabbath that they had forgotten the purpose of Sabbath. Men were focusing on how to not break the Sabbath rules, so they would not be in sin. They did not have the Scriptures to read, so the priests told them what to do. The common people could not even read, so they were at the mercy of the teachers of the Law. I was grieved over My People, because they were in bondage to rules and not in communion with Me. Sabbath was made for My People to rest and commune with Me. Six days were given for work, but on the seventh day their bodies needed rest and time to talk with Me. I explained to My Disciples what I wanted them to keep Sabbath. I AM Master of the Sabbath. I created Sabbath, and I want all My People to rest and commune with Me. Do you make a list of rules for the Sabbath? Let each man keep Sabbath as he is led by My Spirit. I will convict him of his sins, if he violates My Sabbath. I will show him the way to walk. Have mercy on others, and I will have mercy on you.

Luke 6:6-11

My Beloved, the religious leaders were always watching and trying to find fault with Me. The crowds were growing larger who wanted to come hear Me teach. They were hungry for spiritual food that the religious leaders could not give them. I was changing how the people viewed the Scriptures, and the religious leaders did not like this. They could see that the people wanted more that what they were giving them. The people were following Me and not them. The religious leaders thought the system for the Temple and all its offerings would stop and their nation would be destroyed if the people followed Me. They looked at Me as the enemy, because I was "changing the law" in their eyes. They were in bondage to tradition and blind to the Truth. As I was teaching in the synagogue a man that wanted to be healed came to Me. The religious leaders were watching to see what I would do. "Would he break the Sabbath laws?" they wondered. I knew their thoughts, so I brought the man in front of them. I asked them, "What is better to do on Sabbath-good things or bad things?" It was one of their laws that if a man needed help you should help him even on the Sabbath. I asked the man to stretch out his hand, and his withered hand became whole. He was healed. The people were amazed and rejoiced for him, but the religious leaders were furious because I had sinned against the Sabbath. The people could see this was doing a good thing, but the religious leaders were in bondage to the traditions of men. Are you in bondage to the traditions of men? Question everything that you do. Is this biblical or a tradition of man? If you cannot find it in Scripture, then it is a tradition. Take another look at your life. How do you keep Sabbath? Be led by My Spirit.

Luke 6:12-16

My Beloved, I went to a quiet place, so I could be alone and pray. I prayed all night over the decision of who should be My Twelve Disciples. These men had to be brave, bold, and strong. These men would endure suffering and hardship. These men would die for Me. These men would be the foundation of the faith. These men would leave their families and follow Me. I chose men who wanted to cling to Me. They had found their strength in Me. They wanted to love others and show mercy to others. They were not perfect, but they were righteous before Me. I chose these men, but there were others who wanted to be part of the twelve. I knew their hearts and limitations. I knew who would die for Me and who were not strong enough to stand up under persecutions. These men walked beside Me every day for three years. They were like family to Me. I loved them all deeply. I loved Judas, but I knew his heart was troubled. He wanted to cling to Me, but he wanted his own way. He wanted Me to take over My Kingdom at that moment. He was part of a movement to overtake or bring down the Roman Government. Judas could not see that judgment was on My People for their sins. No man could stop the judgment I had declared on My People. They must pay for their sins against Me. Are you under judgment today due to past sins? Repent of your sins, and cleanse yourself. Call on My Name, and I will deliver you from all your problems.

Luke 6:17-23

My Beloved, the crowds of people grew larger. They came with their sick and wounded. They came with those who needed to be delivered. They came to hear My Words of comfort. They came to receive hope and encouragement. They pierced Me with their eyes. They were looking at Me as their Savior. My Heart was merciful and compassionate to all of them. I called them to repentance. I healed all their sick and delivered those who were possessed with demons. The people were filled with joy and danced and sang. They looked at Me as their Messiah. I spoke to the people and told them how to draw closer to Me. They listened and received. I told My Disciples to look at these people. Blessed are those who are poor, because they will inherit the Kingdom of Light. Blessed are those who are hungry, because they will be filled and never hunger again. Blessed are the ones who are weeping with sadness, because they will be filled with joy in My Presence. Blessed are the ones who will suffer persecution for Me, because they will be given great rewards in My Kingdom. These people were poor and had nothing. Their enemies oppressed them. They came to Me for hope, and I gave them the hope they needed. Are you oppressed today? Are you poor? Are you lacking what you need to survive? Call on My Name, and I will give you what you need. I will never let you go hungry. I will open My Hand to you. You are My Beloved.

Luke 6:24-26

My Beloved, there were some rich among the crowds of people who came to hear Me. There were some prominent people who came to learn from Me. I addressed these people for the entire crowd to hear, "If you are rich now and do not give generously to those who are poor, then you are doomed for destruction. If you are full and have abundance and do not share your food with others, then you will become hungry and not have enough. If you are living in laughter giving parties to all your friends, then you will have nothing and cry and mourn. Your old friends will also have nothing. You will have no one to help you. You ignored the poor and needy while you were living in abundance. You must do what I tell you to do and not what you want to do." The rich were offended by what I said. The poor had hope for the future. I came to bring hope to My People. Do you feel hopeless today? I will come to you and comfort you. You may be all alone and no one seems to love you or care if you live or die. I care for you. I love you. I have a plan for you to make your life successful. You must come to Me, and I will show you the plan I have for you. Do not delay. Have you fallen into self-pity? Lift your eyes off yourself, and look at Me. I will bring to you all you need. I am faithful. Others may have deserted you, but I will never desert you or leave you even for a moment. I AM always close. Cling to Me, and I will help you walk on solid ground again. I will give you sure footing. You will not fall.

Luke 6:27-36

My Beloved, My People were surrounded by their enemies who mocked them and insulted them and treated them cruelly. I told My People to love their enemies and this horrified them. They did not want to love those who mistreated them. I was showing them a higher level of love. I told them that sinners are nice to people who are nice to them. I wanted My People to treat others as they would like to be treated. Their enemies would take their coat off their backs. They would make them carry their heavy packs for a mile. They would slap them also the face for no reason. They would take without asking. They were cruel people. I told My People to rise above them. If they asked for their coat, then give them their shirt as well. If the asked them to carry their pack for a mile, then carry it two miles. If they asked for something, give it to them gladly knowing that I would reward them for every act of love that they gave to someone. Love will overshadow hatred and change a man's heart. Many of the soldiers heard My Words and believed in Me. My People are filled with love and compassion for others. They are everywhere scattered all over the world. Do you love others? Do you love those who hate you? Do you treat others with kindness? Watch carefully over your words. Always let your words build up a man. Never tear down a man with your words, because this grieves Me. Walk in peace, and love those around you, and then I will reward you greatly.

Luke 6:37-38

My Beloved, Have you forgiven those who wronged you? Forgive others, and I will forgive you. If you are unwilling to forgive, then I cannot forgive you for your sins. If you judge others harshly, then I will judge you harshly. If you are merciful to others, then I will be merciful to you. If you condemn others for every little thing that they do, then I will condemn you also for every little thing you do. The measure that you give to others is the measure that I will give to you. If you give generously to others, then I will give generously to you. How you love others is how I will love you. You must realize that this is a Law of Heaven. Whatever you sow, you will reap. If you are mean to others, then others will be mean to you. If you steal from others, then others will steal from you. If you are critical to others, then others will be critical of you. You must treat others the way you would like to be treated, and then others will treat you in the way you treat them. The Law of Heaven is constant and does not change. Whatever you do, it will come back to you. Do you guard over your mouth? Speak with love to others. Do not talk about others behind their back, because they will talk about you behind your back. If you do not honor your parents, then your children will not honor you. If you kill someone, then you will be killed in the same way you killed the one you hated so much. Find wisdom in these words. If you want a good life, then live a good life every day.

Luke 6:39-42

My Beloved, it is easy to see the mistakes of others. When you see them you may become irritated and want to rebuke your brother. If you love your brother, you will be patient with him. You will love him continually and not be harsh with him knowing that he is not perfect. He is being transformed into My Image just like you are being transformed into My Image. Are you looking at yourself and trying to change yourself? You see the faults in others, because you are very aware of your own faults. You would rather say to yourself that you are better than your brother, but no one is better than another. I made each of you individually. Each of you has your strengths and weaknesses. You can help others in their weaknesses by loving them and supporting them. They can help you with your weaknesses. Together you are strongly braided and can never be undone. If you bind together with your brothers and sisters and stand with them building them up instead of tearing them down, then you will be a strong community of believers. Your prayers will come up as a flame before Me, and I will move on behalf of you. If I see you fighting among yourselves, then why should I listen to your prayers? Love others around you and I will bless you greatly. Allow Me to work out the weaknesses in others. If you continually point them out to your brother, then he will become weaker and hopeless. If you build him up and stand beside him, you will make him strong. Be willing to help your brother, and I will help you when you call on My Name.

Luke 6:43-45

My Beloved, what is in your heart? Do you love others? Do you want to help others? Do you love only yourself? Do you want to serve only yourself? How do you spend your money? Do you spend your money on others or yourself? Are you looking for ways to help others? Are your eyes only on yourself? I look at a man's heart. I know who you are. Even you do not know who you are. You are struggling with your flesh daily. I know what you will become. If you love others, you will not say mean things to others. If you love others, you will display your fruit of love, patience, compassion, and understanding with others. No one is like you. You will have to overlook the faults and weaknesses of others. Sometimes they will disappoint you and hurt you. You must rise above the situation. You must forgive them and love them. You must realize that your love will overcome what has happened and bring healing to the situation. If you continue in bitterness and hatred, there will be no peace for you. Come to Me if you struggle with unforgiveness, and I will help you overcome. I will give you peace. Others hear the words you speak, and they know who you are. If you speak badly of others, they will hear your words and think badly of you. If you only build up others, then you will be a blessing to all around you and an example of love to those who are watching you.

Luke 6:46-49

My Beloved, do you listen to My Voice and do as I tell you to do? Are you listening to hear if I will give you an order? Each day I want to talk with you and tell you what you should do for the day. Each day you can touch someone in prayer or through your acts of love. Each day listen to Me, and I will guide you so you can show your love to others. Many say that they know Me, but they do not listen to My Voice. They say they are a Christian, but they do not obey My Commands. Only those who talk with Me and love Me are those who are My Servants. If you do not know Me, then you will not be listening for My Voice. A man that obeys Me and listens to My Directions will stand on a firm foundation and not be moved in the darkest of days. He will be strong and mighty. He will be a man of prayer and supplication. He will be a man of faith and trust. He will be a man of love and compassion. He will be a man that knows his enemy and is always on guard to not allow him to be a foothold in his life. A man that says that he knows Me and does not follow My Commands is like a man who built his house on the beach. When the storms come, the house is washed away and he loses all he owns. Do not be foolish, but study My Words and obey My Commandments. Listen for My Voice and obey Me immediately. You will be blessed greatly in My Kingdom. You will be blessed here on earth with overflowing blessings, because I love you so much.

Luke 7:1-10

My Beloved, one day some of the Jews came to Me and asked Me to heal a Roman soldier's servant. The Jews said the man was good to them and had built a synagogue for them. The Jews pleaded with Me to heal the man's servant. I usually only healed My People, because the Roman Government oppressed My People and caused them grief. Since My People asked Me to have mercy on this man, I went to the man to heal his servant. Before I arrived the man sent one of his servants to tell Me not to come to his house, because he was unworthy of Me coming into his house. He told Me to just give the command, and he knew that his servant would be healed. This was a man who understood authority. If you understand the authority that you have, then you can speak and move mountains that hinder you. If you move mountains on behalf of My Kingdom, then you wreak havoc on the enemy and shake the ground that he stands on. Very few people understand their authority over the enemy. I have taken the world away from the evil one and given it to you through the shedding of My Blood. You have authority to ask in My Name and have whatever you want as long as you are in right standing with Me. If you have sin in your life or curses on your family, then your prayers are hindered. You must repent of your sin and walk in the Truth. You must break the curses over your family through fasting and prayer. Once you are in right standing with Me, you can stand before Me blameless and ask and it will be given to you.

Luke 7:11-23

My Beloved, as I traveled from town to town teaching My People, My Disciples and a crowd of people would follow Me. When I was approaching one town, I saw a woman weeping over the loss of her son. The people of the town told Me that he was her only son and she was a widow. I had compassionate for the woman, because I felt her pain and loneliness. I stopped the coffin and spoke to the man inside the coffin to get up. The man woke up and spoke to Me. He was surprised to be inside a coffin. The woman and people around her rejoiced over her son coming back to life again. This was a day of great celebration! News of what had happened traveled around the area. More and more people came to see. Me and listen to My Words. The whole area was hearing about My Miracles, and they wanted to come see who this man was. Even John heard about My Miracles and sent his disciples to Me to ask Me if I was the Messiah. I told him that the prophets spoke of Me and said that I would do working the work of My Father. I was healing the sick, raising the dead, delivering those possessed by demons, healing the blind, deaf, and dumb. I was preaching the Good News to the poor. John could see that signs and wonders were following Me wherever I went. He knew that I was the Messiah. He told all his followers that I was the Messiah and sent them to Me to follow Me. John had completed his mission here on earth to prepare the way for Me to come. What is your mission here on earth? What are you supposed to accomplish before you die? Call on My Name, and I will show you what to do and when to do it.

Luke 7:24-35

My Beloved, John came to prepare the way for Me. He came to fulfill the prophecy that one would be crying in the wilderness to get prepared for the Messiah. John was a simple him who lived in the wilderness not eating bread or drinking wine. He kept a Nazirite vow all his life obeying what the angel Gabriel had told his parents. He lived only to serve Me. He studied the Scriptures to find confirmation that I was indeed the Messiah. I came from a large family, but even My siblings did not trust in Me until I died and arose from the grave. I asked the crowd around Me, "Who did you expect to see when you went to be baptized by John? Did you expect to see a rich man with expensive clothes? Did you expect to see a prophet?" The crowd expected to see a man that was set apart from society living like their other prophets had lived. Many opposed being baptized by John. They said that he had a demon. These same people opposed Me and said that I was a glutton and drunkard who loved to eat with sinners and tax collectors. These people did not want to see the Truth. They ran from the Light. They were blinded by their own religion. Are you blinded by traditions of men? Open your eyes and seek Me. Read the Scriptures and search for Truth. You will find Me and know that you have found a great treasure.

Luke 7:36-50

My Beloved, one of the religious leaders invited Me to his house to eat. He wanted to hear Me teach the Scriptures. While I was there a woman from the town sat next to My Feet and wept over Me. She was a sinful woman who had heard My Words and wanted to turn away from her sins and live a life of righteousness. She was very grieved over her life and what she had done to others. She wanted to change her life and walk in righteousness. She brought a very expensive box of perfume and poured it on My Feet. She wanted to give Me a gift in thanksgiving. The man who had asked Me to come to his house thought to himself that if I was a prophet that I would know that the woman was a sinner and would not allow her to touch Me. I asked the man a question, "If a man had two people who owed him money and he forgave both of their debts, which man would love him more?" The man understood how the story applied to him. He knew that I was teaching him a lesson. The man had given Me very little hospitality when I entered his house, but this woman had honored Me with her gift. I told the woman that her sins were forgiven, because I knew she had repented and wanted to change her life. The religious leaders were outraged that I forgave her sins. I told the woman that her faith in Me had saved her. They did not like this either. They did not know who I was. They looked at Me as a fraud and liar. They could not see who stood in their midst. Do you look at others and judge them by their sins? Put their sins behind them. If they have repented and are trying to walk in righteousness, then forgive them and allow them to not have to relive the past. Do not bring up past sins, but encourage them to continue to walk in the way of love and compassion. You can make them strong by supporting them with your love and not condemning them.

Luke 8:1-15

My Beloved, I traveled from town to town with My Disciples and some women who loved Me and wanted to help share the Good News with others. They were wealthy women who gave generously to Me from what they were given. Wherever there was a crowd of people who wanted to hear Me teach, I stopped and gathered them around Me and taught them. I spoke to them in parables, because many could not receive the Truth. My Disciples asked Me why I taught in parables and did not explain everything to the people. I told them that only those of the righteous seed would receive the hidden jewels from My Kingdom. If a man has the seed of righteousness firmly planted in his heart, then he will gladly receive the Truth and even during hard times he will not turn from the Truth. Some men love to sin and there is no righteousness in them. Some men struggle with their flesh, and do not overcome their flesh and fall short of the mark. Some men have the ability to have faith in Me, because the seed of righteousness is strong within them. They desire to do what is right in My Eyes. They want to please Me. They want to love others and have compassion on them. Many times the seed of righteousness is planted deep within a man due to the blessings on his ancestors. If his ancestors walked in faith and loved Me, then he was taught My Ways at an early age and he adhered to My Words. Do you teach your children to have faith in Me? It is so important to teach your children to walk in faith and serve Me with all their heart. If you love Me, you will give Truth to your children and prepare them for the days ahead.

Luke 8:16-21

My Beloved, I AM the Light. Any one that comes to Me comes to the Light, and the Light exposes his sins. If a man repents and turns from his sins, then he can draw closer to the Light. The more you turn from your evil ways, the more you can draw closer to Me. Once you have received the Light, you must shine it brightly for those around you. Do not try to hide it, but display it so all will know that you love Me and want to walk in My Ways of love and kindness. One day when I was teaching at someone's house, My Mother and brothers wanted to see Me. I was given a message that they were outside. I told those around Me that only those who loved Me and wanted to serve Me were My Family. My Brothers did not believe in Me until I died and rose again. They could not see that I was the Messiah. They could not see clearly, because I was in their house for so long unnoticed. They were blinded to the Light. They knew there was something different about Me. They thought I was a prophet sent from heaven. They did not understand who was in their midst. My Mother knew from the beginning who I was and held it in her heart. She did not tell others about Me, but she kept My Identity safe from others. She lived among her enemies, and she knew that I could be harmed if she told anyone. I revealed Myself to My People and showed them who I was. I gave them evidence with signs and wonders. Those who wanted to draw close to Me believed in Me. Do you believe in Me? You may not see signs and wonders, but you have Truth all around you. Open your eyes and I will show you the Way to go.

Luke 8:22-25

My Beloved, the men who were with Me were mostly fishermen. They had boats on the Sea of Galilee that they used to fish at night. One day I asked them to take Me out in the boat away from the crowds. I was tired and needed a rest, so I fell asleep in the boat. The weather became rough on the sea. The water was filling up the boat, and My Disciples were afraid. They told Me to get up and help with the boat. When I awoke I could see their dilemma, so I rebuked the weather and the sea became still. My Disciples were awestruck. They wondered who I was, "Who could have control over the weather?" They had never seen anything like this before. That is because they had never encountered Me before. They were beginning to realize who was in their midst. I allowed My Disciples to see who I was. I told them about Me and showed them signs and wonders. I brought confirmation to My Words. They became strong men full of My Wisdom. They remembered all My Words and what I taught them. They shared these things with others, and many turned to Me and followed Me. The Truth was spread from place to place until it reached most of the people in that area. They were very blessed to receive the Truth and have the Truth walk in their midst. Are you receiving Truth today? Are you trying to find Truth in My Words? My Disciples asked Me questions and obtained knowledge from Me. Ask Me questions, and I will bring you knowledge. Call on Me, and I will bring you whatever you need.

Luke 8:26-39

My Beloved, after sailing across the Sea of Galilee I came to a man who was possessed by demons. I commanded the demons to leave him, but they begged Me to not send them to the Bottomless Pit. There were many demons that had possessed the man. The man was evil and did not resist the evil inside of him, so more demons came to dwell inside of him until he had no control over himself at all. He did not wear clothes or live in a house. He lived among the dead in the burial graves and sought to scare and torment anyone who came close to him. The people of the town had tried to chain his hands and feet, but he broke the chains and could not be contained. The demons in him were strong, but they had no power over Me. I created the demons. They were the ones who rebelled against Me, and I sent them out of My Kingdom. Now they were confined to earth and a constant existence of wandering the earth. They tried to find as many people as they could to torment. They attached themselves to their bodies of those who were sinful, so they could have a dwelling place. They love to destroy man and find him unworthy to enter My Kingdom. Even though I knew their plan, I allowed the demons to enter into a herd of pigs. The pigs ran over the cliff killing all of them. When the people of the town saw all the carnage at the bottom of the cliff and the man sitting quietly dressed in clothes, they were afraid and asked us to leave. They were not interested in knowing who I was and the Truth that I could give them. They just wanted us to leave, so we left the area. Are you sinful and allow demons to oppress you in sinful areas of your life? Wake up and open your eyes. If you give a place for the enemy to stand, he will stand in that place and try to torment you. Stand firm and do not sin, and I will help you overcome the enemy around you.

Luke 8:40-42, 49-56

My Beloved, as I returned from across the sea the crowd of people was waiting for Me. One man's daughter was dying, so he had been waiting for Me to come back so and heal her. He was desperate to find Me before she passed away. As soon as I arrived he grabbed him and begged Me to come to his house and pray for his daughter. As I started towards his house someone from his house came to tell him that the girl had died. I told the man not to lose faith. He had come to Me in faith knowing that I would heal her. I wanted him to continue to believe in Me, and he did. The crowd was pressing on all sides of Me. They did not want to leave Me. They followed Me to the man's house where all the mourners had already gathered to grieve for the child. I told them that she was only asleep and they should stop mourning, but they only gave Me looks of disgust. I entered the house with Peter, James, John, and her parents. I spoke to the little girl and told her to get up. Her spirit returned to her, and she got up. Her parents rejoiced over her. I told them not to say what happened to her, and they honored this request. I told the mourners to go home that she was only sleeping. Once they saw the girl they left. This man had faith in Me. He had waited by the shore for days for Me to return and heal his daughter. He was grieved inside knowing that she could die before I returned. I honored the man's faith and healed his daughter. Do you think I can heal you? Do you trust Me to heal you? Arise, sleeper! Open your eyes and see your healer before you. Put your trust in Me, and I will bless you greatly.

Luke 8:43-48

My Beloved, when I returned to shore a crowd of people was waiting for Me. They had seen the boat in the distance and gathered to meet Me when I arrived. I saw the crowd waiting for Me. I knew they were lost and without a shepherd. I knew that they needed someone to guide them. They crowded around Me and pressed on Me. There was one woman who had been bleeding for 12 years and no doctor could help her. She had spent all she had to stop the bleeding. Her continued bleeding made her unclean, so she was not allowed to go into the synagogue. She was an outcast and under a curse. She was desperate, so she pushed her way close to Me to touch My Robe. I instantly knew that someone had been healed through her faith in Me. I stopped and wanted to know where she was. She was afraid, but she finally came and threw herself at My Feet. I told her to arise and continue in her faith. She looked to Me for her healing. Do you look to Me for your healing, or do you look to doctors? Who is the first one that you call on? Do you come to Me first for healing? I AM faithful to those who are faithful to Me.

Luke 9:1-6

My Beloved, I took My Twelve Disciples aside and talked to them. I wanted them to go out by themselves and teach the Good News to others. I wanted them to be able to stand on their own once I was gone. I gave them the power and authority over demons, so they could cast them out and heal the person of his disease. I gave them the ability to speak the Truth to others and bring repentance. Once the person repented, then he could be healed. There are two things that keep you from being healed. One is the enemy has a foot hold over you from previous sins of your ancestors or you have sinned and not repented. If you are seeking healing today, then repent of your sins and be free of the bondage of the enemy. If you have curses on you from your ancestors, then fast and pray that you will be released from these sins. If you have a disease that is carried by most of the members of your family, then you may have a curse on your family from their previous sins. Call on My Name, and I will reveal them to you. Trust in Me, and I will set you free from these sins. My Disciples went out and set many free from their bondage to sin. Many were healed and delivered from demons. They came back to Me rejoicing over what had happened when they told others the Truth and they received it. Are you are My Disciple? You are My Hands and Feet. You are the one that I have chosen to spread My Message across the world. Lift up your eyes and allow Me to show you the mission I have chosen for you. I will send you out with power and authority, and you will set many free.

Luke 9:7-11

My Beloved, My Twelve Disciples left to go to other towns to tell the residents about Me and My Love for them. They delivered the people from demons and healed them of their diseases. They told them the Truth, and the people repented of their sins and were healed. They showed them the way to the Truth and baptized them in the water of redemption. My Disciples were very excited when they returned to tell Me about all the miracles that they did in My Name. My Name had authority and power. The demons left when My Disciples used My Name to deliver those who were possessed. I wanted them to go out and see that they could also minister to the people, so once I left they would have confidence in going out and telling others about Me. When they returned they saw that the crowds had gotten even larger and more miracles were being done. Herod heard about all the miracles that I was doing, and he wanted to see Me and talk to Me. I did not go to him, because I knew that he would not receive Me. He would have to come to Me and find Me just like everyone must do. Do you want to know Me? Do you search for Me? Search for Me and find Me. I will make Myself real to you, and you will begin to know your Creator. I will show you hidden things, and you will rejoice in them. I send you out like I did My Disciples to bring Truth to those who are lost. Go forth boldly and rejoice that you have found the Truth, and the Truth has set you free. Rejoice that you are no longer in the bondage of sin, but you have been released. Rejoice that I love you so much and have made a place for you in My Kingdom of Light. Rejoice and be glad today!

Luke 9:12-17

My Beloved, I was teaching My People and My Twelve Disciples came to Me and told Me that it was late. They wanted My People to go to the surrounding towns to get food. We were in a remote area and the people would have to walk to the towns before it was dark. I did not want to send My People away without food. They had been with Me all day listening to My Words. I wanted to bless them and show them a miracle that I could do all things. I told My Disciples to have the people sit down in groups of fifty. After the people were seated I took the bread and fish that I had and blessed it. I asked for the food to be multiplied, so My People could eat before they left on their journey. There were about 5000 men there, not counting women or children. I blessed the food and it multiplied. My Disciples passed out the food in baskets to My People. My Disciples were amazed! The people around them were full of wonder, "Who is this man that multiplies the bread and fish? Who listens from heaven to hear his prayers? Is He the Messiah?" I heard their questions, and I told them that I was the One they had been looking for. I brought Truth to them from the Scriptures, and they understood that I had come to fulfill the prophecy about Me. Many people adhered to Me and wanted to follow Me. I told them to go back to their towns and tell their neighbors about Me. I wanted all men in the area to hear that I had come, so they would come hear My Words. The religious leaders taught My People the Scriptures, because they could not read the Scriptures themselves. I came to teach them, so that the traditions of men could be broken and the Truth would shine in their hearts. Are you following the traditions of men? Break away from the traditions of men and search My Words for Truth. You will find Me, if you ask Me to help you find the Truth.

Luke 9:18-27

My Beloved, I asked My Disciples who the crowds said that I was. They told Me that the crowds said I was John or Elijah or another prophet. I asked My Disciples who they thought that I was, and Peter said that I was the Messiah. I told him not to tell anyone that I was the Messiah now. I had to suffer much before the world could see that I AM the Messiah. I had to die and rise again after three days. The crowds must wait before they could see that I was the Messiah. I told the crowds that they must say "No" to themselves if they wanted to follow Me. They must die to themselves daily as burning incense before Me. They must want to do what I tell them to do. They must want to be My Hands and My Feet. They must want to be My Servant bonded to Me. Your flesh is strong, but if you say "no" to your flesh, then it becomes weaker. You will never get rid of your flesh, but you can control your flesh and make it tamable. Once you have your flesh under control, you can live in peace and contentment. You will not have fear in your life, but you will trust Me and want to serve Me. You will want to believe in Me for all things. You will look ahead without uncertainty knowing that I have your life in My Hands. I have a purpose for you and the sooner that you have control over your flesh, then I can reveal it to you. Do you long for the world and what it can offer you? The world will pass away, and only what you have done while in the flesh will remain. Build up rewards here on earth by the works you do while in the flesh. You will rejoice on the Last Day.

Luke 9:28-36

My Beloved, one day I took Peter, James, and John with Me to pray. As I was praying Moses and Elijah came to see Me. We were discussing My death and resurrection when Peter awoke and saw us talking together. He saw our glorious forms-our spiritual forms. He was afraid and did not know what to say. He could not comprehend that I was really talking with Moses and Elijah. I spoke to Peter from the heavens and told him that this was My Son, and I wanted him to listen to him. Peter took this to heart and listened to all that I said. He knew I was the Messiah that he had waited for. Unlike Judas he was patient to wait on Me to deliver My People. Judas wanted to push Me to hurry My Deliverance. He was filled with rage over the plight of his people. Do you trust Me? Are you patient to wait on Me? I will free you from the bondage of sin, if you cling to Me. You will be set free and no longer under the power of the enemy. If you choose to go back into sin, then you will be in bondage again. Choose to walk in righteousness, and you will not ever be in bondage. You will always be free in Me.

Luke 9:37-45

My Beloved, when I finished praying I came down from the mountain and saw the crowd of people waiting for Me. A man ran to Me and asked Me if I could heal his son. He told Me that a demon would possess him and throw him down and toss him around. The demon would destroy him if he did not receive help. I saw the boy as he came to Me, and the demon attacked him in My Presence. I rebuked the demon, and it left the boy. The boy had peace and could sit quietly without being tormented. The man was so grateful to Me. My Disciples had tried to cast out the demon, but it remained. My Disciples did not have faith that the demon would come out. They were still learning about the authority that I had given them in My Name. Sometimes the person may be in sin and until the person repents the demon will not leave. You must have discernment before you cast out a demon. Seek Me before you begin rebuking demons. Talk to the person and see what is in his heart. If he does not know Me, then he must receive the Truth first before he can be set free. Then the demon cannot come back once he has left. If he leaves and comes back, he will bring others with him. Demons were creatures that hate men and want to destroy them or make them suffer. They want to show all those looking on that man is not worthy to enter the Kingdom of Heaven. They want man to stay out of My Kingdom and not inherit it or be given My Authority. Are you worthy of inheriting My Kingdom? You must stand firm to the end. You must not waiver even in the darkest of days.

Luke 9:46-50

My Beloved, My Disciples were arguing about who would be greatest in My Kingdom. They were still thinking that I was going to set up My Kingdom on earth very soon. They did not know that I had to go away and leave the work of My Kingdom to them. I took a child and held the child in My Arms. I told My Disciples that the person who was like this child would be first in My Kingdom. The person who is last here will be first in My Kingdom. The person who is humble and not wanting his own way will be the person who receives the most rewards in My Kingdom. My Disciples could not understand this until later. They saw rulers and knew their power and authority. They wanted to rule like earthly rulers. They did not realize that I would rule over them in Heaven as they completed My Work here on earth. They did not know that they would have to lay down their life and ambitions and do only what I asked them to do. They would die for Me, but I would bless them greatly in My Kingdom. Will you lay down your life and follow Me? You must lay down your ambitions and seek for My Purpose for your life. If you follow My Will for you, then you will prosper in all that you do. Do not push against Me and reject what I have for you. If you are obedient, then I will give you the strength you need and bring you all you need to accomplish what I have for you to do. Do not be afraid. I will help you and send people to help you. You will be able to stand firm until the last day of your life, because you are in My Hands.

Luke 9:51-62

My Beloved, I set My Face towards Jerusalem and what I must face there. I sent messengers ahead to prepare a place for Me. They came to a town in Samaria, but the people would not allow Me to stay there because I was going to Jerusalem. The Samaritans hated the Jews in Jerusalem and anyone that affiliated with them. My Disciples were outraged and wanted Me to destroy the city, but I had mercy on them. I knew that they did not want to cause Me harm. I told My Disciples to forgive them and move on to another town. I wanted My Disciples to see that if one door closes, then move ahead because I would be guiding them. People would come to Me daily and say that they wanted to follow Me. I always made them count the cost of following Me. Would they stand up under persecution because they believed in Me? I asked others to follow Me, and they had an excuse why they could not come follow Me. They put other things before Me. They had not adhered to Me in their heart. Those who followed Me were able to leave all they had behind and follow Me. These would stand up during persecution. They would listen to My Voice and be obedient. I would show them where to go to escape their enemies. I would lead them to a better place. Will you listen to My Voice in times of trouble? I will lead you to a better place, and you will remain in safety. I scattered My People across the nations, but I can care for each of you no matter where you are. I will call you back to My Land, and you will be My People.

Luke 10:1-16

My Beloved, I sent out seventy disciples to other towns in the area, so they could tell the residents about Me. I wanted them to share the Good News with others. I told them to stay in one house and bless the house there with peace. I told them to travel lightly, because when they stayed in someone's home the owners would provide all they needed. If the town would not allow them to stay and rejected the Truth, then they were to leave this town. If the town rejected them, then they rejected Me. If they rejected Me, then they rejected the One who sent Me. Woe to the town who rejected Me! Their judgment would be worse than Sodom and Gomorrah! You must remember that when you tell others about Me that they are not rejecting you. They are rejecting Me. Do you tell others the Truth? Do you scorn those who do not listen to you when you tell them the Truth? Do not curse them in your heart. Be careful with the words you say. Continue to pray for them that the seeds of Light will sink into their dark heart. You may not see the results of your words, but the seeds have been planted. You may not know who you are touching by the words that you speak. Always let your words be seasoned with salt and light. Your words will go inside and healing with come to the person. They will turn to Me and receive Me. You must be brave and strong. Remember to call on My Name during days of trouble. I will give you hope.

Luke 10:17-24

My Beloved, the seventy disciples that I sent out came back excited. They told Me how even the demons submitted to them under the authority of My Name. I told them not to be happy that demons submit to them, but that their names are written in the Book of Life giving them eternal life with Me. I saw Satan being thrown out of Heaven, because he rebelled against Me. I told My Disciples that anyone who is Mine will not be harmed by Satan. Satan has no control over you. You are in My Hand under My Protection. He cannot touch you. I was so happy over the seventy disciples that came back rejoicing that I lifted My Eyes to heaven and thanked Father for revealing the hidden things to the common people. These are the humble and caring people. These are the people who are lacking and will call on My Name for help. It is hard for the rich to submit to Me, because they have so much. It is far better to have less and trust in Me than to have more and do not know Me. Do you accept what I have given you and rejoice over My Gifts? I know exactly what you need, so you must always trust in Me.

Rejoice and be glad that I love you so much!

Luke 10:25-37

My Beloved, a teacher of the Law came to Me to ask Me a question hoping he may trap Me in My Answer and shame Me in front of the people. He asked Me how he could obtain eternal life. I asked him what the Scriptures say. He said to love the Eternal One with all your heart, mind, soul, and strength and love your neighbor as yourself. I told him that he answered correctly, but he still wanted to trap me. He asked Me who his neighbor was. I looked at his heart and knew he did not like the Samarians, so I told him a story that would help him understand. A man was robbed and beaten and left on the side of the road. Two of the religious leaders who teach all men to love others walked on by and had no compassion for him. A Samarian man who was hated by many saw the beaten man and had mercy on him and carried him to a place where he could heal. This man took care of someone he did not know, because he was a man that walked in love. He was My Hands and Feet. He knew how to walk in righteousness. I asked the teacher of the Law who was the better neighbor. The teacher had to answer that the Samarian was the better neighbor, because the people were listening to his answer. He knew that he would be trapped if he answered any other way, even thought he did not like the Samarians. I told him to go and walk in mercy as this man walked in mercy. The man left feeling convicted of his sins. Do you walk in love even when you do not know the person? Do you have mercy on others when others don't? Keep your eyes open for ways to love others. I will bless you for each person you show love.

Luke 10:38-42

My Beloved, one day I came to stay in the house of two sisters, Mary and Martha. They were both very loving and kind and desired to walk in righteousness. They had heard Me teach and wanted to honor Me by allowing Me to stay in their house at any time that I wanted to stay with them. One time Mary was sitting at My Feet listening to Me teach while Martha was busy preparing for all the guests. Martha wanted her sister to come help her, but Mary wanted to stay and hear Me teach. Mary was absorbed with what I was saying. She had never heard anyone teach like Me. I explained the Scriptures, so she could understand them. She was enlightened as I revealed hidden things to her from the Scriptures. Her heart was ablaze with My Words, and she wanted to cling to Me. She knew that I was the Messiah sent to earth to bring peace to the world. She cherished every minute that she had with Me. Martha asked Me to send Mary to her to help her prepare for her guests. I told Martha to wait, because Mary was doing what she needed to be doing at that time. Do you get so busy with little things that you do not take time to sit with Me and allow Me to show you the hidden gems in My Words? Do you value the things of the world more than the things of My Spirit? Stop what you are doing and listen to My Voice, and I will guide you down the road ahead. Nothing will take you by surprise. You will be ready for whatever comes your way.

Luke 11:1-4

My Beloved, one of My Disciples asked Me to teach him how to pray. He had seen Me pray, and he wanted to be effective in his prayers. He wanted his prayers to be heard in heaven, so heaven would move on behalf of him and answer his prayers. I told him to begin by praising My Name. I wanted him to tell Me what he was thankful for. I wanted him to think about his many blessings. I wanted him to repent of his sins and forgive those who had wronged him. Your prayers cannot be heard, if you have bitterness or unforgiveness in your heart. Go to the person and work out your differences quickly before the enemy gets a foothold and makes reconciliation more difficult. Pray for what you need. I will supply your food and water. I will provide for you shelter and clothes. Call on My Name and ask Me. I will not give anything to you unless you ask Me to give it to you. I want you to rely on Me and recognize Me as the source of all things. You will be greatly blessed, because you call on My Name. Ask Me to help you stand firm even when you are tested to show that you are faithful. Thank Me for answering your prayers before they are already answered showing that you have faith in Me. You must show faith to have your prayers answered. Are your prayers not being answered? What are you asking Me? Is it My Will for you to receive what you are asking? I hear your prayers. The answer is "no this is not what is best for you" or "yes I will give it to you". The answer may be yes, but the time may not be right for you. You must trust Me to do what is best for you at all times.

Luke 11:5-13

My Beloved, My Disciples needed to learn that they should continue to ask Me for things that they need even after I leave them. I told them a story about a man who came to his neighbor in the middle of the night, because he needed bread. Even though the man was in bed and his children were asleep he got up and gave the man bread, because the man kept banging on the door and would not leave him alone. I love you so much more than this. If you continue to ask Me to help you, I will help you. I will give you good gifts. Even fathers on earth give their children good gifts when their children ask them for what they need. Fathers on earth are far inferior to Me. I will give good gifts to My Children who ask Me. My Gifts may not be seen as gifts. At the time My Gifts may appear to be hardships, but the hard times will transform you into My Image. Do you accept what I bring to you and consider them good gifts? Do you complain and question Me? You must trust Me to always bring you good things. Call on Me to give you strength during your times of testing, and I will help you become strong and mighty. Rejoice that I AM a good Father who loves you so much!

Luke 11:14-23

My Beloved, one day I was driving a demon out of a man who was mute. He had never been able to speak since he was a child. The people were astounded when the man began to speak. They rejoiced over his deliverance. In the midst of his rejoicing there were those who condemned Me. They thought that I drove out demons, because I was the ruler of the demons. They wanted a sign from heaven to show that I received My Authority from heaven. I knew they were a wicked generation, so I told them a story about a man who was strong and had all the weapons he needed to keep his house secure. (This man is Satan.) When someone stronger came even his weapons would not help him keep his house secure. (This One is Me.) I AM ruler over all things. I have conquered all things. I created demons that are now fallen creatures. I created them to serve Me, but they rebelled against Me and now they want to destroy man and make him suffer. I have given you My Authority to cast out demons. If any demon comes against you, then rebuke it and make him leave. He must leave in My Name. No one came touch you, because you are Mine. You are protected by Me. The people I came to teach did not know who I was, but you know who I AM. You know that I AM the Savior of all men who desire to repent and walk in righteousness. I will not turn any man away. It does not matter what your sins are. Will you come to Me grieving over your sins and wanting to walk in righteousness? I will save you from the sins you are in and fill you with My Spirit. My Spirit will guide you into all good things. Rejoice that I love you so much!

Luke 11:24-28

My Beloved, if a demon is cast out of a man, then he is clean. If the man does not turn to Me and ask Me to fill him with My Spirit, then the man is still empty. His house may be clean, but unless My Spirit dwells within him the demon that lived there will come back and want his old home back. Demons do not like to live in dry places, but they like to inhabit the wet places of a human body. They can have power over the human, and this gives them great satisfaction. When the demon is cast out of a body, he leaves and sees other demons looking for bodies, so he takes all of them back to his old home. If the man rejected Me and did not ask Me to fill him with My Spirit, then he is empty and there is plenty of room for all the demons that come. The man is far worse off than before. You must be careful before you cast out demons to tell the person the Truth about Me. The man must receive My Spirit to fill him or he will remain empty. If he rejects My Spirit, then he has rejected freedom. Demons will can back to him and torment him more than ever. Beware, because demons are all around you. Do you walk in righteousness? You cannot ever be touched by demons if you are righteous. If you do sin, then repent quickly. Resolve your differences and make reconciliation as fast as you can. If you delay and do not repent, then you open a door for the enemy to torment you. Keep all My Commandments, and you will be free from the enemy. He will have no authority over you. You will stand firm and never be moved.

Luke 11:29-36

My Beloved, everywhere that I went the religious leaders asked Me to give them a sign that I was the Messiah. If they had read the Scriptures, they would know that I had been giving them many signs already. I had healed the sick, raised the dead, cast out demons, and healed the blind, deaf, and lame. I taught the Truth to the people. The signs were before them, but they were blinded and could not see. I told them that the only sign I would give them is the sign of Jonah. Jonah died and was in the belly of the whale three days and three nights. I brought him back to life, and the fish spit him up on the shore. He had rebelled against Me, but he repented from his sin. I had mercy on him and allowed him to continue to go tell the people at Nineveh to repent. I was in the grave three days and three nights just like Jonah. I conquered death and set the captives free. The people in Jerusalem were blinded by the traditions of men and could not see the Light before them. I told them that a man is judged by the light within him. If he has a good eye, then he will be generous to others. If he has an evil eye, then he will be selfish and only want to serve himself. You can look in a man's eye and see the Light that radiates from him. You can tell if he is a loving, kind man or a selfish, greedy man. Does your Light shine for others, so they can see your loving, kind acts and how you walk in My Ways?

Luke 11:37-44

My Beloved, one of the religious leaders asked Me to come to his house to eat. He rebuked Me for not washing My Hands in a certain way before I ate. This was a tradition that was established by the religious leaders for My People that was not necessary, but now it was a law. I told the religious leader that cleaning the hands is not what is most important. Cleaning the inner man and making him clean is most important. I was outraged, because they were so careful to tithe a tenth of everything even the herbs in the garden, but they did not love others. They did not walk justly, but despised the poor. They wanted to be honored with the best seat at banquets and in the synagogue. They wanted to feel superior to others, because they were more religious than others. They appeared to be righteous on the outside, but they were full of dead men's bones on the inside. They were totally defiled. My People are loving and kind and think of others before themselves. They are not puffed up, but they are humble. They do not seek fame and power, but they seek Me and want to do things to love others. This is how to walk in righteousness. Do you want you to keep My Laws? Just keeping My Laws is not enough. You may keep all My Feast Days and Sabbaths, but if you are not walking in love you do not please Me. Arise, and wash yourself! Be clean before Me. Repent of your selfishness and extend your hand to others. You will rejoice and be glad that you have changed your ways and become a new person.

Luke 11:45-54

My Beloved, one day I ate at the house of a religious leader. I rebuked him for his lack of love for others. One of the Torah teachers who was there heard these remarks and did not like them. He asked Me if I was insulting the Torah teachers also. I told him that they were putting a burden of laws too heavy on My People. They were adding to My Laws and making a law for every little thing. Even today it would be impossible to keep all the laws that the Torah teachers have put in their Talmud. There are so many laws that the common man does not even know all the laws that the Torah teachers have written. This is an abomination to Me. I want you to follow only the laws that I gave to Moses. Do you keep the laws I gave to Moses? If you do, then you will love others and treat them with respect. I want you to love those around you and treat them fairly. If you do these things, then you will prosper and have success. The Torah teachers killed the prophets, because they did not like what they said. The scribe wrote down all the words of the prophet and when his words came to pass, then they declared him a prophet and made a large monument to him. They murdered My Prophets, and then they honored them. The blood of the prophets is on their hands. They must pay in full for shedding innocent blood. They even killed Zachariah, John's father, in the Temple. They had no mercy, and they will receive no mercy. The sins of their ancestors are on My People. They will pay in full for their sins against Me. Rejoice that you know the Truth, and do not sin against Me. Woe to the men who rebels against Me!

Luke 12:1-3

My Beloved, the crowds of people that wanted to hear My Words were around ten to twenty thousand. They trampled over each other trying to get to Me. I had to sit them all down, so they would not hurt each other. It was draining to see so many desperate people that needed a touch from Me. I looked across their faces. These were poor people who were burdened down by unnecessary laws and oppressed by their enemies. They were not treated fairly, but pushed down at every turn. I came to lift them up and encourage them. I came to bring them hope. They wanted to believe in Me, and I wanted them to understand who I was. I told them that everything would come to the surface. The Truth would be known and shouted from the rooftops. I told them that the things that were hidden would be revealed to My Servants who love Me. Even this day the eyes of My People are being opened, and I AM preparing them to leave exile and come live in My Land. You will begin to see My People healed and delivered as they come back to My Land in obedience to Me. Their journey may be difficult. Some will come to My Land rejoicing, and others will come bruised and beaten. Those who listen to My Call and leave immediately will come to Me rejoicing. Are you listening for My Call? Be ready!

Luke 12:4-12

My Beloved, I told My Disciples not to fear men, but only fear Me. Once a man kills you, there is nothing more he can do. I will declare judgment on that man, and he will go to eternal damnation. Do not be afraid to confess that you love Me and serve Me to men. They cannot touch you. I hold you in My Hands. I will give you the words to speak when you stand before men and testify in My Name. My Spirit within you will speak through you. Do not be fearful of men but fear Me. Do you fear Me? If you fear Me, you will walk uprightly and not sin against Me. If you fear Me, you will be an obedient servant and listen for My Call. I give generously to those who are obedient. I give generously to those who love those around them and open their hands to them. I will help them in all that they do. Men will rise up against you in the future and condemn you to death, if you say you serve Me. Do not allow these men to cause you to fear. Have faith in Me, and I will help you stand even in the darkest of days. Your life is short. Fulfill your purpose in this life. You are not here to find your own satisfaction. You are here to please Me and be My Servant. Live your life day by day for Me. I will reward you for your sacrifices.

Luke 12:13-21

My Beloved, as I was teaching My People a man asked Me to talk to his brother about sharing his inheritance. I told the man that I did not come to be a judge over My People. I came to teach them the Truth about the Scriptures. I came to tell them the Truth about Me. I told the people to walk in love and kindness. I wanted them to see a better life for themselves instead of being burdened with too many laws. I told them not to be greedy. If you store up money for yourself and do not give to others, this does not please Me. I see some people doing all they can to prepare for their retirement. They want to live a life of ease once they retire. They spend all their money on themselves, and do not give to others. I will strike them down with sickness, and they will not be able to enjoy their life of leisure. I will cut their life short. They work hard, so they can retire and live the good life. They will end up with nothing, and all they worked so hard to obtain will go to someone else who does not appreciate it. Those who inherit the fortune will waste it and end up with nothing. The life of the man who worked so hard for himself was meaningless. How do you live your life? Do you give to others? Do you only spend money on yourself? Do you give from your heart or because you feel like you have to give? I look for the man with a giving heart. I bless him in all he does. He does not value money and what it buys. He sees the needs of others and wants to help those who have needs. Look around you. I will show you when to extend your hands. Be faithful to listen, and I will guide you.

Luke 12:22-34

My Beloved, do not worry about having food or clothes. I will provide all that you need. I take care of all the animals. I give them all they need. Do you believe that I will give you all that you need? Call on My Name and ask Me and I will give to you. If you do not ask Me, then you will be lacking. I do not want you to worry about anything. I will help you at every turn in the road and tell you what to do. I will light the path before you, and you will see clearly the way to walk. Do you seek Me first in all you do? Call on My Name first before you seek the advice of man. Call on Me, and I will help you. There will be times of trouble, but I will give you a way out. If you stay righteous before Me, I will hear your prayers. If you are in sin, then repent and trust in Me with all your heart. Men will pass away, and their wisdom is limited. I AM eternal and I hold all Wisdom in My Hand. Rejoice that you know the Creator of the universe. Rejoice that I hold you in My Arms. Whatever you value most is your treasure. Your heart will lean towards whatever you treasure. What do you value most? Where is your heart?

Luke 12:35-40

My Beloved, be ready! I AM coming soon. Be dressed in your robe of righteousness. Stand firm in the faith. I will come when you are not expecting My Arrival. For those who will die before I return, I will come swiftly and take you when you are not expecting Me. For those of you who will see My Return look for the signs along the way. I will leave My Road Marks. I will show you that the time is near. You will read My Scriptures and put all the pieces together. I will pour out on My People wisdom to interpret My Words. I will give them insight, so they are enlightened. Be ready and turn from the things of the world. Get your house ready. Clean out all but the necessities, and give them to the poor. Keep only the basic things that you need. I will call you to leave your home and come to My Land. You will reside on My Land, and I will put a hedge of protection around you. No one can touch you. You will be in the Ark of My Protection. When will all this happen? It will be soon. You must remain clean before Me. You must love those around you. Do not allow yourself to become defiled, so you cannot hear My Voice. Repent of all your sins, so you can hear My Voice clearly. I will speak, so you can hear Me. You will hear and obey. You will come to Me in a time that I will make the pathway clear. Are you worried about having the money to make such a long journey? Do not worry. I will give you everything you need, so you can come to Me. Have faith in Me.

Luke 12:41-48

My Beloved, I AM the Master of the house and you are My Servant. I have left you in charge of My House while I AM gone. I want you to take care of the servants and make sure they have all they need. If they are discouraged, then comfort them. If they need food, clothes, or shelter, then give them what they need. If they have suffered loss, then surround them with love, so they can be healed. If they are sick, then pray for them and drive their sickness from them. If they are in sin, go to them and rebuke them and ask them to repent. If they are faithful and just, then put them in charge of others so they can also be My Hands and Feet. You are placed here to support the members of the House. If you tell yourself that I AM not coming back soon and you are not prepared for My Arrival, I will punish you with many lashes. You know the Truth, and you have rebelled against Me. If someone does not know the Truth, then their lashes will be few. Do you tell others the Truth? Do you walk in love and compassion?

Be righteous in all your ways, and I will bless you greatly.

Luke 12:49-59

My Beloved, I came to bring fire to the earth. I brought the fire of My Presence. I brought My Fire at Pentecost and filled those who loved Me and wanted to serve Me. You too can receive that fire from heaven and be filled with My Spirit. There will be those who come against you, because you love Me and want to serve Me. Even the members of your household will come against you, because you want to serve Me with your whole heart. They will want to cling to the traditions of men and not change their ways. You will want to obey My Commandments and do what pleases Me. You will see them turn their hearts against you, because you want to walk in righteousness. I tell you that those who stand up for Me on earth, I will stand up for them in My Kingdom. Those who fear man and fall under his reign will not stand up for Me. Do you fear what man can do to you? Fear only Me and what judgment can fall on you while you are in sin. If you do not repent, then you will certainly be punished. Many sin, and they enjoy the sin. Others sin, and they feel the presence of My Conviction and do not enjoy the sin. They feel remorseful, and they repent. These are My Children who want to serve Me and do what is right. If you love Me, you will serve Me and walk in My Way. When I was on earth many came to Me repenting, but when persecution came they quickly scattered. Many say they love Me now, but when men rise up against them they will quickly fall. They will not be strong enough to stand firm.

Arise! Stand! The end is near.

Luke 13:1-9

My Beloved, while I was teaching My People someone came to Me with a question. The man heard that some people had been killed by the Romans while they were sacrificing animals in the Temple. They wanted to know if these people were the worst of sinners, because they died so horribly. I told them that everyone sins and all are sinners. One sinner is not worst than the others. If you are not serving Me, then you are a sinner bound for destruction. It does not matter what your sins may be, because you are in rebellion against Me. If you are not in sin and want to serve Me, then I will care for you and give you the very best. I gave an example of a man who owned a vineyard and there was a fig tree that did not bear fruit. The owner wanted to cut down the fig tree, but the man who cared for the vineyard said to give it a little more time. I have given you a little more time to repent and produce fruit. I will return soon, and once I return you will have no more time. Have you repented from your sins? Have you turned from your sins and do not want to walk down that path of evil anymore? Repent now and walk in righteousness, so you will not be cut down and thrown into the Lake of Fire. Repent and stand firm!

Luke 13:10-17

My Beloved, I was teaching on the Sabbath in the synagogue and many had come to hear My Words. There was a lady who had been crippled by the Adversary for eighteen years. She could not stand erect. She was in bondage, and I had compassion on her. I told her that her sins were forgiven, and she was healed. All the people around Me were so happy to see the lady standing upright again. The lady was rejoicing and praising Me for healing her. Some in the synagogue rebuked Me for healing on Sabbath. They said that I could heal her on another day, but not on the Sabbath. I told them that they do work on Sabbath. They must take care of their animals and children on Sabbath. I took care of one of My Children on Sabbath. She was a child of Abraham that had been abused for years by the evil one. Sabbath is a day to do good things and deliver the oppressed from bondage. What kind of good things should you do on Sabbath, so you will not sin against Me? If you tell others the Truth or help others who are in need on Sabbath, then you are doing good things. Listen to My Voice. If I tell you to stay in your home and commune with Me during Sabbath, then obey My Voice. If I show you someone in need, then I will tell you how to help them even if is on Sabbath. You must not be like the hypocrites. You must be loving and kind. You must always be ready to be My Hands and Feet. You must be ready to be My Voice and share the Truth with others. Lift up your eyes and focus on Me. I will guide you in the way of Truth, so you will never be deceived. You will have keen discernment and never be misled by the enemy. You will be a Light and road marker for those who cannot see as clearly. You will guide others into

righteousness.

Luke 13:18-30

My Beloved, I told My People about My Kingdom. I told them that I start with a very small seed planted within a man. I water it with My Spirit and Truth. The seed grows and the man begins to become strong and mighty and blesses others that come to him. In the shade of his presence he will bring comfort and shelter to those who need him. He will tell others about the Truth, and they will also tell others the Truth. Spreading of the Truth is like yeast as it penetrates throughout the dough, so all the yeast rises and makes bread for all to eat. You must walk in Truth, and then you will walk into My Kingdom through the narrow door. Many will want to come in, but they rebelled against Me in this life. They will tell Me that they did great things in My Name, but I do not know them. They did not come to Me and commune with Me. They wanted their own way. They continued in the traditions of men, because it was easier. They did not want to stand up for Me, so I will reject them before Me on the Judgment Day. They will grind and clench their teeth seeing what is before them. They will call out for mercy, but it will be too late for mercy. They will not be counted worthy to enter My Kingdom. Are you worthy to enter My Kingdom?

Luke 13:31-35

My Beloved, as I was teaching My People some men came to Me to tell Me to leave the area, because Herod wanted to kill Me. I was not afraid of Herod. He was just a man. He had been placed in a position of power, and he used this power to punish My People. I used him to pass judgment on My People. After he had been My Rod of punishment I would completely destroy him. I planned to go to Jerusalem where I would fulfill what I came to do. Nothing would stop Me from this difficult task. Many prophets had been killed in Jerusalem. Jerusalem rejected My Words and would not repent. They turned to pagan practices just as you have turned to pagan practices. You are celebrating Easter and Christmas, which are not My Feast Days. These are days created by the enemy to keep you from obeying Me and receiving My Blessings. Are your eyes open? Do you see how the enemy has tricked you into believing a lie? The sins of your ancestors are curses upon you. If you call on My Name to forgive your ancestors, I will forgive your ancestors and deliver you from the curses on you. I will lift you up, so you can see clearly and restore your relationship with Me. I will bring you back to My Land and give you the best of the Land. Listen for My Call to return to My Land. I will call all those who want to serve Me. They are obedient servants who will listen to My Voice and come when I call them.

Luke 14:1-14

My Beloved, the religious leaders were constantly looking at what I was doing to find fault with Me. I was invited to a to religious leader's house. A man was there whose body was filled with fluid. He was swollen and in pain, and I knew he was suffering. I looked at the man and wanted to heal him. I asked those around Me if it was a sin to heal on the Sabbath. I told them that they would go get their son or ox out of a well on Sabbath. No one answered My Question, so I healed the man. He was relieved from his suffering and everyone rejoiced. I was invited to many banquets. I was disgusted by the pride in the people invited to the banquets. Each man went to the best seat in the house. The men wanted to be lifted up and made important in front of everyone. I told the men to sit in the lowest seat in the house. When the host of the house saw them, they would be brought to a higher seat and honored. Those who are prideful on earth will be humbled. Those who are humble on earth will be rewarded in My Kingdom. I noticed that those who came to the banquet were the rich. I told the host to invite the poor, disfigured, blind, and crippled people who could not repay him to his home, and then he would have great rewards in heaven. Do you want great rewards in My Kingdom? Seek first the Kingdom, and the rest will be added to you.

Luke 14:15-27

My Beloved, as I sat at the banquet table I told the people a story about a man who called all those around him to come to his banquet table. The rich made excuses why they could not come, so the man invited the poor, blind, crippled, and disfigured into his home so his table would be filled. There was still room at his table, so he sent his servant out into the fields to ask whoever he could find to come fill the banquet table. I asked the religious leaders to come eat with Me, and they rejected Me. I asked the poor, blind, crippled, and disfigured to come eat with Me, and they received Me. I even went out and asked those who had not heard of Me to come sit at My Table, and they came also. They came to Me rejoicing and glad to sit at My Table. Those who knew the Scriptures rejected Me and even those who went to the synagogues rejected Me. Those who had the greatest needs received Me, because they were lacking. They knew they were sinners, so they repented and received Me gladly. Each man must put Me first before anyone else. If your mother, father, sister, or brother tries to keep you from serving Me, then turn away from them and have nothing to do with them. They will burn in the Lake of Fire. Only those who sacrifice their flesh daily will enter into My Kingdom. Only those who walk in righteousness and want to please Me will enter My Kingdom. Have you sacrificed your flesh today? Have you tried to please Me today? Look at your life and decide if you are living a life worthy of entering My Kingdom of Light. Rejoice that I have called you, and you are My Own.

Luke 14:28-35

My Beloved, I told My People to count the cost of following Me. I told them that before a wise man builds a building he estimates the cost of the building. He doesn't start the building, and then realize that he does not have enough money to finish it. His neighbors would laugh at him and call him foolish, if he ran out of money and had not finished his building. A wise king looks at his enemy and measures his forces against the enemy that he will wage war against. He considers his people, and if he should sign terms of peace or not. A foolish king goes to war and his army is defeated and slaughtered and he loses his kingdom. You must decide if you will lay down everything in the world and follow Me. This means that your life is not your own. Are you My Bond Servant? Do you want to please Me? You must be listening to My Voice, so you can obey quickly. Many men say that they follow Me, but they do not know My Voice. They have not come to Me in the quiet hours and communed with Me. They have not taken the time to talk with Me and get to know Me. I AM not important to them. It is more important to entertain themselves and do what they want to do. You are supposed to be the salt of the earth. If you have lost your favor, then you are worthless. If you no longer share My Love with others and tell others about Me, then you are worthless. You must continue to fight the battle daily, so you can draw closer to Me and stand firm in these Last Days. These days will be dark, and many will oppose you. You must be able to hear My Voice and obey quickly.

Listen!

Luke 15:1-10

My Beloved, everywhere I went I was invited to eat at the homes of the people in the town. All kinds of people came to Me and invited Me into their homes. I ate with sinners and tax collectors who were hated by My People. The tax collectors put a heavy burden on My People. They collected for the Roman government and also added extra tax to put money in their pocket. They were despised by all My People, yet I knew that they needed to hear My Words. I welcomed them to sit around Me. The religious leaders were furious that I allowed these people to hear Me teach. I told them that a shepherd who lost of one his sheep would go search for the lost sheep until he found it. Once he had found the sheep he would take it home and celebrate. If you lost a coin, you would sweep the house until you find the coin that you lost. You would tell your neighbors that you found your lost coin and celebrate with them. So it is when one sinner repents. The angels in heaven celebrate and rejoice that one sinner has turned back to Me and will not be lost in the Lake of Fire. It is more important that you love those that sin and share the Truth about Me with them. If they listen and repent, you have saved a life. If they reject your words, then they reject Me and will be lost into eternal destruction. Do you love the sinner and hate the sin? Do good things for all men and share the Truth with them.

Luke 15:11-32

My Beloved I told My People about a man who had two sons. One was an obedient son, but the other was a rebellious son. The rebellious son wanted a better life. He no longer wanted to take care of his estate, but he wanted to be able to do what he wanted to do. He was selfish and greedy, so he asked his father for his half of the inheritance. His father reluctantly gave him his share. The son converted it into cash and went away to have some fun. He spent all he had on reckless living. He had parties and got drunk and fornicated with immoral women. When his money was gone everyone deserted him. They only wanted to help him spend his money. The rebellious son got a job caring for pigs. The pigs had food, but his stomach was hungry. He thought about his foolishness and how he had lost all he owned. Even the servants in his father's house had food to eat. He repented of his sins and went back to his father. His father had watched for him to come home every day. He longed for his son and wondered if he was dead or alive. When he saw his son coming towards him, he told his servants to prepare a great feast. The obedient son was furious that his father would celebrate his brother's return. The father was happy that the son was not dead and wanted to celebrate his life. The obedient son had all the inheritance, and the rebellious son only had a place to live. If you are obedient to Me, you will have great rewards in My Kingdom. I will accept a man who repents into My Kingdom even if he repents with his last dying breath. I will rejoice over his repentance, but he will not have the rewards that I give to those who are obedient to Me every day. What rewards will you have in My Kingdom?

Luke 16:1-18

My Beloved, I told My People about a wealthy man who employed a general manager to take care of his properties. The manager was wicked and was stealing from the wealthy man. When the manager found out that the wealthy man knew about his sins against him, he went to each of the men who owed debts and cut them in half. In this way the debtors would feel indebted to him and welcome him into their homes. The wealthy man was impressed how the manager handled the charges against him. Worldly people know how to handle the people of the world. My People trust others, and sometimes they trust people they shouldn't trust. My People are not of this world, so dealing with the people of the world is difficult. You must allow Me to guide you in all business decisions. Partner with people in business that you know will follow Me and not sin against you. You cannot serve two masters. You must serve Me and obey Me. If you love money and want only to make money, then you do not serve Me. Love Me not money! If you love the things of the world, this is an abomination to Me. I know those who really love Me. Do you love Me or money? Make your choice.

Luke 16:19-31

My Beloved, I told My People a story about Lazarus who lay at the door of a wealthy man's house in pain covered with sores. There was no one to help him get food, so he died on the wealthy man's door step. The wealthy man walked by him many days and had no compassion for him. The dogs in his house were fat from all the scraps from his table, yet the wealthy man did not offer Lazarus one piece of food. Lazarus was buried and rested. The wealthy man died and was in torment. He had no rest. He knew that his day of destruction was coming. He called out to Abraham to send someone to his house to tell his brothers, so they would repent and not be so greedy. I gave My Laws to Moses to guide you. If you obey My Laws, then you will love others and do good things. It would not matter what kind of sign that I send to a man, if good is not in his heart then he will not want to do good things. My People have the seed of righteousness within them. When they hear the Truth, the seed grows within them and they become strong and mighty. They can fight against the enemy and never be moved. Those who do not know Me will be judged on the Day of Judgment. They will know that their end is soon and will be in torment over it. It will be too late for them to repent. Do you repent quickly from your sins? Do you serve only Me? Do you love those around you? Be ready to leave this earth at any moment. Keep your eyes on Me and obey My Words.

Luke 17:1-10

My Beloved, I told My People to be careful, because the enemy would set traps for them. If you are quick to forgive, then you are ahead of the traps. If someone sins against you, go to him and rebuke him and make reconciliation. If is much better to have peace with your brother than to live in unforgiveness. Unforgiveness leaves a door open for the enemy to take hold of you in some area of your life. My Disciples asked Me to increase their trust in Me, so they could forgive quickly. I told them that they are My Servants. They should think of what I want them to do first and watch out for the traps set before them. Every man has weaknesses, and the enemy knows what they are. The enemy watches you and knows where you are weak. The enemy will test you at every turn. Soon you will overcome that weakness, because you have resisted him and become stronger. Are you My Servant? My Servant does not want his own way, but he only wants to please Me. Are you willing to do whatever I ask you to do? Do you want to please only Me today? Lift up your eyes and see clearly the days ahead.

Luke 17:11-19

My Beloved, as I traveled between Samaria and Galilee there were some lepers who called out to Me to have pity on them. They were supposed to stay away from everyone by law, so they would not give anyone their disease. They were desperate men who needed to be healed from their sins. Many days they had looked for hope, and there was none. Many days they had dreamed of starting their lives over again, but there were no signs that they could do this. They had heard that I was a healer, so they had been looking for Me. When they found Me their hope was restored. They called out from a distance, and I had compassion on them. They begged for pity, and I healed them. I told them to go to the priest and let him declare them clean. As they ran towards the priest their skin was healed. One man noticed his healing and came back to praise Me. He fell at My Feet and worshipped Me. This man was a foreigner not even one of My Own. Yet he received Me and knew Me and had faith in Me. He went back to his family and shared the Truth with them, and they rejoiced and also believed in Me. Do you feel like you do not have hope? Look to Me, and I will restore your hope and show you the way to go. Do you feel that you have lost your dreams? Your dreams were not in line with the plan I have for you. I have changed the direction of your life, and I am taking you down a different path. I will restore you and make you strong again, so you can complete what I want you to do. Rejoice that I love you so much!

Luke 17:20-37

My Beloved, one day I was asked by the religious leaders when the Kingdom of Heaven was coming. Many wanted to know if I was the Messiah. I told them that I would leave and return again. When I return the whole sky will light up with flashes of lightning. All men would be able to see My Return as I transfer from the spiritual realm to the physical realm. I would make Myself real at last. All men will tremble at My Coming, if they did not know Me. My Children will rejoice and shout for joy. Men will be going about their normal activities of buying and selling, marrying and having children when I return. They will not realize that the end is near. They will not be able to read the signs. My Children will see the signs and know that I AM coming soon. Cities do not realize when judgment is coming on them. Do you live in a wicked city? Judgment will be passed on that city soon. Cry out to Me for mercy. I will guide you to another place, so you can escape the coming judgment. No man can escape the judgment of the world. Men build tunnels under the earth, and I laugh. When the end comes no man can escape My Wrath. I will burn the earth and prepare a new heaven and earth for those who love Me and have proved themselves faithful to Me. Be ready. Stand firm. I will return soon!

Luke 18:1-8

My Beloved, I told My Disciples to never stop praying or give up. Sometimes prayers are delayed until the time is right for the request to be brought forth. I use the delay to increase your faith or to develop patience. I hear all your requests, and I weigh them to see if they will be good for you or not. Sometimes you do not understand why I linger and do not open My Hand to you. Rejoice that I love you so much and only give you good things. You are here to be transformed into My Image. You are like a child in his mother's womb. You are enclosed in flesh and developing each day. Soon you will be birthed and emerge a glorious creature. You will no longer carry around your heavy coat of flesh, but you will be bright as the stars. You must look at your life in perspective. You are here to be tested to be found worthy, so you can enter My Kingdom. You must realize that I will provide all you need, and you will never lack for anything. If you call on My Name and ask Me to help you, then I will help you and your children. I will cover your house with protection. I will help you by guiding you in every decision you make, if you call on My Name to guide you. Are you discouraged because you do not hear an answer to your prayer? I am not ignoring you. I AM waiting for the right time to answer you. I may tell you that this is not good for you. I may close the door. Rejoice when a door closes, because I will open the door that is good for you. Be patient to wait. I AM faithful.

Luke 18:9-14

My Beloved, I saw many among the religious leaders who looked down at others, because they thought they were more righteous than those around them. Two men went to pray. One religious leader looked at the people around him and said to Me, "I am thankful that I am not like these sinners around Me". He did not praise Me or thank Me for the blessings I had given him. He was happy to compare his life to others and puff himself up. He was not a humble man who could see his sins and repent. He looked at all the good things that he did and felt like he was better than others. A tax collector came to pray, and he asked Me to forgive him for his sins. He praised Me for all the blessings I had given him. He was humble before Me and truly repentant. He went away and was forgiven for his sins. The religious leader had no forgiveness nor was he seeking any forgiveness. In his own mind he was perfect. In the mind of the tax collector he knew he was sinful and begged for mercy. Which man pleased Me the most? When you come before Me in prayer, do you repent of your sins? Do you humble yourself before Me? I look at the heart of a man and know who is humble and who is prideful. Humble yourself today or My Hand of wrath will be upon you.

Luke 18:15-17

My Beloved, as I taught My People they would bring their babies and children to Me to bless. They wanted Me to lay My Hand on them and bless them, so they would walk in Truth and be strong and mighty. So many people brought their children to Me that My Disciples knew I was tired and turned the children away. I told My Disciples not to turn the children away but allow them to come to Me. These children would realize that the Creator had touched them. They would realize that they had looked into the eyes of the One who would give them eternal life. These little ones were the future of My People. These little ones would see Jerusalem destroyed and the Temple taken from them. They would have to be brave and strong and flee from persecution. The remnant of believers was saved through these children. You must stay humble like a child before Me. You must realize I know what is best for you and obey what I tell you to do. Are you haughty and want your own way? You do not know what is best for you. You do not know the path you should take. I will guide you. Take My Hand like a little child, and I will guide you every step of the way. Have you allowed yourself to fall into pride? Keep yourself humble or I will have to humble you, so you can look to Me once again. A faithful servant is always listening. Listen for My Call.

Luke 18:18-27

My Beloved, one day a very wealthy man asked Me what he could do to obtain eternal life. I looked into his heart and knew that he gained many things by buying them. He could buy whatever he wanted. He could not buy eternal life. He told Me that he had kept the commandments of Moses since he was a child. He always kept Sabbath and the feast days. He gave his tithes and brought his offerings to Me. He was careful to keep all My Laws. He lacked love and compassion for others. I asked him to sell all he had and give it to the poor and come follow Me. He did not want to give up his riches, because his wealth meant so much to him. He went away very sad, because he had heard My Words and knew they were true. I told My Disciples that it is very hard for a wealthy man to follow Me, because he relies on himself and does not depend on Me for his needs. He looks to his money and does not call on My Name. Once a man knows Me and develops a relationship with Me, then I can give him wealth so he can share his wealth with My People. Do you think that I will give you wealth to spend on yourself? I will give wealth to you, so you can help the poor. In these Last Days men with wealth will be humbled, because all their riches will be taken away. They will cry in agony, but it will all be lost. They will have to call on My Name to help them, and if they don't they will suffer loss. Open your eyes and see that all you receive is from My Hands. I give and I take away. I will give to you as you need. I AM faithful to provide for you. All things are possible through Me!

Luke 18:28-34

My Beloved, My Disciples wanted to know what they would receive in My Kingdom. They had given up their houses and all they had to follow Me. They were with Me day and night, and I provided for all their needs. They would deeply miss Me when I left them. I told them that their rewards in heaven would be great! They had faith in Me and followed Me when I called them to come. I told them about what would happen to Me once we reached Jerusalem. I told them that the Gentiles (pagan worshippers) would take Me and abuse Me. They would beat Me and kill Me through a very painful death. Even though I was filled with the Spirit of My Father, I could feel the pain in My Flesh. I was like any man as far as the flesh was concerned, but I was filled with the Spirit from Heaven. I could see into the hearts of men and know if they wanted to follow Me or not. I told My Disciples that I would die and rise again after three days. They did not understand this. They hear Me saying that I would die, but they kept hoping that this was not true. They wanted Me to stay with them and teach them more about the Kingdom of Heaven. My Time was short here. I fulfilled My Purpose. I came and died and delivered you from your sins. What do you have to do to be saved from eternal destruction? All you have to do is call on My Name, repent of your sins, and ask Me to dwell within you. If you receive Me, then I will dwell within you and you will be lead by My Spirit. You must be faithful to Me every day. You must trust in Me daily. Remain humble before Me, and call on My Name. You will see Salvation come to you!

Luke 18:35-43

My Beloved, as I was traveling down the road one day, a blind man heard the crowd coming and asked his friend what was happening. Thousands of people would travel with Me as I walked from town to town. As I passed a town many would come out to see Me, and they immediately followed Me. They longed to hear more about Me and My Kingdom. My People were without hope, and I brought them hope. They were trampled on by their enemy and burdened by their religious leaders. I was the first ray of hope they had seen in a long time. The blind man called out to Me as I walked by, "Have pity on Me, Son of David". The people around him told him to stop shouting, but he shouted even louder. He knew that if he could get My Attention that I would heal him. He had heard about the miracles that I had done for others. He heard that I could heal the blind. He cried out for mercy, and I hear his cry. I looked into the eyes of a desperate man. He wanted to have his eyesight restored, so once again he could provide for his family. He was a broken man-humbled and poor. I took pity on him and healed him. He rejoiced over his healing. He praised Me over and over again. The crowd rejoiced also for him. The man had repented of his sins and wanted to start a new life and care for his family. He ran home and told his family all that happened, and they believed in Me and worshipped Me. This man did not give up when others told him to stop. He tried even harder to see Me. Do you give up when someone tells you that you cannot do something? If I have told you to do it, then I will provide all you need to succeed. Listen for My Voice, and I will guide you. I will give you all you need every day.

Luke 19:1-10

My Beloved, on My Way to Jericho I saw a man in a fig tree waiting to catch a glimpse of Me. I knew his heart and how much he wanted to meet Me. He had heard about the miracles I had done and the love I had shown to others. He had been convicted about his greediness, and he wanted to change. I called out to him as I approached him, "Zacchaeus, come down, because I am coming to your house today!" Zacchaeus was so excited to have Me come visit him. He felt very unworthy, so he confessed his sins to Me and wanted to change his life. He wanted to make restitution to those he had cheated and give half of what he owned to the poor. He was a very wealthy man, and he wanted to share with others. He ran ahead to prepare a place for Me at his table. He told his servants to prepare the best for Me. When I came to his house he was rejoicing and so willing to share his hospitality with Me. Others looked down on Me, because I came to a sinner's house to eat. They did not know the heart of this man. This man had changed before My Eyes. He wanted to change his life, so when I called his name he immediately told Me about the changes he wanted to make. Are there changes that you need to make in your life? Today is a good day to start those changes. I will help you as you battle to make these changes. You are not alone. I AM always with you.

Luke 19:11-27

My Beloved, as I began My Travels towards Jerusalem, I told the people a story. They were expecting Me to set up My Kingdom in Jerusalem. They wanted Me to become King and take over the Land. They wanted Me to drive out their enemies so they could dwell in peace. They wanted Me to keep them safe from surrounding people who would war against them. They wanted to live in prosperity as in the days of King David. I told them that a hard man gave money to his servants to invest for him until he returned. He urged the servants to use it to prosper his estate. The man's countrymen hated him and did not want to obey him. The man left to be crowned king. He told his servants that he would return, so be on guard at all times. The man was gone for years, but his servants were faithful. He brought his servants before him, and they told him what they had done with his money. The first servant had ten times as much money. The second servant had five times as much money. The last servant only had what the man had given him at first. The man praised the first two servants, but he rebuked the last servant. I have given each of you gifts. Are you using your gifts wisely for Me? Will you have many rewards in My Kingdom? Take the gifts I have given you and show your love for others. Tell others the Truth about Me. Give to the poor and needy. I record in My Book all the good things you do for Me. I will return and judge you and reward you according to your works.

Luke 19:28-39

My Beloved, I turned My Face toward Jerusalem and began the upward ascent. My Followers were traveling with Me to Jerusalem to celebrate Passover. They were all expecting Me to reclaim My Kingdom and set Myself up as King. They were all every excited, but they did not understand what I must face first. I sent two of My Disciples ahead to get the colt of a donkey that no one had ever ridden upon. I rode on the colt into Jerusalem. The people knew I was coming and had thrown their clothes in the road for Me to enter the city. In this way they were showing homage to Me. They praised Me with shouts of joy. Their King was coming! They thought they would be free of their enemies at last. The whole city was filled with My Followers, and they were praising Me with all their hearts. The religious leaders told Me to tell them to stop, but did not stop them. I wanted My People to praise Me. I wanted them to know who I was. They danced and sang before Me. Many wanted to touch Me and rejoiced that they could see Me passing by. This was a glorious day! Do you rejoice over Me and praise Me for all I have done for you? Do you need hope? Are you discouraged? Lift up your eyes, and see what I have done for you. Lift up your eyes, and see the signs of Me everywhere. Do not walk in fear, but walk in faith. Know that I care for you every minute of the day! Rejoice that I love you so much.

Luke 19:40-44

My Beloved, as Jerusalem came into sight I could see what would happen to this great city. I began to weep over the suffering that the people would endure here. The enemy would come in and kill their men, rape their women, and take their children into captivity. These people would see their Temple destroyed. Not one stone would be left upon another. Everything about their religious system would be destroyed. There would be no more sacrifices or priests. There would be no one to teach them the Scriptures. There would be no more feast days. My People would be scattered everywhere without a shepherd. They would lose sight of who they are. They would forget all My Words. They would be in exile not knowing about My love and kindness. I wept for all those who would die there. I wept for all My People who have rejected Me. If only they would receive Me, then I would have spared them all this suffering. They are stiff-necked people who wanted their own way. Even now My People want their own way. They want to do as they please. Are you My Servant? Do you want to obey Me and walk in My Ways of love and kindness? If you really love Me, then you will serve Me. You will stand firm and not give in to temptation. You will want to overcome darkness, and walk in the Light. The flesh can be very dark. Rise above the darkness around you, and walk in the light. Be a Light to those around you!

Luke 19:45-48

My Beloved, after I entered Jerusalem I came into the Temple to teach. I saw the money changers and the merchants treating My Temple like a market. I was furious, because I knew they came to make a large profit from My People. They did not come to benefit My People, but to rob them. I drove them all out of the Temple and rebuked them. This made the religious leaders angry. They were determined to get rid of Me. They wanted to kill Me, and stop the people from praising Me and following Me. They were selfish people who wanted all the people to be under their power of authority. I was grieved for My People. They needed a Shepherd to lead them away from this religious system. Soon it would all topple down, and the Temple would be destroyed. My People would be scattered all over the world. To those who receive Me, I will always be with you. I will never leave you no matter where you go. I taught My People in the Temple every day. They were hungry to hear My Words. They wanted Me to proclaim My Kingdom and deliver them from bondage. They did not realize that I had to die first before I could save them. Once I rose again and overcame death, I would fill them with My Spirit if they received Me. Look to Me, My Child, and call on My Name and receive Me. I will give you only good things. Are you in bondage to your religious system and its man-made doctrines? Be separate from them! Walk in My Ways and not the ways of the world. I will bless you greatly for your acts of kindness.

Luke 20:1-8

My Beloved, I taught My People in the synagogues on Sabbath. All the people wanted to hear what I had to say. I interpreted the Scriptures, and I healed the sick and diseased. I healed the lame, blind, mute, and deaf. The people rejoiced over what I was doing for My People. The religious leaders and elders did not like what I was doing, because I was teaching the people a different way to look at the Scriptures. I was telling them the Truth and delivering them from the bondage of the many laws that the religious leaders had piled upon them. The religious leaders could see their authority and power over the people dwindling away. They did not like My Words, and they wanted to find fault in Me. They came to Me asking questions trying to trap Me in front of the people, so the people could rebuke Me and find fault in Me. They asked Me by what authority did I speak and heal. I knew what they would say if I said it is My Own Authority received from heaven. They would try to make Me a false prophet and turn the people against Me. I asked them a question about where John's authority came from. Of course they could not answer that question without causing turmoil among the people, so they declined to answer the question. I also declined from answering the question and beat them at their game. These were wicked men who wanted to gain as much power as they could over the people. They were not honest or fair judges. They ruled under their own power and did not seek Me to guide them. I was going to put an end to their power and their Temple. Only then could My People serve Me in Spirit and Truth. Are you led by My Spirit? Are you walking in Truth? Do you ask men for the answers to your questions? Ask Me for the answers to all your questions. I will give you guidance and advice, and you will be able to prosper in this life.

Luke 20:9-19

My Beloved, I told My People many stories that had hidden meanings to them. When the religious leaders questioned Me about My Authority I told them a story. I told them that the owner of the Land planted a vineyard and left if to tenants to take care of. The owner sent a servant to collect his portion of the profits from the vineyard, but the tenants beat the servant and sent him away. The owner sent more servants to tell them to repent and each was treated shamefully. The owner then sent his son to them. The tenants decided to kill the heir and keep the vineyard for themselves. When the owner returned he killed the tenants and chose others tenants to care for his vineyard. The religious leaders knew that I was calling them the wicked tenants, so they wanted to seize Me and kill Me. They did not seize Me, because they were afraid of the people. The people loved to hear Me teach and wanted to continue to have Me heal their sick. They knew that I was a very special person, maybe a prophet or even the Messiah. The religious leaders could not see any good in Me at all. The religious leaders had killed My Prophets sent to them to tell them to repent, and now they would kill Me. These rebellious people would be killed and another people would come in and tend the Land that they loved so much. They despised the Truth and rejected the Light when I walked among them. Do you reject the Truth? Search the Scriptures for the Truth. Question everything that you have been taught. If you cannot find it in My Scriptures, then you have been taught a lie. Open up your eyes, and do not be deceived any more.

Luke 20:20-26

My Beloved, the religious leaders hated Me. They were afraid of Me taking the people away from them and their false doctrine. The religious leaders had led My People away from the Truth by adding numerous laws to rule over everything they did. I gave Moses the Laws I wanted My People to obey. One of My Commandments is not to add or delete any of My Laws. The religious leaders sent spies to catch Me in a lie or find fault with Me. The religious leaders would send questions for these spies to ask Me to trap Me. I saw through all their traps. They could not trap Me, because I only spoke the Truth. They asked Me to whom they should pay their taxes. They knew the people hated the Roman taxes. I took a coin and saw the Roman Emperor on it. I told My People to pay what is owed to the Roman government and bring the offerings that are owed in the Temple. I did not want My People to rebel against their enemies that hated them and bring them more trouble. I did not want them to neglect the Temple offerings and disobey Me. I wanted My People to live in peace even in the midst of their enemies. I want you to live in peace also. Do you keep the laws of the country where you live? Pay your taxes to the country you live in, and bring your offerings to Me by giving to the poor. Do not fall into sin, because you disobey the laws of the land. You are in exile, so you must obey the laws set up by a foreign country for now. Soon I will bring you home, and you will walk on My Land and keep My Laws. Keep My Laws while you are in exile, and I will bless you greatly.

Luke 20:27-38

My Beloved, one of the religious leaders asked Me a question about the life after death. He asked Me if a woman was married to seven brothers whose wife she would be after she died. The people did not understand that they would not marry nor have children after they died. You will live one life in the flesh where you will marry and have children, and then die. You will have one life to live and be judged if you are worthy to enter My Kingdom or not. You will not be given a second chance to live life in the flesh again. You must strive everyday to do your best to walk a righteous life before Me. You must make sacrifices of your flesh, so you can walk humbly before Me. Many of My People had been taught pagan ideas about the afterlife. I told them that they would be like the angels neither marrying nor giving birth. The angels are only My Messengers from My Kingdom. I send My Messengers everyday in all different directions. You may not know that you have spoken with an angel. You may not see the angels, but they are there. They guard and protect over you daily. While you are on earth you will be transformed into My Image and be counted worthy to enter My Kingdom. All My People who love Me and have died have been preserved in a sleep of peace until the Judgment Day. They will then arise from death and stand beside Me in My Kingdom. Do you walk in righteousness? Will you stand beside Me in My Kingdom? If you are not sure, then come to Me and let us reason together. I will show you how to live your life.

Luke 20:39-47

My Beloved, I asked the religious leaders a question, "If the Messiah is David's son, the why does David call him Lord or Master?" David looked into heaven and saw Me seating at the right hand of My Father. He saw Me in heaven on My Throne. David knew that I would come through his seed, but he never called Me son. The religious leaders could not answer this question. They eventually stopped asking Me questions, because they continued to be lessened in front of My People. I told My People to only listen to the religious leaders who walked in righteousness. If they were not humble, then do not listen to them. If they wanted the best seats in the synagogue or at a banquet, then they were not humble. If they called attention to themselves as they fasted or prayed, then they were not humble. If they were dishonest or unfair with the widows, homeless, or the poor, then they were not righteous. I wanted My People to judge their religious leaders and not obey them unless they were worthy of the authority that they walked in. Many of My People could see clearly that the religious leaders were not an example for them, and they did not seek their counsel any more. They did not go to the synagogues, but they sought My Disciples after I returned to My Throne in Heaven. My People met in small groups in private homes to learn the Scriptures as led by My Spirit. How are you learning the Scriptures? Are you searching the Scriptures for yourself or with a small group of believers who love Me? If you are listening to a man give you advise and you are not searching the Scriptures for yourself, you will be mislead and fall short of all the things that I want to show you in My Words. Open your eyes and see the Truth.

Luke 21:1-4

My Beloved, I watched as each person came to the Temple to present their offerings. I saw the rich give from their abundance and the poor give what little they could spare. I saw one woman give two coins and that was all she had. The rich looked down at her for even giving Me the two coins. They shunned her and did not want to associate with her. I looked at her with compassion, and I wanted to give generously to her. I brought blessings to her house that day. She praised Me for the blessing knowing that it came from above. She glorified Me, because now she had all that she needed. Even when you give a little I will bless you. If you give generously, I will give you more. I look at the heart. Some give abundantly, but they only want a tax write-off or a way to make themselves look better in others' eyes. Some give secretly and want to remain anonymous. I know who really loves Me and wants to give to Me. I know those who only want attention from those around them. Look at your heart. What are the motives of your heart? Why do you give to others? Do you want to give to Me and My People? Do you desire to have a generous giving heart? Call on My Name if you are selfish and wish you could change. I will change your heart and help you give freely to others. I will open up your hand to others, so I can bless you. Do not hold back from others. If you see a needy person, then help that person.

Remember that you are My Hands and Feet.

Luke 21:5-19

My Beloved, one day some of My Followers were commenting on the beautiful Temple. I looked at the Temple and could see its destruction, because I could always see the future. I knew how much bloodshed and loss of life would come with the destruction of the Temple. I told those around Me that the Temple would be destroyed and Jerusalem would be taken over by her enemies. I told them not to be afraid, because men would hate them because of Me. They would have to testify in front of judges and governors concerning their relationship with Me. This would give My Followers the opportunity to tell those who were listening about Me and My Love for them. I would give them the words to say, so that those listening would be pierced to the heart by My words. Times would be difficult for anyone who wanted to serve Me. They would flee to new places to live, so they would not be hunted down and killed. Judgment will be passed on the nations for how they treated My People. There will be earthquakes and famine and destruction by war. The whole world will have to pay for the sins against My People. I wanted My People to stand firm and know that I would avenge them. They did not have to do anything but bear My Name and testify on My Account. I would care for them and guide them and show them the way to go. Even today the world hates Me, but My People continue to testify in My Name. Rejoice that I love you and care for you in the midst of a very dark and troubled world. Do you testify in My Name of what I have done for you? I will bless you greatly for your faithfulness.

Luke 21:20-28

My Beloved, My People asked Me about the future, and I told them what would happen. They loved their Temple and their lifestyle, but that was all about to change. I would send in armies to destroy the Temple and take over Jerusalem. Jerusalem would pay for her sins against Me. I told those around Me that they would see armies surrounding Jerusalem. I warned them to escape as soon as they could. I told them not to wait or they would be taken captive or killed. Those who had ears to hear listened to My Words and escaped Jerusalem before this happened. Many did not want to leave their homes, so they were killed or taken captive to a land they did not know. They cried and mourned over their fate. Those who listened to Me left with what they could carry and went to find a better life. I helped those who called on My Name and wanted Me to guide them. I kept a remnant for Myself to remain close to Me. Are you listening to My Voice today? I will be calling My Children home to My Land. If you listen to My Voice you will escape persecution and possible death. You must stay one step ahead of your enemy that wants to destroy you. I know the future and I will guide you, if you listen and obey My Voice. It will be hard to leave all you have and go to another land that you do not know. It will be hard to leave family and friends that do not want to leave. They will try to persuade you to stay, but you will be obedient to Me. Lift up your heads and focus on Me. I will show you the way.

Luke 21:29-38

My Beloved, I told those around Me that just as the fig leaves appear on a tree that means summer is near. Just as you see all the signs in the heavens and all My Words coming to pass the end is near. You must be alert and watching for My Coming. You must not enter into partying and living a loose life. You must remain steadfast and anchored. You must teach your children the Truth and prepare them to be strong and mighty. They must be able to stand firm in these Last Days. All those around Me would see the Kingdom of Heaven come to earth. As soon as I died and resurrected from death, I would conquer death and be able to give My Children eternal life. All those around Me would witness this event and know that I had changed the world. I had brought liberty to those who received Me. Those who received Me also received My Spirit to come dwell within them. They would become strong and mighty and be able to stand against the powers of darkness. Those around Me did not know what a miracle was about to take place that would change their lives. They would be transformed into a new creature when I filled them with My Spirit. They would be able to fight the fiery battles ahead. Do you think that you are alone? I am always with you. I am by your side. You are never alone or forgotten. At times you may think I am very far away, but I am close. Call on My Name, and I will come close to you and surround you with My Presence. I will keep you safe.

Luke 22:1-6

My Beloved, I continued to teach in the synagogues in the day and sleep and pray at night in the Mount of Olives. The people would rise at dawn to come hear Me teach. They were searching for Truth. My Words brought life to their being. The High Priest and his guards wanted to kill Me. Satan also wanted to kill Me, so he entered into the weaker disciple Judas. Judas wanted Me to stand up and declare My Kingdom on Earth. He wanted to overthrow the Roman government and set My People free. This was his plan, but this was not My Plan. He tried to press Me in this direction, but I told him that now was not the time. He thought if he put Me in the High Priest and his guards' possession that I would be forced to change My Plan. He did not realize that My Plan could not be altered, and now he was becoming part of My Plan. He would betray Me to My Enemies and set Me up for My Death. Judas did not want Me to die, but he did want his own way. He did not accept My Plan. Have you accepted My Plan for you? If you do not accept what I am doing in your life, then you are rejecting Me. Your plan may be an excellent plan and may help many people, but if it is not My Plan for you it will fail. Trust Me that I can guide you and show you the best way to go.

My Plan for you is a far superior plan designed to change you into My Image.

Luke 22:7-13

My Beloved, I came to Jerusalem to keep the Passover festival with My People. My Disciples asked me where we were going to celebrate the Passover, so they could prepare the meal. This was the Day of Preparation and all My People were preparing for the Passover Seder. I had already spoken to a man's heart to allow us to stay in his house in his upper room. I saw ahead the man carrying his water jug getting water for the meal. I told My Disciples to go to the man with the water jug and tell him that I needed a place to eat the Passover Seder. The man was moved to let them use his upper room to prepare the meal. My Disciples had learned that all they had to do was ask Me, and I would go before them and prepare the way. You must learn this also. Do you have a need today? Ask Me, and I will show you the way to go and help you at every turn. If you need to find shelter just call on Me, and I will provide you a place to stay. If you need food just call on Me, and I will provide you food to eat. The food may come to you or you may be taken into another's house and he will feed you. You must realize that I control all things. I move on a man's heart and prepare him to provide for you when you come to him. He will open his hand to you and not even know why he is helping you. You will be given favor with the man, and he will be generous to you sharing all that he has. You are My Beloved, and you will have all you need if only you ask Me to help you. Once you realize this principle that you must ask to receive, then you will understand that I love to give to you and bless you. Ask and receive, so that your joy may be full.

Luke 22:14-20

My Beloved, when all My Disciples were around Me at the Passover Seder My Heart went out to them. I knew what they would suffer after My Death. I loved each one of them and delighted in them. They would be made strong after My Death, so they could carry the weight of teaching My People how to stand firm and remain in the faith until I returned. I had longed to eat this meal with them. This was the last time I would take Passover with them. I told them that this would be our last time together, but they did not understand My Words. I took the cup and blessed it and passed it among My Disciples. I told them that this was My Blood shed for them. I took the unleavened bread and broke it. I told them that this was My Body broken for them. We ate the meal together and I enjoyed their company. After the meal I blessed the cup of the New Covenant that I would restore. The original covenant with Adam and Eve had been broken through their sin, but I would restore the covenant by shedding My Innocent Blood to cover their sins and the sins of the world. I was going to give the world a great gift, but no one understood what I was about to do. Even the evil one could not see My Plan and used Judas to bring Me to My Death. You have been given a great gift. Receive Me and allow Me to work inside of you. Are you allowing Me to change you daily as you submit yourself to Me? If you listen to My Voice and obey Me, I will change you into a glorious creature that will emerge after your flesh has been stripped away. You will be birthed into a new kingdom as My Bride and reign with Me eternally.

Luke 22:21-30

My Beloved, when I told My Disciples that the one who would be betray Me was at the Passover Seder, they were all very upset. They could not see the evil man in their midst. Judas had been a brother to them. They did not know his sins, because I had not revealed his sins to them. Judas carried the purse and took money for himself as he pleased to support his own ambitions. I saw his heart as he struggled with his feelings towards Me. He wanted Me to stand up and declare My Kingdom, but the time was not right. He could not accept this, and he struggled against Me until he betrayed Me. My Disciples argued over who would be the greatest in My Kingdom. They thought My Kingdom would come to earth immediately, but they did not understand My Plan for them. I told them that being great in My Kingdom is the exact opposite of being great in the kingdoms of the world. I place a man in power and use him to pass judgment on the nations. I chose My People to be servants to those around them and love others as I loved others. I told My Disciples to follow My Example, and I would hold a position for them in My Kingdom. Each of My Disciples would have his own throne in My Kingdom and rule over the tribes of Israel. My Disciples still did not understand until after My Death how I was going to set up My Kingdom. You may not understand how My Kingdom will be set up. Do you know what you are supposed to be doing until I return? I have given you a mission to be a servant to those around you and tell them about Me and My Love for them. Be a faithful servant to Me, and I will bless you greatly in My Kingdom.

Luke 22:30-38

My Beloved, I knew what Peter would face in the coming hours. All My Disciples would be scattered to different places, and they would be afraid they would die. The Roman soldiers wanted to find them, but I would keep them safe. I told Peter that I had prayed for him that he would stand firm and support the others after he repented from his sin against Me. He thought he was strong and could endure anything, but I knew that he would deny Me three times before the rooster crowed that day. Peter followed Me to see what would happen to Me when the others scattered. He did not want to give up hope, but he wanted to see Me released. I had told My Disciples to get a sword and defend themselves against their enemies. The Roman soldiers were everywhere, and My People needed to leave Jerusalem. They needed to find a safer place where they could live and worship Me. Do you need a safer place to live? You are protected by your government now, but soon you will face persecution and you will have to protect yourself and your family. Arise and be strong. Call on My Name, and I will guide you to a place where you will be safe during these troubled times. Be brave. Be strong. Prepare for the days ahead.

Luke 22:39-46

My Beloved, after the Passover Seder I took My Disciples to the Mount of Olives as I usually did at night. I went there to pray and regain My Strength to endure the days ahead. I could see My Sacrifice approaching, and I wanted to remain strong to the end. I wanted to shed My Blood willingly for My People to show My Love for them. I prayed that My Disciples would be able to endure the test before them. They would have to suffer greatly on behalf of Me. I knew that all of them would have to be strong and have faith in Me. These were common men ordained for a great purpose. They would endure and overcome and change the world by the message they brought to others. They were grieved that I told them that we had just eaten our last meal together. The reality of Me leaving was setting in, and they were grieving and weak. They were supposed to be praying with Me that I would endure the test ahead of Me, but their grief overcame them and they slept. I knew their hearts were heavy. I grieved for them having to live without Me. I knew how they would long for Me to return. They thought I would return shortly, but I would leave My Ministry to My People to spread the Good News to all the nations and give all men a chance to receive Me. My People have spread all over the world, and they were a Light to many. Are you continuing My Ministry on earth? Share the Good News with others and spread your Light to those around you. I will call you home soon! Listen for My Voice.

Luke 22:47-53

My Beloved, Judas came to betray Me while we were on the Mount of Olives praying. Suddenly a crowd of people arrived with weapons to arrest Me. My Disciples were all surprised and did not know what to do. Judas kissed Me on the cheek to tell the ones with him that I was the one they wanted to arrest. I looked into Judas' eyes and asked him, "Is this how you betray Me with a kiss?" The words pierced his heart and he became wounded and broken. My Disciples had brought swords and wanted to fight for Me. Peter cut off the ear of one of the men. I told My Disciples that I would go quietly with the men. The men did not need weapons to force Me to go with them. They could have arrested Me any day while I was teaching. Instead they came by night to arrest Me knowing that the people would riot against them during the day if they tried to arrest Me. I told My Disciples that I would complete My Task that I had come to do, and they should not interfere. I told the men to only take Me and leave the others behind, so My Disciples fled in fear as I walked away with the guards. Do you not understand what is happening in your life? Have faith in Me to bring you understanding. I will show you that what is happening to you is for your own good. Do not doubt Me, but trust in Me. I will bring to you all you need, and show you hidden things.

I will transform you into My Image and make you at one with Me.

Luke 22:54-62

My Beloved, the mob of men took Me away to the High Priest, so I could be found guilty. Peter followed Me to see what would happen to Me. He stayed at a distance, but he could hear what was being said. As he sat by the fire warming his hands someone recognized him that he was with Me. He denied that he even knew Me. Again another one recognized him, but he denied that he was with Me. Once more someone recognized him, but he denied that he was with Me. At that moment the rooster crowed. I turned to look at Peter and he saw Me. Peter could not bear to see My Disappointment in him. He was grieved so deeply. He was broken and went away weeping not being able to forgive himself for what he had done. In his fear he had rejected Me. He cried all night asking Me to forgive him and make him stronger and overcome his fear. I heard his prayers, and I made him a strong mighty man. Once he was filled with My Spirit he was determined that he would never deny Me again. He would make up for all the words he said against Me. Peter was a strong support for the other believers around him. He stood firm for Me and even gave his life for Me. He had a moment of weakness, but he repented and overcame. Have you had a time of weakness in your life when you fell into sin? Repent, and ask Me to forgive you. I will hear your voice and forgive you and lift you up. I will help you overcome and become strong. You do not have to be afraid, because I will help you all day long. Just call on My Name, and I am there.

Luke 22:63-71

My Beloved, when I was taken to the High Priest I was falsely accused. I was brought to him, because the religious leaders hated Me. They did not want to listen to My Words, because they would have to repent and change their lives. They wanted to rule harshly over My People and walk in a false authority. I wanted the priests to be an example of love for My People. They were chosen to teach My People My Words, so My People could have a good life. These priests were not worthy of being called My Priests. They had killed all the prophets before them that had called them to repent. Now I came to them, and they even rejected Me. They blindfolded Me and mocked Me and asked Me to prophesy to them. They surrounded Me like wolves wanting to destroy their prey. They beat Me and insulted Me and laughed about their actions. Not one of them told the others to stop. Not one of them stood up for Me. They led Me to the Sanhedrin in the morning to stand before the elders. Not all the men in the Sanhedrin were against Me. There were some who wanted to follow Me, but they were afraid of their elders. They asked Me if I was the son of the Most High, and I told them that I was. They took Me to Pilate to deliver Me up to be killed, because I was blaspheming. They did not understand nor did they want to understand. They were all condemned at that moment for killing Me. They all suffered horrible deaths, because they did not repent of their actions towards Me. Their sins fell on their children and on their children's children. Some are still under that curse. Have you accepted My Salvation? Rejoice that you have not rejected Me, but have accepted Me as your Savior. Rejoice and be glad.

Luke 23:1-12

My Beloved, the High Priest and the elders took Me to Pilate. They made up lies about Me saying that I told the people not to pay taxes and incited the people to rise up against the state. They poured lies out of their mouth to try to get Pilate to condemn Me to death. He knew that the religious leaders were jealous of how the people followed Me. The people saw the good in Me and wanted to hear Me teach, but the religious leaders wanted to keep the people in darkness and under their control. The High Priest told Pilate that I had spread lies form Galilee to Jerusalem. When Pilate found out that I lived in Galilee he sent Me to Herod. Herod was very glad to see Me. He wanted Me to perform a miracle. When I wouldn't perform a miracle for him he mocked Me and said that I was a fraud. He put an elegant robe on Me and called Me "King of the Jews". The High Priest did not like this, but Herod did not care what the High Priest wanted. Herod was enjoying mocking Me and laughing at Me. I could see the wickedness in the heart of Herod. He loved to see the misery of others. He loved having power and authority. He was destroyed by his own wickedness. Rulers are set up to pass judgment on a nation if they are in sin. If your nation has a righteous ruler, then that nation is blessed by My Hand. Are the rulers over your nation wicked? Do not be afraid, because I will protect you from all wicked rulers. I will call you out of that wicked nation. I will keep you in the palm of My Hand. No one can touch you. You are My Beloved.

Luke 23:13-25

My Beloved, after Herod was tired of making fun of Me he sent Me back to Pilate. Herod did not want to sentence Me to death, because he feared the people. He knew the people thought I was a prophet or the Messiah. He did not want a riot from the people. He was supposed to keep peace in his area not provoke a riot. He would let Pilate make that decision. Pilate did not want to sentence Me to death either. He knew that I was not guilty. The High Priest and elders stirred up a mob of people to make a disturbance, so Pilate would listen to their demands. They screamed out, "Kill him! Kill him!" Pilate could see that they would not stop yelling and screaming no matter what he said, so they turned Me over to be crucified. He had unrest in his heart over this matter. He told the High Priest that this was their decision not his, and the blame for My Death would be on them. The High Priest and elders accepted the responsibility for My Death, which brought a heavy curse on them and their children. These men died horrible deaths and their children were taken into captivity by their enemies. They carried a terrible curse on them that lasted for hundreds of years. Their ancestors have been hunted down and killed like animals. They have had no peace. They have not been able to prosper. They have bore My Blood on their heads. These families were completely wiped off the earth. They will face Me on Judgment Day for their sins against Me. What sins are on your head? Repent today of your sins and become righteous before Me. Are you committing the same sins that your ancestors did who rejected Me? Walk with Me and love Me, and you will be blessed by My Hand.

Luke 23:26-31

My Beloved, Pilate turned Me over to the Roman soldiers who took great pleasure in watching Me suffer. They beat Me and stripped Me naked. They wanted to humiliate Me. They beat Me so badly that I could barely walk. They wanted Me to carry the stake that I was to be crucified on, but I fell under the weight of it. They grabbed a bystander to carry the stake for Me. Crowds of people followed Me crying and yelling out in agony. I was their only hope of salvation. Now their enemies had beaten Me and wanted to kill Me. There was no more hope for them left. I told the women not to cry for Me, but to cry for Jerusalem that the people would repent of their sins. If Jerusalem did not repent, the people would be punished so harshly that they would cry out to die. They would want the rocks to fall on them and kill them, so their lives would be over. I was grieved for My People who loved Me. I knew their sorrow and how they wanted to help Me. Great crowds watched Me as I walked down the street beaten and bleeding. Their grief was almost too much for them to bear. It was a dark day in Jerusalem and for the nation of Israel. Darkness had fallen on the Land, and the people would have to pay for its sins against Me. How often I cried out to them to repent and turn from their sins, and they did not listen. Listen to My Cries today. Repent from your sins and walk in righteousness. Have you turned away from the world? Focus on Me and not the things of the world. Draw near to Me, and I will help you at every turn.

Luke 23:32-43

My Beloved, I was taken to the place called The Skull. This was the place where the Romans crucified criminals. That day two other men were crucified for their crimes. They were guilty, but I was innocent. I was without sin, and I laid down My Life willingly for you. Crowds of people watched Me as the Roman soldiers nailed Me to the stake. They cried before Me. The soldiers and men of authority mocked Me in front of the people, "If you are the Messiah, then come down from there and save yourself". They wanted to show the people that they had their hopes in a man not the Messiah. My People were hopeless. They waited to see what I would do to save Myself. Even one of the criminals mocked Me and told Me to save Myself and him. The other criminal had heard about all the good things I had done, and he believed on Me. He asked Me to remember him in My Kingdom. I received the man into My Kingdom, but the other criminal will be thrown in the Lake of Fire along with all the others who rejected Me. As I hung on the stake My Body was weak, and I could feel the life flowing out of Me. I knew that soon I would no longer be here with My People. I had come to die for them, and I had done what I came to do. Are you accomplishing what you came to do? What is your purpose for this life? You are My Servant-My Hands and Feet. Listen to My Commands every day, and walk in what I tell you to do. Love those around you, and share the Truth about Me with others.

Luke 23:44-49

My Beloved, when it was around noon darkness covered the land until about three o'clock in the afternoon. The Land began to shake, and the graves were open. My grief was being expressed through the heavens. A host of heavenly beings looked on in anguish at My Suffering. Great crowds watched and waited to see what would happen to Me. I called out to My People, "It is finished!" I had finished My Work here on earth. It was time to go back to My Throne. My People could see the power all around Me. Even the soldier said, "This must be the Messiah!" The Land was grieving as it received My Blood. My People went home in agony once I was dead. Their grief was so heavy. Their hope was gone. They were confused. They had trusted in Me to be their Messiah and deliver them from their enemies. They did not realize that I would give them a great gift of My Spirit to all those who believed in Me and received Me. Are you confused about what I am doing in your life? Sometimes you cannot see what I am doing in your life, but you must continue to trust Me. If the situation looks hopeless, then turn to Me and ask Me to help you. I will comfort you and bring you peace. I will deliver you from your hopeless situation. I will show you the way to go. You must trust in Me. There is always hope in Me. In Me you can stand firm and never be moved. I am your Rock.

Luke 23:50-56

My Beloved, I died on the stake, and My Blood spilled on the Land covering the sins of My People. The Land quaked in agony as it received My Blood. The Land was covered in darkness, because the people could not see their sins against Me. It was a very dark time for My People who loved Me. One of My Disciples named Joseph went to Pilate and asked for My Body. Sabbath was approaching and he wanted to take down My Body and not have it defiled. Pilate gave him My Body. Joseph took down My Body and wrapped it in a linen cloth. He took My Body to his own tomb and placed Me there. He rolled a large stone over the tomb, so no one would bother Me. Roman soldiers were placed around the tomb, so no one would steal My Body. The women who followed Me from Galilee trailed behind Joseph to see where he would take Me. The women went home to prepare spices and perfumes for My Body for burial. Sabbath was upon them, so they rested on the Sabbath. Sabbath began at sundown, so they did not want to violate the Sabbath by touching the dead. My People were in their homes grieving. It was not a Sabbath of rest for them, because their grief was so heavy. My People did not understand the timetable of My Death and Resurrection that I had told them about. They were confused. You may seem confused at times and not know what is happening in your life. Call on My Name, and I will show you the answers to your questions. The answers may not come that moment, but in time you will see all the answers to your questions. Are you questioning what I am doing in your life? Have you lost hope in having a better tomorrow? Be patient and see what I will do for you. My People had to wait to see what would happen. They were able to rejoice in a few days that I had done so much for them. Rejoice and be glad that you have salvation through My Blood. I have given you a great gift, so rejoice in it.

Luke 24:1-12

My Beloved, the women prepared the spices and perfumes for My Burial, but Sabbath was upon them so they rested in their home. Sabbath is from sunset to sunset, so they did not go out at night. They stayed inside their homes until sun rise on the first day of the week. Their land was full of their enemies, so it was dangerous to go out at night. At the first sign of light they took their spices and went to the place where Joseph laid Me. When they came to the large stone it was rolled away, and My Body was not there. They were filled with grief. Two of My Angels were there to deliver them a message from Me. The angels reminded them that I taught them that I would be crucified and then rise from the dead. The angels asked them, "Why are you looking for the living among the dead?" The women remembered My Words and rejoiced over the Good News. They ran back to the other disciples and told them what the angels had said. No one believed that this could happen. They were too filled with grief to receive their words. The women were very upset that the others did not believe them, but in their hearts they were glad. They knew that My Words were true, and I had done exactly what I said I would do. What should you do when others will not receive the Truth? There will be those who do not want to believe that I AM alive and I AM your Savior. Even if they do not believe your words continue to rejoice and pray for them. You have planted seeds of Truth within them. You will be blessed, because you believe in Me and share the Truth with others.

Luke 24:13-32

My Beloved, all of Jerusalem was in an uproar over what the High Priest and the eiders had done to Me. My People were outraged over their sins against Me. After the women had gone to the Tomb and found that I was gone, the women reported to My People that I had been raised from the dead. As two of My Disciples were walking along the road outside of Jerusalem, I heard that they were discussing all these things. I came to them and walked along with them. I asked them what they were talking about. They were both very confused but hopeful. I explained to them the Scriptures that revealed that I would be crucified and resurrected for the sake of My People. As I explained the Scriptures to them they burned inside receiving the Truth of My Words. They came to their house and begged Me to stay with them. My People were celebrating the Feast of Unleavened Bread. They prepared a meal for Me, and I broke the unleavened bread and blessed it. As soon as I blessed the bread their eyes were opened, and they knew who I was. They rejoiced over Me, and then I left them. They wanted to go tell the other disciples immediately. They left to bring the good news to My Disciples in Jerusalem. This was a great day for My People. Good news had come at last! Last night they were in pain and suffering over the loss of their Messiah. Today they would have hope again. Are you grieving today? Call on My Name and allow Me to help you. I will bring you comfort and peace. Trust in Me, and know that I will never leave you. I AM always near. Sometimes the night may be dark. Light will break in the morning, and My Presence will guide you into only good things. Trust in Me to bring it to pass.

Luke 24:32-42

My Beloved, My Disciples immediately left for Jerusalem. They were so happy to bring good news to the other disciples. They rejoiced as they went along the road. They told everyone along the way that I had risen from the dead. They came to the other disciples and told them that I walked with them along the road and explained the Scriptures to them. Their hearts burned inside as I told them the Truth. As the disciples were sharing their story I appeared in their midst. I asked them, "Why did you have so little faith in Me?" I had explained before I died all the things that had to happen to Me, but they did not understand what I was saying. I explained all the Scriptures to them and showed them how the prophets had prophesied everything that would happen to Me. As I unveiled the Scriptures to them they rejoiced and were glad. They looked at My Hands and Feet how they pierced Me. They could see how I had to die for them, and they worshipped Me. These were common people who I gave a great gift. They believed in Me and wanted to receive My Gift. Do you want to receive the gift of salvation? Do you want to share this gift with others? Be brave and bold and open your mouth. I will fill your mouth with My Words as you tell others about Me. I will give you the words of Life.

Luke 24:43-53

My Beloved, after I was resurrected from the dead I appeared to My Disciples in different places. I had disciples in Galilee and Jerusalem and the surrounding areas. I wanted to explain the Scriptures to My Disciples that loved Me, so they could also share the Good News with others. I told My Disciples that I must go back to My Throne in Heaven, but I was leaving them to continue My Ministry on earth. They were to go to all the nations and tell them the Good News. The tribes of Israel were scattered among the nations, and I wanted all My People to know that I had died for them so they could receive My Spirit. I told My Disciples not to leave Jerusalem, because I would send My Spirit to them to comfort them and guide them. While they were waiting in Jerusalem they worshipped Me in the synagogues and told My People the good news. My People rejoiced and were glad. They sang and danced in My Presence. It was a joyful time for My People who loved Me. I want you to rejoice and be glad also. Are you allowing the cares of the world to overtake you? Rejoice that I have given you so much. Rejoice that you have eternal life in My Kingdom. Worship Me and praise Me for all My wondrous works!

Acts 1:1-11

My Beloved, I appeared to My Disciples many times after I was resurrected and explained the Scriptures to them. I visited with them until the 40 days were completed. I did not visit with them again after I brought My Spirit to dwell in them. My Spirit was within them, and they could talk with Me all day. John immersed in water, but I brought My Spirit filled with fire. This fire would bring a cleansing for the person and prepare him for the days to come. My People look forward to the Feast of Pentecost, because they can celebrate the day that I immersed My People with fire. I taught My People with an urgency to know My Words. I taught them as much as I could, and then I had to leave them. I left them My Example and My Love. I told them that I wanted them to go tell the Truth about Me, so others could receive salvation. I went up into Heaven and left them looking up for Me to come down. My Angels told them to stop looking for Me to return. I would return at the end of the age. Now they must tell the Good News to all the people around the world. My Disciples could not believe that they would not see Me again. They had leaned on Me for everything while I was with them. Now they would stand with each other and support each other. Are you standing with your brothers to encourage them and strengthened them? Do not give up on them, but rejoice in all the little things that they do.

Acts 1:12-26

My Beloved, after I ascended into heaven My Angels told My Disciples to leave and go tell the nations the Good News. My Disciples went back to where they were staying in Jerusalem and devoted themselves to prayer. They searched the Scriptures for evidence that I fulfilled all the prophecies while I was on earth. They wanted to show the other believers that I was the Messiah sent from Heaven and I would return again to begin My Kingdom on Earth. The disciples were grieved over Judas and how he betrayed Me. They could not understand how he could do such a thing. They realize that what he did was also prophesied and recorded in the Scriptures. Judas died a horrible death as a sign to all those around him that he was a traitor. The disciples wanted to fill his place, so they prayed and asked Me to guide them. They wanted to choose someone who had been faithful to Me from the beginning of My Ministry. They wanted someone that they could trust. They chose two men, and they asked Me to choose the man who was worthy of the position. Only I knew the man's heart, so I choose the new Disciple to fill Judas' position. This act brought healing to the rest of the Disciples. They were now whole and complete again. Have you lost someone in your life and feel empty? I can make you feel whole again. Come to Me and ask Me to help you. I will bring someone into your life to fill that empty place. It may not be exactly like it was before, but the person will bring you love and care for you and stand next to you in times of testing. There will always be testing, so you need each other to encourage and bring you strength to stand. Call on My Name, and I will bring you comfort once again.

Acts 2:1-21

My Beloved, My Disciples and the other 120 believers were waiting in Jerusalem for the gift of My Spirit to be poured out when the Feast of Weeks (Shavuot) arrived. The room where they were staying was filled with the roar of a violent wind. Fire from Heaven came down and baptized each one of them with My Spirit. My Spirit manifested as tongues of fire over their heads. Each one could feel the fire of My Presence within them. They were made clean, and they began to speak in a heavenly language that they did not understand. There were all kinds of nationalities in Jerusalem at that time that had come for the festival. When the people in Jerusalem heard My Believers praising Me in their own language, they were confused and did not understand what was happening. Peter tried to answer their questions by telling them that this was a fulfillment of Joel's prophesy that in the Last Days My Spirit would be poured out upon My People. When I ascended into heaven this was the beginning of the Last Days on earth. My Spirit was poured out onto My People to help them be able to stand firm during these Last Days. Are you afraid of what will happen in the coming days? Do not be afraid, because I am with you always. I have sent the Comforter to help you endure until the end. Be strong. Be brave.

Acts 2:21-41

My Beloved, when My Spirit was poured out on My Believers those around them could not understand why they could hear the believers praising Me in their own language. Peter explained to them that this was prophesied in Joel that I would pour out My Spirit on all men who believed in Me and received Me as their Savior. Peter explained why I had to come and die to save them from their sins. King David was a prophet and he looked into heaven and saw Me ascending from the grave and was restored back to My Throne. He praised Me for overcoming death and establishing a new reign on earth. David was promised that one of his descendants would always reign on earth. I came through the seed of David, and I established My Reign on earth and will continue to reign in the hearts of men. David did not understand what he saw, but he knew that I had showed him that I would be established and reign forever. Peter explained how I fulfilled the Scriptures, and I was the Messiah sent from Heaven. The people who were listening were pierced to the heart. They were grieved over what they had done to Me. Three thousand repented and were saved that day. They were filled with My Spirit and spoke in a heavenly language. They were filled with the fire of My Presence. They burned inside with the Truth, and they wanted to tell others about what I had done for them. The new believers left Jerusalem and went to all parts of the world telling others how I came to earth to save them from their sins. You also are called to tell the Truth to others. Are you filled with the fire of My Presence? Ask Me to immerse you in My Spirit and you will speak in a heavenly language. You will burn inside with the Truth, and you will want to share it with others. Call on My Name, and I will baptize you with fire.

Acts 3:1-26

My Beloved, Peter and John were going to the Temple one day to pray when they saw a crippled man. I told them to heal the man and restore him. Peter looked at him and love rose up in his heart for him. The man reached out his hand to Peter for money, but Peter did not have money to give him. Peter took his hand and told him that he was healed in My Name. As Peter pulled the man up healing came into his body, and he was restored. The man leaped and shouted and praised My Name. Those around him knew him only as the cripple, but now they saw him praising My Name. Peter and John shared what I had done for them. They told the people who were in shock over this miracle that I had brought healing to this man, "The One who you put to death is the One who came to save you from your sins". Peter reminded them that Moses said that I would send a prophet from among their own people to guide them. If you rejected Him, then you would be cast out from My Kingdom. The people remembered the prophecy, and it burned within them. Peter explained the Scriptures to them and how I fulfilled all the prophecies written about Me in the Scriptures. Many people repented and turned to Me. Are you looking for the miracles that are happening all around you? Many times miracles happen around you, and you do not recognize them as miracles. You must open your eyes and see what I do for others every day. I answer the prayers of My People. Lift up your prayers to Me, and I will answer every one of them.

Acts 4:1-22

My Beloved, Peter and John healed a crippled man in My Name, and everyone around them was in shock, "How did this happen? This man is 40 years old and has been crippled all his life." Peter and John were able to testify in My Name who healed this man. They told them, "The One you nailed to the stake is the One who healed this man. You killed the Author of Life!" The religious leaders did not like what they were telling the people, so they sent the Temple guards to arrest them. Peter and John stayed in custody over night. In the morning they appeared before the Sanhedrin, so all the religious leaders could hear their testimony. Peter and John spoke about how I fulfilled the Scriptures with boldness and authority. I spoke through them, and the words amazed the members of the Sanhedrin. Even though they heard the Truth, they still rejected Me and told Peter and John not to talk about Me again. Peter and John told them that they would continue to talk about Me and share the good news with others. They were released from custody. Five thousand men plus women and children had heard their message and received it. Those who had ears to hear came to Me and received Me and were saved from their sins. Do you have ears to hear My Voice? Do you want to know what I am saying to you? Open your ears and I will speak to you.

Acts 4:23-37

My Beloved, Peter and John were released from custody and went back to their friends and told them how they spoke with boldness in front of the Sanhedrin. All the believers praised Me for their release. They all prayed to have the same boldness to speak the Truth no matter where they were. They wanted to be strong and stand firm until I returned. As they were praying I sent My Spirit to them. As it rushed into them the whole house was shaken. They were filled with boldness and the fire within them continued to burn for Me. The believers sold their properties, and all they had, and shared it with each other. There were no poor among them. All the believers considered themselves brothers and sisters, because they all came from My Blood. They were one family now, and they would care for each other. They knew that the religious leaders would be against them, and they would have to suffer persecution. They would need to be one community to be able to endure the days ahead. Do you not feel part of a community like this today? You are in exile, and you may not have any other believers around you. I will help you remain strong. I will be the Strength you need to stand. Just call on My Name, and I will help you. Soon I will call you back to the Land, and you will be part of a large community once again. You will be like this community sharing with each other. There will be no poor among you. You will carefully guard over each other with love. Be encouraged for the time grows near for you to leave exile and enter into your Land once again.

Acts 5:12-42

My Beloved, all My Disciples began to do miracles in My Name. People all over the area brought their sick for My Disciples to heal. Some even thought that the shadow of Peter passing over the sick may heal them. Whenever My Disciples were told to heal the sick they obeyed My Voice and healed them in My Name. I wanted to continue to heal My People and set them free from demons. I told My Disciples to heal all those around them and deliver them from the evil one. The Temple guards arrested them again and put them in prison. I sent My Angels to open the doors of the prison and lead them out without the guards even seeing them. I closed the eyes of the guards, and they did not even see them walk by. I told My Disciples to continue to teach in the synagogues, so in the morning they continued to teach My People about Me. The Temple guards brought them in front of the Sanhedrin to explain to them why they continued to tell the people about Me. My Disciples said that they would never stop sharing the Good News with others. One wise member of the Sanhedrin spoke his concerns. He could see that this uprising was different than the others, because it was followed by signs and miracles. He wondered if the Eternal One was really behind this movement. He persuaded the council to allow the disciples to teach in the synagogue. The Temple guards whipped My Disciples for disobeying their commands and sent them home. My Disciples rejoiced that they suffered in My Name, since I had suffered so greatly for them. Are you suffering today? When you do suffer rejoice that I AM transforming you into My Image. I suffered for you, so rejoice in your suffering for Me.

Acts 6:1-15, 7:51-60

My Beloved, My Twelve Disciples became involved in caring for all the new converts who needed to be fed. My Twelve Disciples realized that they needed more help, so they chose seven other men as led by My Spirit to help them. They laid hands on them and My Anointing came on them to minister in My Name. One of these men was Stephen, who was filled with My Spirit. He was a man of faith and continued My Ministry on earth. He healed the sick and delivered those oppressed by demons. He taught others about Me wherever he went. The religious leaders knew that he was changing the hearts of the people, so they devised an evil plan against him. They found wicked men who would testify against Stephen accusing him of telling others not to keep the commandments of Moses any more. Stephen was dragged before the Sanhedrin where he testified in My Name. Some of the religious leaders did not want to hear that they crucified their Messiah that had been prophesied in the Scriptures. Stephen told them that they killed all the others prophets and now they killed the Messiah also. The religious leaders were so angry that they took him outside and stoned him. He asked Me not to hold their sin against them. He delivered his spirit into My Hands and he was gone. This was the beginning of great persecution for those who testified in My Name. My People began to flee to other regions to escape the persecution. Do you want to honor Me and testify in My Name? You will see others come against you, but stand firm. Persecution will come to My People, but this will drive them back to My Land and into My Arms of protection. If you truly love Me, you will listen to My Voice. I will guide you every day even though you have to endure difficult situations. I am always with you. I will help you endure to the end.

Acts 9:1-22

My Beloved, there was a man named Saul who was taught from a child to memorize all the Scriptures. He taught others the meanings of My Words. He was against My People and wanted to stop the uprising against his religion. He could see how the believers were causing division between My People, and he wanted to stop them. He received letters giving permission to arrest all those who testified in My Name. He was fervent to make sure the believers were punished for disobeying Me. He was confused and did not know the Truth about Me. I came to him as he was heading to Damascus to arrest some of the believers. I asked him, "Why are you persecuting Me?" He did not know who I was. I told him who I was, and My Words cut deep into his heart. He was extremely grieved. He was blinded by the Light of My Presence. He saw that My Hands and Feet were pierced. He understood that I was the Messiah crucified for his sins. I told him to go to Damascus and stay there. I spoke to one of My Disciples in Damascus and told him to pray for Saul to be healed. This was very hard for Ananias to do, because Saul had arrested other believers and sent them to jail. Ananias was obedient Me and healed Saul and taught him all about Me. Saul saw how I fulfilled the prophecy written in the Scriptures. He was filled with My Spirit and burned with love for Me. He taught everywhere he went telling others about My Love for them. I can call any man to come to Me. I know the heart of a man. Even if the man is deep in sin, I can touch him and open his eyes and bring him to Me. Are you giving up on someone because he is in sin? Do not give up on any man. Continue to pray, and ask Me to open his eyes to the Truth. I will hear your prayers.

Acts 10:1-48

My Beloved, there was a man named Cornelius who was a good man and gave generously to My People even though he was a Roman solider. I knew this man's heart that he would receive Me and love Me. I sent an angel to him and told him to send for Peter. I wanted Peter to know that the Good News was to be shared with all men not just the Jews. I sent Peter a vision of unclean food. In the vision I told him to eat it. He was disgusted by this, because he had never eaten unclean food before. I spoke to him and told him to go to the Gentiles and tell them about Me. He understood that the unclean food in the vision was a symbol of the Gentiles. He had never associated with the Gentiles, because they were unclean. He was obedient to Me and went to Cornelius' house and told them about Me. As he was speaking My Spirit descended upon them, and they began to speak in tongues. Peter was amazed that My Spirit was being poured out on the unclean Gentiles. He realizes how much I loved all men, and all men were equal in My Sight. Cornelius and all his household and friends were baptized in water and cleansed from their sins. Do you judge a man by the color of his skin or his religion or his nationality? Share with all men My Love and how I want to deliver them from their sins and save them from eternal darkness. Share with others as I lead you to tell them about Me. I will open their heart, and they will receive Me. Listen and I will guide you to those who have ears to hear My Words.

Acts 12:1-17

My Beloved, King Herod began to persecute My Believers. He killed James and this pleased the religious leaders, so he began to kill more of My Disciples. He arrested Peter and put him in prison. Herod was going to bring him to trial and kill him, but I sent an angel to Peter to release him from prison. King Herod thought that his sixteen guards could hold Peter against any force that came against them. These guards were highly trained to kill anyone. King Herod and his guards were nothing to Me. I sent an angel to release Peter. Peter and the angel walked past all the guards, and the guards did not even see them. I blinded the eyes of the guards, so they could not see. Peter was released, so he could continue to tell others about Me. Peter went to the believers who were praying for his release. I heard their prayers and sent an angel to help Peter. Do you believe that I near your prayers? Nothing is impossible with Me. Pray and believe for the impossible to happen. These praying believers wanted Me to protect Peter from death, but I did more than that. I released him from the clutches of Herod and showed Herod who was more powerful. Pray and believe. I will hear the prayers of faith for the believers.

Acts 14:8-18, Acts 12:21-23

My Beloved, as Paul and Barnabas continued on their journeys many Jews and Greeks believed in Me and were saved. In one city Paul saw a crippled man who had faith to believe in Me to be healed. Peter took his hand and healed him in My Name. The people thought Paul and Barnabas were one of the Greek gods. The Greeks worshipped Hermes and Zeus. The priest of the Temple of Zeus came to offer sacrifices to Paul and Barnabas. This greatly upset Paul and Barnabas. Paul and Barnabas told the Greeks not to worship them, but to worship Me. Paul and Barnabas told them about Me and how I came to save the world from their sins. The worshippers of Zeus were blinded and could not see the Truth, but many citizens of the town did believe and were saved. I blessed Paul and Barnabas, because they accepted no praise for themselves, but they humbled themselves and glorified My Name. King Herod had invited some men to his palace, and they called him a god not a man. He received their praise, and I struck him down immediately by an angel. Herod was filled with worms that ate him up until he died. Those who glorify My Name and walk in humility will be blessed in My Kingdom. Those who seek glory for their name will be brought low and humbled. Do you set yourself up as a god and serve only yourself? Do you seek your own pleasure and do what you want to do? You will be punished for your wickedness. If you listen to My Voice and are a humble servant, I will lift you up and reward you greatly.

Acts 16:16-40

My Beloved, I continued to guide Paul and Silas into different regions to tell others about Me. Many received Me gladly and rejoiced in the Good News. One day a female slave who had a snake spirit followed behind Paul and Silas yelling and screaming. She was telling everyone that Paul and Silas were from Me and would tell them how to be saved. She never stopped calling out to them and pointed them out to others. Paul became tired of her constant yelling, so he delivered her of the spirit in My Name. The owners of the girl were very angry, because she could tell the future. The owners dragged Paul and Silas before the authorities and had them whipped for ruining their source of income. Paul and Silas were locked in prison. They sang songs to Me and worshipped Me and prayed to Me. I heard their prayers, and I shook the earth and all the doors of the prison broke open. The jailor knew that he would be killed for allowing the prisoners to escape, but Paul and Silas told the man they were still there. They told the jailor about Me and My Love. The jailor and his whole household were saved. These new believers told many more in the region how I had saved them and filled them with My Spirit. Since Paul and Silas praised Me and believed in Me to deliver them from their enemies, I shook the earth to protect them. I can do all things! Do you have faith to believe in Me to answer your prayers? Call on My Name, and I will hear your prayers. Have faith in Me, and praise Me even in trying situations. I will deliver you and take you to a safe place, because I love you so much.

Revelations 1:1-20

My Beloved, I sent an angel to deliver a message to John while he was exiled on the island of Patmos. I allowed John to look into Heaven and see Me and My Glory. I stood in the midst of seven menorahs and seven stars. I radiated Love as bright as the sun. I wanted John to deliver a message to each of the seven communities of believers. They needed to be encouraged during these Last Days. I wanted them to know that if they endured to the end that I would give them great rewards. Most of these communities were under attack by the evil one, so I had an angel guarding over every community of believers. I had given each community a Menorah in My Throne Room burning before Me as a symbol of their loving devotion towards Me. These believers were precious to Me. They fought daily to stand firm in the midst of those who hated them. They were kept out of markets and the citizens of towns would not trade with them. Most had very little, but what they did have they shared among themselves. They encouraged each other and were fervent in prayer and fasting for the believers. Their life as a believer was difficult, but I rewarded them greatly. You may not have any believers around you. Do you have to stand by yourself? Are you looked down upon or mocked because of what you believe? If you continue to believe in Me and allow Me to guide you, you will be greatly rewarded for your acts of faith. Continue to love those who are mean to you. Your love will be a strong example to them, and they will be pierced by your loving ways. Speak words that will build up My Name, and I will help you endure to the end.

Revelations 2:1-7

My Beloved, I sent a message through John to all the communities of believers that had been persecuted and persevered. I walked in the midst of them and sent messages to them through the angels over them. I protected them by My Right Hand. They were precious to Me. I loved how they hated the wicked and tested those who wanted to become a believer. They tried the new believers and found them to be faithful, or they were sent away from their community of believers. There were those who wanted to come into their midst and divide them and cause confusion. These people were from the evil one. The community was very cautious, because there were those who hated them and wanted them to fall into destruction. These believers stood firm and did not grow weary. They continued in the faith, but their love for Me had grown dim. They were going through the motions, but not worshipping and praising Me as they did before. I did love them, but I wanted them to love Me with all their heart. I told them that if they endured to the end I would allow them to eat from the Tree of Life. You will also eat from the Tree of Life and live eternally with Me in My Kingdom, if you endure to the end. If you love Me and want to serve Me, I will guide you and you will remain close to Me always. Are you standing firm today? Have you lost your first love that you had for Me? Allow Me to renew you and draw you close to Me again, so you can rejoice in My Love for you.

Revelations 2:8-11

My Beloved, I sent an angel to John with a message for each community of believers in a certain area. This message is still in effect for you. If you listen to the words that I spoke to them and walk in what I told them to do, you will also receive their blessing. They were suffering under a rule of people that hated them. They were ridiculed by the Jews who were some of their own people. These Jews were not My People. They said that they were My People, but they were from the evil one. They tested My People and made them stronger. They said that they followed My Commandments, but they rejected Me and My Ways of love and kindness to others. If a man says that he follows Me and there is no love in his heart for others, then he is not My Child. He does not know Me, if he judges others harshly and mocks others. Are you My Child? My Child has mercy and compassion. My Child loves others and wants to help them no matter who they are. My Child listens to My Voice and obeys Me. My Child wants to be a servant to others and not seek his own position and authority. If My Child has authority, it is because I gave it to him. My Child does not fight to have power and wealth. I give to My Child, and I take from My Child as needed. If you endure to the end, you will not face the second death. Your flesh will die in the first death, but you will not be thrown into the Lake of Fire and no longer exist. You will receive a crown of eternal life in My Kingdom.

Revelations 2:12-17

My Beloved, I have sent a message to you by an angel. This message is the same message that I sent to the other communities that wanted to serve Me. They confessed My Name and said that they served Me. Even when one of their believers was killed for confessing My Name and sharing his testimony of faith in Me, the community stood firm and continued believing in Me that I would keep them safe from destruction. They lived in a region dominated by the Adversary. They were under constant attack in the spiritual realm, and they stood firm. Yet they did not know how to worship Me completely. They still had followers that followed customs from all forms of religions. You have other forms of religions in your midst. There are those who keep Christmas and Easter and say that they are worshipping Me when I did not declare these celebrations as My Feast Days. These are pagan feast days. I did not command you to keep these celebrations. Look at their source and see where they come from. Do My Scriptures command you to keep these celebrations? Search My Scriptures! My Scriptures command you to keep Passover, Feast of Unleavened Bread, Feast of Tabernacles, Pentecost, Feast of Trumpets, and Day of Atonement. Do not look to man to tell you what to do. If it is not in My Scriptures, then do not do it. Follow only My Commands and you will receive hidden manna. You will be given a white stone with a new name written on it that only you and I know. If you endure to the end, you will see My Face and know who I AM. I AM the sharp double-edged sword dividing the Truth from darkness.

361

Revelations 2:18-29

My Beloved, I come to you today and tell you that I am pleased with how you are standing firm and not giving into the enemy. Just as in the days when I sent a message to John, there is still a spirit of Jezebel who tries to seduce the believers. This spirit wants you to fall into sexual immorality and violate your covenant with Me. This spirit wants you to celebrate pagan feasts and eat the meals associated with these feasts. This spirit tells you that it is okay to have sex before marriage. This spirit tells you that you can go to someone's house and enter into their celebrations and eat their unclean food. If you are eating Christmas and Easter meals with others, then you are entering into their celebrations and this does not please Me. If you are entering into sexual immorality before you take your marriage covenant and are not keeping yourself pure, this does not please Me. I AM jealous over you. You must not fall under the spell of the seducing spirit of Jezebel. Whatever spirits rule over your city, fight against them and do not allow them to seduce you into darkness. Are you keeping yourself pure and in right standing with Me? I will allow you to rule over nations and have authority in My Kingdom. I AM the Morning Star. I will shine over you and in

you.

Revelations 3:1-6

My Beloved, wake up! You say you are alive yet you are dead inside, if you are not walking as led by My Spirit daily. If you are going your own way and doing as you please, then you are not in covenant with Me. You are not following close to Me. You are not My Servant listening for My Commands every day. Walk close to Me and follow in My Ways, and I will allow you to be clothed in white. I will not blot your name out of The Book of Life. I will acknowledge you before My Father and the angels. I will say that you are My Beloved, and you are a treasure to Me. You have been found faithful and have endured until the end. You have been tested and tried and been transformed into My Image. You are worthy of bearing My Name and of being called My Child. You will inherit My Kingdom of Light. Wake up those who walk in your own ways! Wake up and listen to My Voice, and do as I tell you to do. Are you fulfilling your purpose for this life? Do not do what makes you happy! You are here to serve Me!

Revelations 3:7-13

My Beloved, I open doors and I shut doors. If I open a door, no man can shut it. I will open a door for you that no man can shut. Do you believe that I will make a way for you, so you will not be harmed by the Adversary? If you continue to call on My Name and confess your love for Me, I will keep you from severe testing in these Last Days. If only you will walk close to Me, I will protect you from the evil one. I will make you steadfast and firm. You will not bend. You will be like a pillar in My Temple. You will hold up the others around you. You will be faithful until the end and bring a host of others with you. You are the faithful ones who I smile upon. You do not want to enter into the celebrations of the world, but you only celebrate My Feast Days. You read My Scriptures and only keep the commandments that I have given you. You follow My Commandments very closely and cling to My Words. No man's words can make you turn from Me. You will enter into My Land dancing and singing. You will listen to My Call and follow Me. I know that others try you daily, because they say that they serve Me and they do not. You do not understand how they bend in the wind. You want to please Me in all you do. You have been found faithful when others around you are not faithful. You will be given a safe place while the unfaithful will have to be tested harshly in these Last Days. Rejoice that you have not fallen to temptations and have remained strong and unbending. You are sealed with My Name.

Revelations 3:14-22

My Beloved, you think you are rich in the things of Me. You say, "I am blessed. I am rich. I have so many possessions". I want to vomit you out of My Mouth. You are focused on your material possession and how much you have. You do not want to give to the poor. You do not want to listen to My Voice. You think you are rich, because you measure up to what the world defines rich. You have money in the bank for your security. I AM not your security. You love your money and what money can buy. You are poor, naked, and blind. You need to come to Me and want to be clothed in righteousness, and I will give you white clothing. You need to come to Me and ask Me for wealth, and I will refine you by fire and give you gold from My Kingdom. You need to come to Me and ask that your eyes be opened, so I can rub salve into your eyes and allow you to see again into the spirit. You have forgotten what is important. Pleasing yourself is not important. You must please Me and serve Me. You must fulfill your purpose in this life. What are you doing to serve Me? Are you obeying Me daily? Do you want to walk in My Ways and not the ways of the world? You need to think with a spiritual mind and not a worldly mind. Come to Me, and I will give you the keys to life eternal. Come to Me, and I will allow you to rule with Me as I rule from My Throne. Come to Me and I will lift you up, so you can see once again. You have lost sight of Me. Come let Me take you by the Hand. I will guide you into My Presence and into the Light. Walk hand and hand with Me.

9 781771 431965